Us, Relatives

ETHNOGRAPHIC STUDIES IN SUBJECTIVITY

Tanya Luhrmann, Editor

Us, Relatives

Scaling and Plural Life in a Forager World

NURIT BIRD-DAVID

University of California Press

University of California Press, one of the most distinguished university presses in the United States, enriches lives around the world by advancing scholarship in the humanities, social sciences, and natural sciences. Its activities are supported by the UC Press Foundation and by philanthropic contributions from individuals and institutions. For more information, visit www.ucpress.edu.

University of California Press
Oakland, California

Library of Congress Cataloging-in-Publication Data

Names: Bird-David, Nurit, 1951– author.
Title: Us, relatives : scaling and plural life in a forager world / Nurit Bird-David.
Other titles: Ethnographic studies in subjectivity ; 12.
Description: Oakland, California : University of California Press, [2017] | Series: Ethnographic studies in subjectivity ; 12 | Includes bibliographical references and index.
Identifiers: LCCN 2016036900 (print) | LCCN 2016038991 (ebook) | ISBN 9780520293403 (cloth : alk. paper) | ISBN 9780520293427 (pbk. : alk. paper) | ISBN 9780520966680 (Epub)
Subjects: LCSH: Hunting and gathering societies—South Asia. | Families—South Asia. | Human-animal relationships—South Asia.
Classification: LCC GN388 .B57 2017 (print) | LCC GN388 (ebook) | DDC 306.3/640954—dc23
LC record available at https://lccn.loc.gov/2016036900

Manufactured in the United States of America

25   24   23   22   21   20   19   18   17
10   9   8   7   6   5   4   3   2   1

Contents

Illustrations

TABLES

Prologue

One of Us

Ootacamund (Ooty) was a thriving hill station in the Nilgiri heights during British rule in India, its residents not just colonial functionaries but their wives and children as well. Few white women, however, ventured onto the forested slopes below the station. When I first trekked down those slopes in 1978, a white woman was still a novelty to those who lived there (and remains a rare sight even today). Curious laborers crowded around me, my partner, and our guide as we walked across the tea plantation where they worked and, crossing its lower boundaries, began the steep descent into the forest. A few followed us, intently observing our gear and our behavior, until we were swallowed up by the thick forest and they turned back to their work.

We finally arrived at a tiny hamlet comprising six bamboo and grass huts clinging to the hillside. As we entered the hamlet, its dwellers continued to go nonchalantly about their affairs. Two men eventually approached us in a leisurely fashion and struck up a conversation. I vividly remember today their ease and laughter as they teasingly encouraged frightened children to approach me and accept the sweets I had brought with me and as they made their own offer of wild honey to us. The contrast between the approach of these forest foragers and that of their uphill neighbors (mostly Hindu and Muslim rural wageworkers and roadside traders) could not have been greater. And it was reinforced a few visits later, when my partner and I moved into one of the forest huts. This time, entranced by the tantalizing idea of a white couple on their way to stay with the forest people, the plantation laborers followed us right down to the hamlet. They surrounded the hut where we unloaded our supplies and possessions, trying through the cracks in the bamboo walls to see what we had and what we did. After they at last had left, one of the hamlet's residents, whom I call Kungan in this

book, matter-of-factly took cups and tea leaves from my rucksack and prepared tea for us. In the evening, he and his family shared their meal with
us; that night, his daughter and one of her friends slept inside our hut.
When my partner left a week later to return to his job, the rest of Kungan's
family moved in with me. I shared the hut with them for the duration of
my fieldwork and closely associated with their several dozen relatives living in their hamlet and in half a dozen other smaller ones (each a three- to
six-hour walk from its nearest neighbor). After a few months, I discovered
that I had become more than just a welcome visitor.

"I live very far away," I told Kungan one morning, chatting casually
with him and feeling homesick. My mind drifted to the stately Cambridge
University Library, where, surrounded by books, I had read about hunting
and gathering societies in preparation for my fieldwork with this man and
his relatives. I was flooded with memories of the three-month search in the
Nilgiris for a suitable study group and, beyond that, of the years of intense
planning and preparation, worries and fantasies, which had ended with the
anticlimax of my simply moving in with them. His voice penetrated my
wandering thoughts. "But you are here," he said, perplexed, "you are living
with us; you are our *sonta* [us, relatives, our own, we who live together]."[1]
I surprised Kungan with my vision of myself as someone "from faraway"
when, for him, I was *there*, being-with his family. He, in turn, surprised me
when, after my initial delight at being accepted as one of "our own," he
showed me that local nonhuman beings also were regarded as *sonta*. I later
learned that *sonta* was the term by which his people communally referred
to themselves, on a par with the kinds of designations by which other indigenous groups around the world are known to refer to themselves, terms
that translate as "real people," "humans," "kinspeople," and the like.

. . .

I could have told this story simply to provide a sense of the methodological
basis of this book and to begin to thank Kungan and his relatives for making my work possible. I also could have told it to forestall the question
ethnographers working with such peoples learn to expect: "How did they
accept you?"—those posing it prepared to hear of locals' fright and wonder
at seeing white people, their expectations projecting onto locals their own
senses of the unknown, different Other. But if one acknowledges a multiplicity of ontological options for being-with others—which is to take differences seriously but not, as one currently popular view does, to entertain the
existence of altogether divergent worlds—then this story raises a set of
serious questions. Beyond questions about participatory fieldwork in the

tiniest of communities and the putative universality of "us-them" divides, my first encounter with these foragers has left me with a lingering wonder about modes of experiencing and understanding belonging. My first field encounter has never ceased to intrigue me in the years since. Yet anthropology has only recently offered me a conceptual basis for seriously developing and discussing the questions it raised, and so I have previously written about other issues and only now feel able to address those questions. I elaborate on the theoretical grounding of this shift in perspective—the discipline's and my own—in my introduction. Here I share a few general thoughts on my perspective and on the questions this book addresses and how they developed.

. . .

An anthropologist's arrival among exotic, faraway people continues to be the stuff of scholarly and popular fantasy, persisting today in a rapidly shrinking, technologically mediated global village. It has a place of honor in a family of encounter scenarios with Others, whether strange primitives in Herodotus's time, savages and barbarians in the European era of discovery, or, more recently, extraterrestrial life in yet unknown parts of the universe. A core leitmotif of all these scenarios is the titillating sense of an encounter with beings that, although corporeally present, are imagined to be from elsewhere, at once faraway and different. The paradoxical state of being copresent with such an Other is emotionally and cognitively stirring. And generating this unsettled state, to no small extent, is the capacity of the imagined community to which the Other belongs to command attention *over and above* the vivid being who is copresent. Yet consider, as a thought experiment, another option: one in which living with and corporeally experiencing other beings, each in his or her uniqueness, takes precedence over typifying and categorizing those beings in terms of imagined communities of belonging. Suppose, in a first encounter, that de facto corporeal being-together is given primacy and that attention is directed to what can be learned about the distinctiveness of a newcomer through unmediated experience of him or her. Suppose that differences *are* observed and taken seriously, not for sorting beings into classes as a primary means of thinking about or dealing with them but rather as an effort toward good diplomacy (to borrow Bruno Latour's term) and skillful management of interaction. This option has generally hovered in my mind for a long time even as I have pursued other issues.

For many years, I focused my scholarly energies especially on examining how Kungan and his relatives regarded and engaged with nonhumans (hills, elephants, birds, lizards, stones, etc.). My work was in sync with a new anthropology of animism that looked at indigenous challenges to Western ideas about people's place in the world, particularly the divide—some would call it opposition—between the nonhuman and the human, Nature and Culture/Society. But what if, I wondered, engaging with a particular vivid being precedes imagining its class? What if one observes the vivid lizard one encounters on the forest path *before* one reflects on the attributes shared by all those creatures classed as lizards and on what traits (if any) distinguish lizards from humans? What if copresence and engagement, and not imagined sameness of form and essence, constitute the prime register of belonging?

Kungan's and my mutual surprise—his at my vision of myself as someone "from far away" when, for him, I was *there*, being-with his family, and mine at his inclusion of me within "our own, relatives" alongside lizards, elephants, and hills—suggested to me that maybe not only things but also communities of belonging can be other than we initially perceive them. Maybe the way anthropologists frame "peoples" a priori as their cultural units of study, each unit distinguished from the others (not to mention from nonhumans), obscures alternative senses of peoplehood and community. A group of influential scholars (primarily students of Amazonian ontologies) has argued for the "radical alterity" of indigenous peoples and their worlds, an argument that I have always found at odds with my vivid memories of living with Kungan's family and of joining them on forays into the forest and in engagements with spirits. I asked myself whether a profoundly plural world is possible, one consisting of communities of heterogeneous copresent beings who are not serialized into classes of things, societies, and ontologies. And I wondered if *sonta* does not, in fact, show us a heretofore unexplored style of imagining community (in Benedict Anderson's sense).

For several decades now, anthropologists have explored modes of figuring and experiencing the singular being other than in terms of the modern "individual." Thirty-odd years after I first met Kungan and his relatives, I decided the time was ripe for me to begin exploring their ontological options of we-ness, their ways of "being many," their modes of figuring community. To ethnographically explore how a "people" perceive their own peopleness is a somewhat paradoxical project and, when a people include nonhumans in their "us," not an easy one. It took me still more years to figure out how to do it, as I experimented with various architectures and strategies for this book.

In the course of those years, the search for a solution brought into relief another issue that anthropologists of indigenous communities have often overlooked in their analyses: the scalar gulf separating the imagined modern West from the peoples whose options we explore as challenges, subversions, or alternatives to modern Western certainties. No ethnographer who has worked with a tiny forager-cultivator community can forget the all-pervasive sense of living with so few people, surrounded by forest, tundra, or desert. Yet, analytically, the scalar context of such communities has usually gone unacknowledged in anthropological studies, whether of gender, equality, marriage, childhood, contact with outsiders, or other issues—even ontology. I asked myself whether sociocultural anthropologists have not overreacted to modern evolutionary scripts that entangle the small-scale with "early" and "less developed" forms of social life. Have we not ignored, even been altogether blind to, the minuscule context of indigenous experience? Suppose concealment of the intimate context of their lives and worlds opens the gates to Trojan horses that insinuate anthropology's intrinsic large-scale communal terms into our analyses? Suppose those terms cripple ethnographies of indigenous groups and, in turn, the insights to be gained from comparing them with Western society? What if our scale-skewed ethnographies of indigenous communities and worlds, however well motivated, adversely affect their political struggles and futures? Didn't Kungan's puzzlement at my statement that I was "from far away" arise from his scalar context, one that anthropologists more often than not overlook?

Kungan and his relatives did not share in the tradition that gave birth to the classic anthropological interest in peoples like them. They were not moved by the spirit that led Europeans to explore the imagined far corners of the earth and beyond. Their horizons of attention did not stretch to "the world" at large as an unknown realm but one assumed to be knowable through exploration. If they did not focus their cultural energies on places they imagined to exist, that they could travel to and live in, places that strange beings lived in, what did they focus on? Writing this book required me to look for fresh theoretical perspectives on scale/ing, which I found in the anthropology of large-scale and global phenomena and adapted to my subject matter. It forced me to take scale and scalability seriously to the point that they came to constitute a major theoretical issue for me alongside the indigenous sense of we-ness. Scalar context, bias, and distortion became a subtext for all the issues I touch on in this ethnography as well for my primary pursuit: delineating Kungan and his relatives' senses of community, their modes of "being-with" and "being many."

I was well into the second and third drafts of this book, and at a stage when scale-sensitive analysis had become second nature to me, when, like thunder on a clear day, the realization hit me that in all the time I stayed with Kungan and his relatives and lived in their hamlet, I never saw a face-to-face encounter in the literal sense of the term: two persons facing one another, oblivious to those surrounding them. In a tiny community like Kungan's, it would be a gross impropriety to interact in this way. Didn't the same hold true, I wondered, for certain contexts within the multiscalar modern world (at home with intimate family, in a pub with friends, in gatherings with relatives)? For the most part, in a tiny forager camp, one's actions are not oriented vis-à-vis a "significant other" and occur not in the presence of disinterested "third parties" but in the presence and sphere of awareness of close relatives. In a tiny forager community like Kungan's, the *manyness* of *few* relatives is omnipresent. Their manyness is pregiven, and (dyadic) relations and individualities are distinguished within that plurality. Moreover, that manyness of few is not singularized as a hyperexistent homogenized collective.

In previous work, I labored to help relationalize the study of hunter-gatherer personhood, animism, childhood, and other facets of hunter-gatherer life; I was happy with the capacity of the relational approach to redress the limits of (predominantly Euro-American) individualist language and ideology and, thus, bring clarity to this field of study. Recognizing that one simply cannot ignore the fact that these are communities of "few-many," I wondered whether the relational approach reaches its limits in these cases. What if the worlds of tiny communities, with their essential "manyness of few," fall through the sieve of individualist, relational, and groupist languages? Suppose relational tools by themselves are not sharp enough to delineate the dominant contours of life in foragers' intimate plural contexts?

Neologisms, I feel, should be cautiously introduced and only as a last recourse. Yet, in finalizing this book, I found it necessary to do just that: what I call "pluripresence" ultimately became my framing analytical concept, and it lies at the core of my multiscalar and multiontological study of an intimate forager community. Instead of projecting the community as radically alter, this concept and the perspective it denotes opened a conceptual space for me to discern scalar ontological options and, in turn, patterns that we who inhabit the "Westernized" world share with indigenous peoples, at least in certain niches of our multiscalar and multiontological modern lives.

· · ·

Entry stories like mine have a special appeal, popularly and in classrooms. But they must be taken seriously, I suggest, if only for the simple reason that they are not exceptional. Many ethnographers of tiny-scale indigenous communities have been adopted by the people they have studied. The anthropology of such communities could not possibly be what it is, or offer what it does, had they not been. Beyond their appeal as personal anecdotes, as evidence of good rapport with informants, and as indications of successful fieldwork (see Kane 2001), such entry stories call for probing the local ontological terms and sensibilities that underscore them. As one way of thanking Kungan and his relatives for including me among "our own," and for the lifelong intellectual challenges they have posed for me, I offer this book as an exploration of the "we" senses, imaginations of community, and modes of "being many" that are embodied in their complex notion of *sonta*.

Introduction

Scalar Blindness and Forager Worlds

The ten-volume *Encyclopedia of World Cultures* (Levinson 1991–2001) is organized by major world regions, each region's cultures presented without regard to population size. Cultures of many millions of people and those of a few hundred are presented alphabetically by ethnonym, the large populations identified by widely agreed-on names and the tiny groups assigned one or another of the multiple ethnonyms outsiders have bestowed on them. The criteria governing the length of each volume's summaries are very clearly stated by the editor, the principal one being the total number of cultures to be covered in a volume's allotted pages, adjusted by such factors as the availability of authoritative sources and the extent of information for a particular culture, the degree of a culture's similarity with other cultures, and its scientific or political importance (3: xv). Population size is irrelevant. In fact, cultural parity is lauded, and inclusion of the tiniest groups is explicitly extolled because of such groups' rarity and sociocultural import.[1]

The *Encyclopedia*'s contents illustrate the democratic ethos of cultural anthropology that developed partly in reaction to the modern association of the small-scale with early (and supposedly less developed) forms of human sociality, and it is expressed at its fullest in cross-cultural comparison wherein, rather, all cultures are given equal standing regardless of group size. Comparing hunter-gatherer-cultivator groups whose populations are estimated on the order of "a few hundred to a few thousand inhabitants" (Smith and Wishnie 2000: 493)[2] and Western cultures of hundreds of millions is now standard practice in the discipline. These comparisons are the bread and butter of the profession. Anthropology owes its key insights and unique perspective

---

(Facing page) A honey collector. Photographed by the author (1978–79).

and appeal to them. Highly influential agendas in recent years have been generated by comparisons of, for example, Western and Melanesian ideas of gender (Strathern 1988), Western and hunter-gatherer perceptions of the environment (Ingold 2000), and Western and Amazonian ontologies (Viveiros de Castro 2012). The huge scalar disparity between the cultures being compared does not trouble anthropologists as much as the fact that the comparison itself involves essentializing the systems involved, overdrawing the contrast between them and overhomogenizing each side (61).[3] Indeed, Philippe Descola (2013 [2005]) has recently expanded the scale-blind comparative charter to all cultures with his proposal to analyze human approaches to the nonhuman world using four universally applicable categories.

I contend that anthropology's multiculturalist and democratic ethos, well-meaning as it may be, has interfered with attempts to understand the cultures and ontologies of extremely small populations. Imagine, if you will, a handful of forest huts and, between them, fires burning in closely spaced hearths. Darkness is falling on the forest around you, yet you can observe small clusters of relatives, men, women, and children, about two dozen in all, seated around the fires, dancing flames lighting their faces. Their voices carry from hearth to hearth, and you find yourself listening to a generalized conversation that links everyone present; no one addresses anyone in particular, anyone can join the conversation at any time. The fewness of these people and their relaxed togetherness cannot fail to impress you. When an ethnographer lives with such people, she becomes aware of the depth of each person's presence to all the others—not just to one or a few others but to all of them, all of the time, throughout a lifetime. This intimate community is the core of their daily experience, the context for much of what happens in their lives: what they do and think, how they interact with each other, and how they engage with the nonhuman world that surrounds them. Yet this fundamental experience has not been central to anthropological analysis of their cultures. How can it be when scalar disparity goes unacknowledged in the normal practice of cross-cultural comparison—and equally, of ethnographic writing?

Demographic surveys of such societies are logistically challenging, in some cases politically charged, and often conceptually murky (cf. Kelly 1995: 208–9). But unreliable population estimates do not justify analytically ignoring their order of scale. Cultural ethnographies of such groups often generally provide an order of size but then do not pursue its implications. Often in monographs, a single line of text provides a rough estimate of the population of interest, and another, with more surety, gives the size of the specific group the ethnographer lived with. If these figures are mentioned again, they are rarely integrated into the analysis. They are hardly ever repeated in the ethnographer's subsequent articles and are almost never cited in theoretical comparisons drawing on those works. For the most part, sociocultural anthropology has left the miniscule size of forager groups to the purview of its sister branches of evolutionary and ecological anthropology (which discuss group size in relation to foraging efficiency, environmental carrying capacity, reproduction parameters, etc.)[4]—and with it the conditions and experience that it potentiates and limits. Notably, Robin Dunbar (1993), an evolutionary psychologist, has argued that the human brain's neocortical processing capacity sets the maximum size of a group within which each person can vividly know every other person and how all are related at 150 people. Dunbar (1998) has further argued that language and gossip evolved to transcend this limit. On its part, cultural anthropology's preoccupation with parity, I contend, has effectively hidden the intimate communal basis of foragers' lives, and ethnography has not explored the social, cultural, and ontological concomitants of that intimacy.

Scale-blind analysis, in fact, is not scale-blind but is biased toward the large-scale for the simple reason that anthropology's terms, forms, and architecture of inquiry are drawn from the scholarly traditions of modern, large-scale society; those traditions ultimately shape ethnographic research. The attendant analytical problems are generally well known, the effect of cross-scalar distortions far less so. One large-scale bias concerns topical research. Ethnographers focus on discrete realms of knowledge (e.g., ecology, politics, gender, suffering, morality, ontology, etc.), products of the contemporary large-scale world that tend to continually subdivide and multiply in that world (Strathern 1991, 1995). One outcome of such categorical proliferation is that the number of foragers in a local group often does not exceed the number of cultural domains ethnographers expect them to inhabit!. A second bias involves naming. Even though the members of many tiny indigenous groups do not formally name themselves, ethnographers refer to them by ethnonyms, as they would any other (larger) population, neglecting locals' identity categories and own scales of practice and imagination. As other outside "identity experts" do, scholars ethnically pigeonhole the people they study, amalgamating them with others who are supposedly the "same" but whom the study people do not know or may not even imagine to exist.[5] Haphazard assignment of ethnonyms is one reason estimates of indigenous populations are so erratic. These and other large-scale biases discussed in this book are, I contend, Trojan horses that steal their way via scale-blind anthropology into the ethnography of tiny indigenous communities, distorting our understanding of them.

My main comparative category in this book comprises those indigenous communities that have since the middle of the twentieth century been labeled hunters and gatherers (and are also known as modern hunter-gatherers, gatherer-hunters, foragers, and post-foragers), but my argument is not restricted to them. One reason for my focus on these communities is that they constitute my own field of specialization, and another, more general reason is that their cases illustrate my scalar concerns especially vividly. Never have so few carried so much theoretical weight! They are among the tiniest communities studied by ethnographers.[6] With the average local group size estimated at 28.4 men, women, and children (the "magic number" for modern foragers' local group size is 25–50 men, women, and children; see Kelly 1995: 211; Lee and DeVore 1968: 8), its members are fewer than the number of students in an average-size university classroom; whole societies, estimated at several hundred to a few thousand, are smaller than a large apartment complex. The depictions of these minuscule groups, who barely register numerically against the millions who live in modern nation-states or against the billions who now make up the world's population, have had unrivaled influence on modern social thought and imagination, from seventeenth-century deliberations on the "natural state" of humankind through nineteenth- and twentieth-century classic theory on property, religion, and kinship to current debates on alternatives to modern environmental understandings and alter-ontologies. Their ethnography serves the understanding of human evolution and prehistory and was undertaken, in Richard Lee and Irven DeVore's words, to elucidate the history of "Cultural Man . . . on earth for some 2,000,000 years" (1968: 3). They are also a popular "court of appeal" with respect to questions of "human nature" (e.g., the innateness of aggression, gender roles, and forms of child care and diet). Their place in the structure of modern thought is so special that, as Tim Ingold wrote, "had they not existed they would certainly have had to have been invented" (1999: 399). It is ironic that so few have mattered so much when the ontological effect of their fewness has scarcely been taken into cultural and comparative account.

Claude Lévi-Strauss remarked on encountering the Nambikwara that their "society . . . had been reduced to the point at which I found nothing but human beings" (1961: 310). Surely the "human beings" Lévi-Strauss met were simply a small group of relatives who all lived *with* each other— very likely chatting every night around their hearths like the foragers I describe above. Lévi-Strauss's observation expresses the limits of comprehending such tiny communities when one measures them against the modern privileged sense of *society*. Recent considerations of the place of nonhumans in indigenous worlds have labored to loosen the tether between those worlds and the modern privileged sense of *nature* (a link deriving from Lévi-Strauss's structural thesis of a universal "nature-culture" binary).[7] Efforts to do the same with respect to the modern sense of *society* have been episodic at best.[8] One of my concerns in this book is to consolidate these efforts and to align them with and integrate them into current discussions of indigenous ontologies. I contend that separately exploring indigenous subversions of modern *nature* and *society* simply reifies the Western "nature-society" binary. When scalar disparity is ignored, the distortive effect of such efforts is exacerbated, and tiny communities are painted onto huge modern canvases as visions of radical alterity. In this book, I focus especially on indigenous subversions of the modern imagination of society as *nation*, a construct that emerged alongside that of *nature*. I look to forager ethnography for ontological possibilities at the tiny end of the spectrum of us-ness, communality, and modes of living jointly with humans and nonhumans (leaving to other studies larger-scale hunter-gatherer-cultivator communities and, more generally, the continuous range of plural forms between tiny-scale and large-scale societies).

Environmental concerns in the late twentieth century have provided fertile ground for anthropologists to explore hunter-gatherers' perceptions of their natural surroundings. However, we have arrived at an era in which humans are recognized as a geological force, shaping the world rather than living dually alongside and in nature. The Internet is undermining old semiotic-structural hierarchies and altering modes of belonging. Globalization and transnational migration are challenging the still-powerful nineteenth-century notion of the national community as naturally given. The "social" is opening up, and scholarly efforts across the social sciences are being directed at studying modes of assemblage and reassemblage (Latour 2005) and to critiquing twentieth-century paradigms such as groupism and methodological nationalism (Brubaker 2004; Brubaker and Cooper 2000; Wimmer and Glick Schiller 2002). Philosophers wrestling with the issue of contemporary social alienation are trying to shake the nostalgia for the view of lost community lying at the core of Western political thinking: a community of common norms and values shared by people with the same identity and background (Nancy 1991). Understanding hunter-gatherers' modes and imaginations of plural life has new purchase, I think, and we must find the appropriate scalar frameworks for their exploration. This book represents my modest effort to start meeting this challenge.

Us, Relatives combines a reading of what I now consider to be a scale-blind literature with ethnography based largely on my work since the late

1970s with a group of South Asian forest foragers that I now scale-sensitively analyze. Below I introduce the conceptual pathways I follow, the language that guides me, and my fellow travelers on the journey, and I outline the journey's itinerary.

REVISITING FORAGER WORLDS: CONCEPTUAL PATHWAYS

Scale/ing and the Other

By the mid-twentieth century, sizing and quantifying as a means of characterizing processes and entities had become a standard everyday practice (Strathern 1992a; Hacking 1990). Modern anthropology extended this standard to its Other in framing forager-cultivator peoples as "small-scale societies" vis-à-vis modern "large-scale societies." This category alluded to smallness within a modern grand narrative that entangled scale with time and both with the progressive development of plural forms. In this narrative, "small-scale societies" grew over time in size, complexity, and sophistication to become "large-scale societies." *Small-scale society* connoted, at once, small size, antiquity, and lack of development. Modernity's temporally infused concepts and discourse shaped the making of the anthropological subject through the early to mid-twentieth century (Fabian 1983). Late twentieth-century multiculturalist anthropology shifted to imagining its Other as equitably comparable cultures drawn from all parts of the world rather than from different times and stages of human evolution. For the most part, anthropologists have since avoided the small-scale category and favored exclusive use of regional and political ones (e.g., Amerindian peoples, Melanesian societies, First Nations, and indigenous peoples). But in the zeal to rehabilitate indigenous communities as contemporaneous and sophisticated, we seem to have thrown the scalar baby out with the bathwater. I question whether excluding scalar issues does not skew cultural analysis of tiny groups, and if so, how to bring fresh theoretical perspectives to bear on scale.

Nancy Howell's (1979) demographic study of the Kalahari hunter-gatherers (then named) Dobe !Kung provides a wonderful parable for introducing my concerns. Howell drew on an exceptionally large database for a hunter-gatherer community, the combined effort of a dedicated team of scholars working between 1963 and 1973, who cumulated close to one thousand individual records. One thousand actual people, she writes, constitute "the group that we have information on ... [but] we want to generalize from this information to the group of which these people are a part: the !Kung people over long periods of time." With the "target population" defined as "the members produced by the ethnic group population . . . no matter where they are" (17), Howell cautioned that valid statistical analysis of demographic trends requires a minimum of five thousand individuals. To achieve that minimum for the small !Kung population, she calculated, she would need records spanning more than a thousand years. So Howell ran a computer simulation that "produced" (mathematical) "individuals" over a thousand-year run, determining their sex and life span randomly and marrying them according to stochastic demographic availabilities at successive points of time. In this way, she produced a large artificial population of which the real study group constituted a segment—a sizable enough population that the "law of large numbers" could smooth out what statisticians lump together as the "random fluctuations" that obscure "regularities." "Regularities" that may transpire from this exercise, however, are external to the "real" members, who are spun into an imagined order of scale exponentially larger than the one they experience and which they, unlike members of nation-societies, do not imagine. For "real" people living in tiny societies, the field of marital options is dramatically affected by haphazard events, and they are fully aware of it. The cultural ethnographer would do better to explore locals' "nanoscale" conditions and experience and to examine their cultural strategies and logic at that scalar plane (see chapter 3).

Cultural analysis can be similarly affected when foragers' (and other peoples') scalar conditions and experience are not considered, though that fact gets easily swept under the carpet of generalizing terms. In this book I develop downscaled analyses of an array of issues in forager studies, touching on both traditional and new topics (e.g., domicile, ownership, mobility, marriage, gender, childhood, cosmos, and relations with others and with the state). Here, I introduce my concerns through one of those issues, the cross-scalar spillage involved in studying forager-cultivators' alternatives to the modern "nature-society" binary. *Nature* came, in the seventeenth century, to mean the abstract singular Nature in which everything (in some versions, humans excluded) exists, rather than a specific singular nature, the nature of something (Williams 1976: 184). *Society* similarly came, in the eighteenth century, to signify an abstract container *in* which people live (Anderson 1991 [1983]), though its root, *seq-* or *seui*, means "following," and it comes from the Latin *socius*, meaning "companion" or "associate" (Strum and Latour 1987: 793–94). Large-scale imaginations and conditions are embodied in the *nature-society* binary, and I question whether inverting modern Western terms (for example, using *naturesociety* rather than *nature* and *society* or *multiple natures and single culture* rather than *single nature and multiple cultures*) can sufficiently correct for cross-scalar confusion.[9] Scale-blind analysis, I argue in this book, opens analytical gates to all kinds of Trojan-horse scalar slippages that obscure foragers' experiences and lifeways. Among these slippages are such basic ethnographic standards as naming groups and their individual members (I address these and other distortive anthropological conventions in Downscales 1–5).

To write forager-cultivator ethnography that is mindful of local scale, I look to new approaches to scale/ing that have proven useful in the study of modern large-scale global society (the "scalar turn" is a full-blown perspective in various social sciences).[10] Rather than view scale as a variable that scholars set *before* doing research, this approach sees scaling as a human activity and the work of scholars as exploring how and what "actors achieve by *scaling, spacing and contextualizing* each other" (Latour 2005: 184). In fact, Bruno Latour unequivocally argues that actors should not be denied "one of their most important privileges, namely, that they are the ones defining relative scale" (ibid.). Not only are humans approached as scalers but anthropologists have shown that large-scaling constitutes a way of seeing and making the world (Scott 1998), that it is a frame of thought and a resource (Strathern 1992a), and it involves certain senses of plurality, complexity, and diversity (Strathern 1991). Ethnographers have begun to describe the intersections of local, national, and global scale-making projects (e.g., see Ferguson and Gupta 2002; Tsing 2005; Jimenez 2005; Xiang 2013). Attendant vocabulary has proliferated in the social sciences (e.g., scalar logic, scalar relations, scalar tropes, scalability, interscalability, sliding scales, multiscalar, etc.) that could help in rewriting scale into cultural analyses of forager lifeways.

This book offers an ethnography that redresses scale-blind cultural analysis of forager communities by adapting this recent approach to "scale/ing" to the tiny end of the social spectrum. Foragers are scale makers, no different in this respect from any other humans. Bringing this perspective to their study, for me, involves pursuing a variety of related questions: Do foragers downscale their spheres of activity? Do they scale down their horizons of imagination? Does downscaling constitute, for them, a cultural resource and a project? What senses of plurality and diversity does their tiny scale/ing afford and limit? With these questions in mind, I focus my exploration on a particular indigenous concept of community: *sonta*, "us, relatives."[11]

Indigenous We-Designations

Sonta belongs to a family of notions by which tiny forager-cultivator groups around the world (and some other peoples) are known to refer to themselves, the vernaculars commonly translated as "real people," "humans," "kinspeople," and the like. These recurring indigenous notions have remained for the most part below the theoretical radar—either because outsiders' names have been used in their stead or, conversely, because the indigenous notions have been used as if they were proper ethnonyms (and in the same ways that ethnonyms are used in any larger population), usage that has numbed attention to their indigenous function and ontological sense. Examples abound, and here I present a selection: the Australian Aboriginal people known as Pintupi call themselves *walytja* (relatives, family; Myers 1986: 110); the East Asian forager-cultivator known as Chewong refer to themselves as *he* or *bi he* (us or people, us [S. Howell 1984: 13]); the North American hunters known as Ojibwa call themselves *Anishinaabek* (people) and are now also known by that name. And moving to examples of known ethnonyms that, in fact, are self-referential vernacular terms (I italicize each ethnonym as a reminder that it is a vernacular word): the Asian *Batek* (person of our group; Kirk Endicott 1979: 3), *Ilongot* (friends [Rosaldo 1980: 37]), and *Ainu* (most humanly beings [Svensson 1999: 132]); the North American *Dene* (people [Asch and Smith 1999: 46]), *Innu* (humans [Mailhot 1999: 51]), and *Inupiat* (genuine people [Chance 1966: 4]); the Australian *Tiwi* (people [Goodale 1999: 353]), and the South African *Ju/'hoansi* (genuine people and real people [Lee 1979: 38]). Many more examples are available from around the world, yet ethnographic discussion of such indigenous terms is scarce, as if their translation as *people, humans,* and *kinspeople* were straightforward and simple. Exceptions suggest that these indigenous categories of identity may have greater cultural significance than assumed. For example, Fred Myers observes that *walytja* is a "key symbol for the Pintupi social order" (1986: 110). He adds (note the scalar implications) that *walytja* refers to "those with whom one grows up, those with whom one is familiar, those who have fed and cared for one, and those with whom one camps frequently" (109–10).[12] It is very difficult to explore these notions, a possible reason for their neglect: to ask how the Pintupi (or any other such group) imagine themselves is a somewhat oxymoronic question, and if the local word is used as an ethnonym, to ask how the Sonta (Batek, Ilongot, etc.) imagine themselves is somewhat paradoxical.

Despite the striking cross-cultural recurrence of such terms, and even though their local uses may express ontological understandings and imaginations of community other than those expressed in ethnonym, few anthropologists to date have paid theoretical attention to them. Lévi-Strauss's (1973 [1952]: 384) attention was caught by the recurrence of what he called "auto-ethnonyms" among Amerindian peoples, many of whom call themselves "real people" and "real humans." Lévi-Strauss suggested that this phenomenon reflects an indigenous version of ethnocentrism, indicating, he proposed, a perception that beyond a group's boundaries humanity ends. Nearly half a century passed before Eduardo Viveiros de Castro (1998: 447; see also 2012: 97–98) challenged that argument by offering a perspectival view on what Lévi-Strauss had perceived as essential bounded groups. Perceptively, if briefly, Viveiros de Castro remarked that indigenous "self-designations" (his gloss) refer to the social condition of personhood. Self-designations like "people," he argued, mean "person" rather than "member of the human species," for which reason these categories of identity have enormous contextual variability and can refer to one's immediate kin, one's local group, or even all beings endowed with subjectivity). These terms function pragmatically (and possibly also syntactically) as pronouns that mark the position of the enunciator rather than as substantives. Like Lévi-Strauss, Viveiros de Castro primarily referred to Amerindian instances translated as "real people" and "humans," but he also alluded to Amerindian peoples who designate themselves "our kinspeople," and for whom "human" and "kin" are interchangeable (Viveiros de Castro 2009: 242, 2012: 98 n. 10, citing Peter Gow).

Whereas Lévi-Strauss's "auto-ethnonym" left undisturbed the universality of ethnonyms (only shifting from outsider- to indigenous-authored names), Viveiros de Castro's "self-designation" gloss opened conceptual space for exploring indigenous identity categories. In fact, he differentiated indigenous terms from ethnonyms. He proposed that indigenous "self-designations" belong to "the category of '*we*,'" unlike ethnonyms, which "are names of third parties" and belong to "the category of '*they*'" (1998: 476). My lingering concern is that the prefix *self-*, though, still leaves undisturbed a modern sense of *many persons* as a singularized entity, a group. It limits exploring ontological alternatives expressed in indigenous identity categories as well as the distinction Viveiros de Castro draws between them and ethnonyms. His distinction can gain depth and complexity when, lifted out of the scale-blind regime in which he offered it, it is considered scale-sensitively.

Ethnonym comes from the Greek *éthnos*, "nation," and *ónoma*, "name," and it commonly means "an ethnic name ascribed to *a* people or group; the proper name by which *a* people or ethnic group *is* called or known" (my emphasis).[13] In modern understanding, an ethnonym carries a particular sense of peoplehood; it refers not just to multiple persons figured as a single entity but to an ethnically based group, one whose members are ethnically the same. In this book, I explore scale-conditioned indigenous alternatives that are expressed through local identity categories, that is, other options of figuring "many" (more accurately, "few-many") people. For this reason, I shift to "we-designations," my gloss for those indigenous categories comparable to *sonta* that, more often than not, are locally used with the first person plural rather than singular possessive (e.g., *nama sonta*, "our own, relatives").

For the anthropologist, choosing a name by which to refer to an indigenous group is far from straightforward. Conventionally understood, naming entails picking the most authentic label of local identity from multiple and confusing names by which a group is known (in the region and the literature), often names insulting to the group. I see a much larger problem here that goes beyond simply choosing this or that name: naming groups is necessary in anthropology's large-scale project. Without proper ethnonyms, a comparative anthropology can hardly be imagined. Without an ethnonym, one cannot write legibly about another people to imaginary generalized readers presumed not to know, or know of, those people. The *proper*-ness of the proper name precisely lies in its effectiveness under these constraints. But naming small indigenous communities can obscure their imaginaries and modes of figuring "many" people, especially in the case of tiny forager communities, each of whose members knows (almost) everyone else—all are close kin.

In researching the literature on the naming of indigenous peoples, I have encountered stories ranging from the banal to the bizarre. These stories are generally related without comment, however, and the names that emerge from them are often perfunctorily applied. For example, Annette Weiner (1988: 11) tells us that the Trobrianders were named after their home islands, which, in turn, were named after Denis de Trobriand, the French first lieutenant of the first European ship to arrive in the islands in 1793. Every anthropology student learns their name, and every time they utter it, they inadvertently invoke the spirit of this Lieutenant Trobriand. Deriving an ethnonym from the name of the territory a people occupy is a reasonable choice in a nationalist era when names of population and territory (and language too) often coincide. When extended to indigenous peoples living in a postimperial and postcolonial world, as this example shows, the strategy can produce absurd results.

Another tantalizing example is a story Signe Howell heard (and confirmed) of how the Malaysian forager-cultivators had acquired the name Chewong by which they are generally known (1984: 12–3). A British game warden was on his way to meet them in the Kraw Game Reserve when he asked a Malay employee in the reserve what they were called. The latter wrongly understood the question to be about the name of the local ranger, his employer, and so provided the ranger's name, Siwang. The "slightly deaf" game warden understood him to say "Che Wong," and so this community has since been known in bureaucratic registers and, through Howell's prolific ethnography, in comparative anthropology. The names by which many indigenous peoples are known were bestowed on them by outsiders and often reflect what outsiders imagined them to be named—or to be.

Stories like the foregoing are legion in ethnographic writing. These stories, in my view, are not simply amusing anecdotes but reflect profound problems in anthropological theory and practice. My special concern is that unthinking use of ethnonyms exports large-scale ontologies into indigenous worlds. Such naming carries a sense of, say, one Chewong, many Chewongs, and Chewong Society—which I abstract as "one, many ones, and many-as-One"—and it conceals options afforded by locals' own scales of perception, especially those of the tiny societies I set out to explore through the case of South Indian foragers known as Nayaka but who call themselves *sonta*, "us, relatives." With an ethnographic focus on *sonta* and Nayaka, I explore what I suggest are two scale-conditioned ontological options of "we-ness," each based on a distinctive mode of "being many" and thus a distinctive mode of "being one." To distinguish between these modes, I turn to discussions of imagined communities.

Modes of "Being Many"

The centrality of the idea of nation in modern life and thought cannot be overemphasized, and one may well ask whether it constrains the study of tiny-scale indigenous communities—their worlds and their futures—as much as (if not more than) the contemporaneous concept of nature, the impetus of so much recent work. The origin of the nation concept and its spread to the point that, today, everyone is presumed to "have" a nationality, alongside a gender and other identity attributes, was the subject of a seminal study by the political historian Benedict Anderson (1991 [1983]) in what he describes as an "anthropological spirit." He approached nationalism in terms of belonging, on a par with kinship and religion, and set its analysis within a comparative framework. His study of the origin and spread of the nation overshadowed the general framework within which he carried it out, and as a result, his notion of imagined community is often used synonymously with its modern mode: the nation. His general framework, though, for my purposes, provides a productive basis for thinking about communities other than as nations. His work offers a trigger, insights, terminology, and a conceptual basis for ethnographically exploring plural modes. Anderson's work has been widely read, and here I explicate what exactly I take from it—for me, his *hau* (return gift) for anthropology's gift to him.

Anderson's approach could be read, in contemporary terms, as ontological and also as scalar. He argued that profound changes during the sixteenth and seventeenth centuries in ontic concepts of time, space, and action "made it possible to 'think' the nation" (1991 [1983]: 28). "Imagining," in his thesis, refers to profound and consequential human action, rather than to superfluous fabrication, a view that resonates with anthropological perspectives.[14] Anderson broadly suggests that *all* communities "are to be distinguished not by their falsity/genuineness, but by the style in which they are imagined" (6). Though he does not formalize the scalar factor in any way, a scalar dimension is present in his work and, once noticed, becomes glaring and profound. A basic condition of the *nation*, as Anderson defines it, is spatial dispersal of members beyond the horizons of personal reach. "Members of even the smallest nation," he writes, "will never know most of their fellow-members, meet them, or even hear of them, yet in the minds of each lives the image of their communion" (6).[15] Germane to the imagination of the nation is the idea of "homogenous empty time," according to which acts are performed at the same time in the same general way by actors who may be largely unaware of one another, a calendrical coincidence linking them through the "remarkable confidence of community in anonymity which is the hallmark of modern nations" (36). Print capitalism, vernacular presses, and colonial, long-distance periphery-center affiliation and pilgrimage were a few of the many factors that complexly combined to generate this new apprehension of space, time, and community. The imagined community that is the nation, then, began to index a new "world of plurals" (32)—*series* of books, newspapers, shops, offices, carriages, and on and on. Moreover, it indexed *series* of persons, each person a stand-alone entity, corporeally and experientially separate from other such entities but groupable with them into categories. Anderson describes this emerging modern mode of solidarity as involving members "who had no necessary reason to know of one another's existence. . . . But they did come to visualize in a general way the existence of thousands and thousands like themselves" (77).

Nation itself is a serial notion; its horizons are humanity at large imagined to be divided into nation-societies. The societies are limited and sovereign, bounded and determinate. Each society is conceived as "a solid community that moves steadily down (or up) history" (26). This imaginary now speaks "with the voice of nature," and not only are communities imagined as entities in time and place, past and future, but their absence has become unimaginable (Billig 1995: 37, 77).

In the second edition of *Imagined Communities*, Anderson expounds on how the colonial map, survey, and museum—essential tools and resources of modern anthropology—consolidated the grammar of national solidarity. In quantifying the members of social-groups-as-categories, the survey reproduced them as series of persons, each having the defining feature of their category (ethnicity, religion, region, etc.). Map-as-logo became a powerful emblem of the nation. The museum produced shared past and tradition. Together, those institutions expressed a style of thinking that illuminated the nation's "warp," a totalizing classificatory grid, and its "weft," "what one could call serialization: the assumption that the world was made up of replicable plurals" (Anderson 1991 [1983]: 184). *Serialization* and *replicable plurals* are, for me, especially productive counterpoints for thinking about the basis of *sonta*, while, terminologically, I shift from Anderson's "styles" to "modes" and from "imagining communities" to modes of "being many." The modern imagination of the nation, and generally of the world, as made up of series of replicable plurals, I suggest, provides a powerful model against which to assess indigenous alternatives.

Ironically, recognizing foraging peoples as "first nations," though it may be politically advantageous to them in a world so imagined, entrenches the nation's ontological and scalar foundations as universal and primordial, denying alternatives.[16] Through my ethnography of *sonta*, I explore scale-conditioned alternative structures of belonging, with special focus on those that subvert the idea of *nation*.

Relatives, the Community of Being

One might think that cultural analysis of a notion like *sonta* would be simple after the resurgence of kinship studies in the late twentieth century, which led to productive means of troubling modern Euro-American understandings of "the person." Anthropologists have cut through the ideologically dominant identification of person with a singular being, the individual. And they have offered alternative concepts in which relations figure prominently: for example, the person as a composite of relations (hence, dividual rather than individual; see Strathern 1992a and Marriott 1976). Of late, analysis has shifted beyond the *singular* being (embodying multiple relations) to, for example, a concept of "mutual person(s)" that recognizes relatives as beings who are "intrinsic to one another's existence" (Sahlins 2013: 2). This model elaborates on the "more than one" modular person. Nevertheless, I argue in this book, understanding belonging in an intimate community of relatives remains beyond the bounds of these concepts, and exploring it takes one through a rough terrain of modern sensibilities of manyness, a landscape of series and replicable plurals disguised in national kinship metaphors.

Nations are imagined through (sometimes gendered) kinship metaphors,[17] and national kinship metaphors serialize kinship entities. For instance, the "children of the nation" (in their "thousands and thousands") are dispersed; they do not personally know each another; they do not all grow up *with* one another as children do in an intimate family. These metaphors also present kinship entities as isolable forms that are linked together in parts-and-whole relations. For example, the father of the nation is a solitary creature (without a wife/mother), and the nation as family, an image so gripping that soldiers die for it, stands in a whole-parts relation to the citizen children who constitute it. The national grammar of replicable plurals seems to have taken over some representations of everyday modern kinship, where one can count relatives, on a par with *persons* and *individuals*, and say, "Sixty-nine relatives came to my wedding." The *relative*, in this view, constitutes a kind of standardized being, many replications of which exist, and if the relative is viewed as constituted by relations, the *relation* is similarly standardized, serialized, and pluralized (cf. Strathern 1995). The locally paramount sense of *sonta*, I show, is easily lost when discussed in English, with its peculiar designations of a singular "relative" and plural "relatives"—the latter suggesting many times "relative" and extending to genealogical "replicable plurals" dispersed across the large-scale world—resonating with the ontological model of the "nation." Through ethnography of *sonta*, and integrating scale/ing issues into analysis, I explore a foragers' option of "being many" relatives, which is about being-*with* different others rather than being *in* society, dispersed from but like others.

"Withness," especially as a state involving more than two, is an elusive condition to pursue within individualist language and ideology and not easy to address within the relational discourse that tries to redress individualist limits. Although I found myself increasingly turning to the idea of "with" instead of "in" as I struggled to bring clarity to my fieldwork materials, I was at a loss to enunciate any analytical grounds for this move, until I stumbled on the work of the philosopher Jean-Luc Nancy. Nancy (1991: 6) goes so far as to proclaim that the sense of *being-with*, of *withness*, lies at the end of philosophy and perhaps logic and grammar. One of the main themes in his prolific and versatile work is how to speak of a "we" or of a plurality without transforming it into a substantial and exclusive entity. He suggests a perspectival shift from "the being of community" (i.e., a community as a single entity, one thing) to "the community of being," in other words, to "the community of existence, and not the essence of community" (1). In *Being Singular Plural* (2000), he analyzes the nature of "being" as "being-with," taking it further than Martin Heidegger and Georg Simmel do. He posits that "being cannot *be* anything but being-with-one-another" (2000: 3). "Existence is *with*," he writes, "otherwise nothing exists" (4). *Being-with* is a pregiven condition, and *being* is abstracted from it; thus, singularity exists *after*, not before, plurality (Simmel, in a similar vein, had argued that being alone is not the absence of social relations but removal from them). No doubt, my understanding and use of these terms reads from the ethnographic context into this philosopher's abstractions more than the other way around, but I use his terms in this book as productive analytical language for investigating foragers' everyday experiences and senses of being *sonta* and the mode of "being many" that *sonta* represents.

Community can be figured as the sum of its individual members, as a hyperexistent entity that is more than that sum, and as, in the relational stance, a composite of relations. Factoring in their scales of imagination, I show (in Nancy's sense) that, for these foragers, the community is an intimate *plurality* of relatives that exists *before* its members, who differentiate their relations and each other within the encompassing plural context of all those "(few-)many" who are present. I show that the sense of *being-with* is as salient in the *sonta* model of plural solidarity as it is obscured in the national imagination. I explore the capacity of *sonta*-grammar to encompass beings of all sorts (both human and nonhuman). Diversity is the touchstone of the *sonta* model, I argue, as much as the nation model's is sameness.

Pluripresence

The presence of relatives few enough for one not to be able to ignore any one of them, few enough for one to be aware of and engage not with one in particular but with all of them at once—a universal everyday experience, I dare say—frames and provides the predominant context for much of what goes on in a tiny forager community. The manyness of relatives who live together in these communities, a manyness of few, evades the modern sociological grammar (deriving from the large-scale) that could be described as "one, two, (indefinite) many-as-One." This grammar impedes analysis of foragers' minuscule societies (and ironically, it mirrors their putative "one, two, many" counting systems).[18] Below, I briefly sketch the roots and uses of this grammar, whose limits I hope to overcome through the introduction of the neologism *pluripresence* and its derived lexicon.

Since the seventeenth century, the singular being has been the touchstone for theorizing society and its emergence. Its pivotal role is captured in one of the best-known and most influential statements on human nature, political philosopher Thomas Hobbes's description of the life of humans in the state of nature as "solitary, poor, nasty, brutish, and short." The last four adjectives have drawn general critical response, not least in the form of the "noble savage" thesis, and the lack of well-being they imply has been questioned in hunter-gatherer scholarship.[19] But the first descriptor is the most startling. The Hobbesian hypothetical scenario of many solitary beings roaming in the wilderness (warring until a social contract vests a sovereign with the right to govern them) is less likely than bands of relatives making their way through a faceless crowd in the business district of a modern city, an early historical version of which probably animated Hobbes's idea and its multiple descendants since. Only strong ideological convictions could lead students of society to overlook their own daily domestic routines with family and relatives—this, and the crucial fact that in modern large-scale society, relatives have increasingly become a tiny proportion of the people inhabiting one's lived and imagined order. There are always many "ones" and still many more "others" within modern, large-scale horizons who have to be anonymized, even some who are proximate. Amid seemingly infinite others, a single being may be and often is held in the center of attention, and others are relegated to the background.[20] Doesn't this experience, reinforced by ideological individualism, resonate with the "singular being" analytical module and, precisely for this reason, ill serve analysis of foragers' communities of relatives? In such communities (and not only them), even if one wanted to, one would not be able to focus on a singular being and push others into the background.

Anthropologists have invested a great deal of labor in trying to break free not so much from the construct of the singular being as from its Western historical-cultural manifestation in the form of the individual. Perhaps the most widely known efforts, though, belong to social psychologists, who, on the basis of experimental evidence, distinguished between predominant models of "self" in two broad cultural areas, the West and Asia, represented, respectively, by the "egocentric self" and the "sociocentric self," the "independent self" and the "interdependent self."[21] Some ethnographers have used these models, and some have offered a range of other concepts as resources for analysis of actual lived experience, whether small-scale or large-scale. Notable examples of recent conceptual coinages include the dividual (reversing indivisibility), the partible being, the fractal being, the composite of substances, the composite of relations, the microcosm of society, and, turning to the image of the cyborg as analogy, a sort of plural singular.[22] Sacrificing conceptual finesse for brevity, it can be said that the mode of "being one" in these sophisticated works at best embodies multiple relations or microcosms of society and at worst conceals the company and presence of other people, including close relatives with whom one lives.

With *pluripresence,* I foreground the salient experience of being-with vivid and proximate others rather than the experience of being one.

Relation figures in an umbrella of current approaches that attempt to go beyond the individualist focus on the singular being (e.g., *relation*alism, *relation*ism, the *relation*al turn). One does not normally think of a *relation* as involving "two" or, more broadly, of two as informing a range of long-standing and cross-disciplinary conceptual emphases on the intersubjective, mutual, reciprocal, dyadic, dialogic, and so on. Likewise, one is not normally aware of two as integral to a host of popular words like *face-to-face, exchange,* and terms generated by adding the prefixes *inter-* and *co-.* However, a modular "two" does lurk behind this lexicon, if only because it is the irreducible, minimal, necessary, and sufficient number of persons these terms apply to and because it is the simplest basis for lucidly explicating concepts that break away from the tether of "one." The phrase *face-to-face,* a popular and sociological currency that is often used to characterize small groups and smallscale societies, illustrates this structuring twoness especially well.

"Face-to-face" is one of a number of bodily metaphors (eye-to-eye, heart-to-heart, mind-to-mind, and the colloquial eyeball-to-eyeball) that, literarily read, foreground two bodies. More than any of the others, *face-toface* has gained a generality of meaning within the large-scale modern context, distinguishing one's direct engagement with another who is physically present from engagement with anonymous passersby and abstract imagined others (James 1996: 23). Its salient sense now derives from this distinction, although it still carries the implicit literal sense of two bodies and, moreover, two bodies that stand not alongside each other, sharing the same view and open to engagement with others, but facing one another, each seeing what the other cannot—what lies behind the other's back—closing onto themselves. Such posture and corporeal experience are rare in a tiny forager community and not as common as might be thought in the ordinary run of normal life elsewhere. *More than two* persons associating with one another is by far a more common daily experience, against which—arising from and subsiding back into it—dyadic face-to-face encounters take place for fleeting moments or sometimes longer (typically in modern public settings and specifically delimited situations like visiting a doctor, paying a vendor, approaching a clerk, etc.).

Relation is one of a host of kinship terms (others include *affinity, reproduction, issue,* and *marriage*) that entered the discourse of logical analysis during the sixteenth and seventeenth centuries. Kinship relations, thus, offered the domain of knowledge concreteness, Strathern (1995) suggests, but equally, the new knowledge of the time gave logical constructs a concreteness that kinship then borrowed. Could this borrowing have included a sense of kinship relations as *dyads*, even though involvement with more than one relative at a time was, and is, an ordinary everyday experience? Kinship terms may appear to describe dyads, but they are predicated on and constitute an intimate community of relatives. A "father" may be individualistically regarded as a particular man or, relationally, as one of the parties distinguished within and constituted by a specific father-child pair. But in ordinary everyday experience, *father* calls to attention relatives beyond the one child (the mother, another child, grandparents, an uncle, etc.) with whom he is often simultaneously engaged. Perhaps, given modernity's large-scale horizons (one's relatives are widely dispersed), partitioned homes (family members have their own spaces), and multiple kinds of relations, both kin and other, one *can* focus on one relation, just as one can on one individual, and push other relations to the background. To disentangle and singularize one kinship relation from others in this way is next to impossible in a tiny forager hamlet. With *pluripresence*, I foreground the salient forager's experience of being-with *more* than one physically present other, being-with several *pluri*present others (an ordinary experience everywhere). To avoid losing sight of this multiplicity through the use of the two-oriented sociological lexicon, I occasionally substitute the prefix *pluri-* for *co-* and *inter-* and reference the hamlet's pluriresidents, their plurirelations, their pluralogues, and so on.

Popularly and sociologically, "many people" can be hypostatized as a hyperexistent entity. John Locke provided an early statement of this idea, describing society as "made up of many particular substances considered together, as counted into one idea, and which so joined are looked on as one" (1900 [1689]: 183). As Strathern suggested for *relation*, perhaps this abstract idea was then applied down to the level of a family of three. This threesome can figure, in the "many-as-One" register, as a supraindividual that, like a single person, is perceived as able to do and say this or that (the family is happy, buys a house, goes on a holiday, etc.). It can figure as three individuals or three dyadic relations or Family (the capital letter denotes the reification)—just as a large, delimited body of people can figure as a multitude of individuals or multiple dyadic relations or Society. The arithmetic ontological jump from two to One drew the attention of turn-of-the-twentieth-century philosopher and sociologist Georg Simmel. He proposed that the dyad is a basic and irreducible form, but once a third person joins the dyad, "societalization" begins. There emerges a completely new figure, a social whole, a "we" that obtains hyperexistent life, independent of the individuals that compose it, characterized by part-to-whole relations.[23]

Anthropologists have elaborated on the "one and many" and "parts-whole" character of the modern Western register of "society,"[24] yet they have paid little attention to subversive options, a contrast to the substantial work that has focused on concepts subverting the modern "individual."[25] Compared with "individualism," the modern idea of "groupism" has only recently been subjected to critique, mainly by sociologists (e.g., see Brubaker and Cooper 2000).[26]

Numerous words in popular and professional use index many-as-One: *band, group, village, collective, corporate kin group,* and *nation* are just a few. In fact, finding a word for an aggregate of people that does *not* evoke many-as-One is difficult. *Community* is a good example to consider because it connotes the idea of shared life (in some contexts standing opposite *society* and in others synonymous with *society*). Its folk etymology (*com + unus:* what is together as one) captures a trace of its sense as "one thing" (Van Den Abbeele 1991). Using *self-* as a prefix for words referencing these plural entities (e.g., speaking of a collective's *self*-identity, *self*-recognition, *self*-designation, etc.) is very common. Through this discursive praxis, these forms of "many" further figure as one entity, as one body, leaving their pluralness and what goes on between their constituents unaccounted for. When peoples are described as Other to the Western self, the "two" and the "many-as-One" modules are combined.

The "many-as-One" idea constrains anthropology right down to the banality of the ethnographer's choice of how to reference his or her study people. The three formal choices that ethnographers face—sometimes forcing recourse to such alternatives as "the people I worked with" and "my friends"—are the same for tiny-scale and large-scale societies: (1) *One,* for example, Nayaka or English society; (2) many ones, for example, Nayaka or English people; and (3) a generalized singular exemplar, for example, a Nayaka or an English person. With *pluripresence,* I index the missing range of few-many, the range between two and an indeterminate many. *Pluripresence* opens conceptual space for exploring subversive concepts of "being many." With Nancy, I use *plurality* as a general term for such "manys,"[27] sometimes also referring to *community of being* (or simply *community*). I often substitute the prefix *we-* or *us-* for *self-* (we-designation is one example) to assist in exploring manyness that is not reified as a self-referential singular entity.

Lastly, *pluripresence* and its adjective form, *pluripresent,* constitute a structuring presence in this study, especially when paired with the notion of community. Pluripresence, here, at once amplifies "copresence," in suggesting the presence of more than two, and it reshapes "imagined community" to encompass a community in which all members are present (as ideal and project, if not always physically) and each engages with all the others. *Pluripresence*, thus, is also a way to emphasize a particular scalar condition that entails the vivid availability of each member of a community to every other member, a situation for which small size is a necessary but not a sufficient condition. The sociological "small-group perspective" shows us that small groups, subsets within large-scale societies, function as crucial mediators between the individual and the social body. These small groups constitute microarenas in which macrostructures are enacted and reproduced.[28] By foragers' standards, these are part-time small groups, segments of large bodies, and they operate with large-scale imagined horizons (they do not necessarily include their members' relatives, their members can belong to other groups and to multiple imagined categories, and members only convene at specified times and for specified periods). The forager pluripresent community, by contrast, engenders and perpetuates many of its own social and cultural structures, relatively free (to the extent of its cultural autonomy) from micro-macro reverberations. *Pluripresence* targets a general human experience and scalar condition, but foragers may show us structures of pluripresence in their most institutionalized and culturally elaborated forms. They can reveal social, cultural, and ontological options of "being few-many" in a way that small groups within multiscalar national societies cannot.

Hunter-Gatherer Ethnography

Hunter-gatherer ethnography is a diverse field, and any brief sketch can only be dismally reductive. But one can broadly discern three anchoring questions, the first dating to the middle of the twentieth century, the second arising since its waning decades, and the third not yet as firmly embedded as the other two, although the earliest studies that can be associated with it date to the first decades of the twentieth century. The first anchor is material and asks, how do people make a living on what the natural environment provides, without recourse to food production, and what are the concomitant organizational, social, and symbolic structures of such a mode of subsistence? The second anchor is cosmological and asks, how do people who hunt and gather perceive their environment and metatheorize the cosmos, and what alternatives to the Western modern binary division between nature and culture, and nonhumans and humans, do they show us? The third anchor is more elusive. Its focus and body of scholarship are not as easily recognized and have not galvanized as much attention. As I develop it in this book, it could be distinguished as social, and it asks, how do people who hunt and gather live *with* diverse others, human and nonhuman; how do they structure, understand, and imagine communities; and what alternatives to the modern world of "imagined communities" do they show us? The focus here is a mode of association, a communal mode—or, as I prefer to call it, a mode of "being many."

The kind of plural life I have preliminarily sketched above has not escaped the attention of students working with communities labeled hunter-gatherers and with other tiny hunter-gatherer-cultivator groups; one simply cannot ignore constant being-with others when one lives among such peoples for a sustained period of time. Beginning in the early twentieth century and continuing today, a stream of eclectic studies has addressed this experience, framing it in terms of varying models, among them, band society, family level of social organization, individualistic society, family-oriented society, autonomy, relatedness, immediacy, conviviality, and recently, accompanied life,[29] and I take up this task here in terms of modes of "being many" and pluripresence. In early evolutionary-oriented models, group size was indexed (e.g., band society was the first rung on a scalar evolutionary ladder). As cultural anthropology became more myopic with respect to scale, size was reduced at best to background information. Hunter-gatherers' modes of being-with others, humans and nonhumans, and their communal modes cannot be persuasively discussed without accounting for scale and without a language of analysis suiting such peoples' "nanoscale" realities. For this reason, I think, the third approach to hunter-gatherer ethnography has not taken off as the other two have. It is my hope that through the (scale-sensitive) concept of pluripresence I can help it do so.

The high-stakes anthropology of hunter-gatherers has undergone many upheavals, not least in relation to what defines a hunter-gatherer people, that is, the criteria of belonging to the class. Obviously, for those who focus on the first anchoring question, subsistence based on hunting and gathering (a gloss for various ways of procuring wild resources that would include, e.g., collecting honey) is as exclusive a defining criterion as possible for membership, despite the continuous variability of the ethnographic field. Strictly limiting attention to groups who *only* hunt and gather is not of the essence for those who pursue the other anchoring questions. Participants in the constitutional *Man the Hunter* symposium decided "to consider as hunters all cases presented" (Lee and DeVore 1968: 4), a principle that Robert Kelly also follows in his well-known textbook *The Foraging Spectrum* (1995: 3). I generally endorse this approach. Eschewing adherence to strict criteria, this approach, remarkably, resonates with the logic underscoring my interlocutors' notion of *sonta*—an unbounded community performed through each member's constant relating to (almost all) the others.

VISITING FORAGER WORLDS: ETHNOGRAPHIC JOURNEY

Kungan and His Relatives: South Asian Foragers

In informal settings, ethnographers sometimes refer to the people they have studied as "my people." This phrase can elicit both smiles at the implied affection and critiques of the claim of possession. In an ironic twist, "my people" more closely reflects Kungan and his relatives' sense of themselves as *sonta* than may be realized, certainly more than any ethnonym does. "My people" only connotes a claiming of possession under the presupposition that *a* group of "people" constitutes an entity *in* the world that the ethnographer can claim as "his" or "her" own. "My people" can be understood in another way, echoing the mode of living plurally that this book explores. In the local vogue, "my people" refers to those with whom I lived, people in their relatedness with me, a relatedness forged during fieldwork. "My people," in this local vein, is an emergent and performed entity, born of shared lives during fieldwork. Usefully, it identifies the subjects of this ethnography neither as *all* imagined Nayaka nor as Nayaka at all times but simply as those I lived *with* and have since kept in touch with. This said, "my people" is an awkward phrase that may be misunderstood, and those whom I so designate, in fact, never used the first person possessive singular but always the plural, *nama sonta*, "us, our relatives." In tune with my pragmatic multiscaled approach, I introduce the people I worked with in pluripresent terms and, then, in terms of the imagined communities they can be associated with.

My analysis moves from the core of relatives with whom I lived outward to their horizons. For a year, I shared a hut with the family of the man I call Kungan. This hut stood in a small forest clearing on the steep side of a gorge that runs from the Wynaad plateau west to the Kerala Plains. During my fieldwork, I focused my attention on this hamlet and four even tinier hamlets, each with two to three huts. The dwellers of these five hamlets, all relatives of Kungan and of one another, constantly visited each other, the journey between hamlets entailing a three- to six-hour walk through the forest. Beyond this core of relatives, my fieldwork extended to other kin who visited the five hamlets and were visited by their residents less frequently. They lived in two "satellite" hamlets at the edges of the local world, within a day's walk of the core; despite their marginal location, they played an important role in reproducing and scaling the core study group (see chapter 3). Relatives living beyond the immediate horizons of those two hamlets received only sporadic mention and had little presence, if any, in the local lived experience and imaginary at the time of my study.

My research also encompassed nonhumans present in the area and migrants who encroached on nearby forestland—all of those whom Kungan and his relatives constantly engaged with and situationally perceived as "our own" (*sonta*). The migrants were wage laborers on a plantation established in the area in the late nineteenth century. It originally produced rubber and expanded to coffee production in the twentieth century (see more in Bird 1983b; Bird-David 1992b). Two plantations devoted to the cultivation of tea also bordered on the local world, but the workers on those properties had few dealings with Kungan and his relatives.

In terms of broad imagined categories, Kungan and his relatives could be introduced as a South Indian people, giving them an easily recognized "address" in comparative anthropology. I suspect, though, that this tag would more likely bring to mind the 250 million inhabitants of South India than the tiny and encapsulated minorities among them. Several categories that more narrowly apply and are used in India include "tribal people" and, increasingly, *adivasi* (original inhabitants). The latter is an umbrella term for a heterogeneous set of ethnic and tribal groups, officially estimated at less than 10 percent of the national population in the 2011 Census of India.[30] Within this category, a very small minority are recognized by the Government of India as Particularly Vulnerable Tribal Groups, or PTGs (this designation replaces the earlier Primitive Tribal Groups). PTGs include communities specified as hunting, food-gathering, and (a few) agricultural people deemed in need of special development programs. Officially recognized as Kattunayaka (*katu* means forest), Kungan and his relatives are a nationally certified PTG.

Downscaling to the district level, I could introduce Kungan and his relatives as a "Nilgiri people," a less immediately recognizable "address" in comparative anthropology but one that places them within a rich regional scholarship.[31] Nilgiris is the name of both a political district in Tamil Nadu and a geographical region in that state and adjacent parts of Kerala. Its roughly 2,500 square kilometers lie mainly in the Western Ghats mountains, second in elevation only to the Himalayas in the subcontinent. It is populated by diverse tribal peoples, who lived there in relative isolation until British colonization started in the 1820s, followed by massive in-migration of people of various castes and religions from the surrounding plains. Cultivator and pastoralist tribal people lived at higher elevations (including the Toda, famously studied by W. H. R. Rivers). On the lower slopes, a profusion of tiny dispersed forest communities have for two hundred years evaded the unceasing efforts of ethnographers and other identity experts—such as colonial and contemporary administrators—to draw clear ethnic divisions between them and to define and identify them by ethnonyms (see Bird 1987; Bird-David 1989). In Tamil Nadu, the Jenu Kurumba have been studied by Ulrich Demmer and P. K. Misra; in Kerala, P. R. G. Mathur, Ananda Bhanu, Seeta Kakkoth, and Anita Varghese have undertaken ethnographic investigations among the Cholla-Nayaka, and Daniel Naveh, Noa Lavi, and I have worked with those named Nayaka (and recognized by the Indian government as Kattunayaka). These ethnonyms may give the appearance of distinct ethnic groups, but whether any per-ceived distinctions go back more than few decades is questionable. These ethnonyms have become everyday currency in marginal areas of the Nilgiris since government organizations and NGOs began working there in the 1980s, so much so that some in these communities now state as their ethnic affiliation whatever appears on their government ration cards (Naveh 2007: 31). These forest groups constitute a tiny fraction of the three-quarters of a million people now living in the Nilgiris (2011 Census of India). They are little-known, exotic, tiny minorities, such that ethnog-raphers working with the larger upper Nilgiri groups can hardly appreciate the everyday banal fieldwork experience and related theoretical concerns entailed in their study. Ethnographers who work with tiny-scale foraging people in other faraway corners of the world, however, can easily relate to those experiences and concerns.

For this reason, in some of my publications I have engaged with regional issues.[32] The bulk of my work, however, has addressed broader issues of hunter-gatherer scholarship. The latter remains the main framework of this study, recent recognition of "South Asian foragers" as a major regional class being a further reason for this framing. South Asian foragers are now regarded as a major subdivision of the world's hunter-gatherers (Fortier 2009a).[33] Peter Gardner (2013) has estimated that they constitute no less than 25 percent of the world's present-day and recent hunter-gatherers (five times as many as in North America and the circumpolar region com-bined, over four times as many as in Australia, and nearly three times as many as in Africa).[34] Few of the more than forty listed South Asian forager groups have been studied today "to current standards" (Fortier 2009a). Those living in South India include Paliyan (studied by Gardner and, more recently, Christer Norström) and Hill Pandaram (studied by Brian Morris) in addition to the above-mentioned Nilgiris groups. South Asian foragers are now semiotically assembled as an emergent entity with an analytically promising presence in comparative anthropology. That does not, however, change the fact that the groups subsumed by this entity are tiny and are widely dispersed across the vast Indian subcontinent.

To these comparative categories, I add a new one dictated by my concerns: "peoples without ethnonyms," indigenous tiny communities who call themselves by terms of kinship and shared humanity. This is an ad hoc working category for investigating modes of "being many" at the tiny end of scaling. I also call these peoples pluripresent communities. Those considered hunter-gatherers belong to this category—but this category does not encompass all hunter-gatherers or only hunter-gatherers.

Late Ethnography

This book is based on long-term study that began with fieldwork in 1978–79 and continued with visits in 1989, 2001, and (briefly) 2012. It has benefited, furthermore, from the fieldwork of my former students, Daniel Naveh and Noa Lavi, ongoing since 2003.[35] This longitudinal study has produced a series of articles, but this is the first full ethnography.

I have chosen to offer in this book what may be termed a "late ethnography," one that looks at my early field experiences but with current anthropological sensibilities. A long-term perspective affords the opportunity to follow up on changes in the field since the baseline study, to examine those changes from the standpoint of the initial observations. But it also permits the development of new readings of the baseline time, taking advantage of ethnographic and theoretical progress in anthropology and using knowledge of subsequent changes in the field setting to understand the baseline observations (the closest equivalent an ethnographer can have to the historian's *longue durée*). I have chosen the latter course.[36]

I find it remarkable how substantially anthropological approaches to hunter-gatherers have changed during the life span of the people I have known personally. Those changes have been far more profound than the changes Kungan and his relatives have undergone, without slighting their experiences in any way. When Kungan's father was born (in the late nineteenth century), anthropologists approached people like him as savages and, in even less accommodating terms, as creatures of nature. When Kungan was growing up (in the early mid-twentieth century), his community's lifeways were explained as cultural-ecological and evolutionary adaptations to nature. By the time Kungan had raised his children (in the late mid-twentieth century), people like him had begun to excite the anthropological imagination as rare populations whose lives could shed light on human evolution and human nature. Now, as his children raise his grandchildren, in the very same forest clearing in which I first met him, students are approaching hunter-gatherers with a view to understanding alternatives to the modern Western nature-culture dualist ontology. In this book, I look to them to provide alternatives to national visions of "being many."

Early data from long-term studies are rarely reanalyzed in a rapidly changing world, and leaving them to early theoretical terms in rapidly changing scholarship is a great loss. What is said of late love perhaps also applies to late ethnography: the experience may be less vivid, but one perhaps is more skilled and knows what he or she is doing. I choose to exploit a rare vantage point afforded by my late-stage ethnography: to reexplore local life at the time of my first study armed with an awareness of changes since then and with new theoretical perspectives. I take this opportunity to revisit precious early fieldwork material (most not previously published), using what the ethnographic method with its ethos of immersion in the field so generously affords: field notes, head notes, and I would add, body notes (i.e., embodied understandings). The latter are especially important in trying to evoke what tiny-scale living entails. The late 1970s, then, provide the temporal focus of this ethnography, with insights gained during the thirty-odd years since incorporated into the analysis as and when they are helpful.

In this book, I explore the plural life of a tiny South Indian forager community a decade before development and government organizations would start working in the area, two decades before they would reach these particular forest people, and a further decade yet before missionaries would reach one of their hamlets. I emphasize, however, that the notion of *sonta* on which I dwell does not belong to the past. People I first met in 1978 who are still alive, and the children of the people I knew then, now move between traditional forest huts and brick-and-mortar houses built for them at the turn of the new millennium by the government and NGOs.[37] But *sonta* is still a powerful local framework within people's increasingly complex local lives. Kungan's descendants still we-imagine themselves as *sonta* at the same time as they increasingly identify themselves as Kattunayaka within the bustling regional "development" scene and the national politics of *adivasi* rights (see chapter 7).

On Reading This Book

Ethnography of a foraging people may hold broad interest, theoretically and popularly. I have therefore worked to make this book accessible to a broad interdisciplinary readership and others interested in the issues I consider. Writing ethnography is generally a complex business, and writing this ethnography has offered its own particular challenges. My goal is to produce a text about a core experience for Kungan and his relatives, who themselves have no tradition of writing or even of formal oral instruction. Theirs is an experience that is grown into and shared, and my job is to communicate it intelligibly to strangers who read about it, whether in a library or a coffee shop, on an airplane or at home, in Cambridge, New York, New Delhi, or Udhagamandalam. The challenges I face are those tackled by all ethnographers, not just those of tiny indigenous communities. But they are exceptionally complicated in the present case. I write in English, the grammatical structure and vocabulary of which inherently carry distinctive senses of self, pluralities, and the world as well as a distinctive perspectival scale. Paradoxically, I attempt to explore the "we" of those I must construct as "they," and I must use ethnonyms to explore plural forms that ethnonyms conceal.

My project may seem subversive, not to mention counterintuitive in the contemporary historical moment, when tiny groups struggle for their place in national and international arenas. My position might be wrongly read as critiquing all use of ethnonyms and other nationalistic conventions that overshadow local worlds—and this by an ethnographer who has already built herself a career precisely by using such conventions and who uses them in this book! I can categorically state that I do not envision ethnography without such devices. I simply argue that, now and then, it is crucial to suspend their use to enable critical reflection on and inquiry into other imaginaries of plural life. If we unreflectively persist in their use and *remain unaware of their nature,* they can, like Trojan horses, surreptitiously introduce a myriad of biases into our research, biases that defeat one of anthropology's most basic endeavors: exploring the full range of options for living plurally, including, and perhaps especially, those of tiny forager societies who inspire so much modern social thought and imagination. It is my hope that my elucidation of Kungan and his relatives' kinship model of communal membership will be of practical use to forager and other tiny communities in India, as they struggle within the complex national politics of distributive justice. I am aware of using new terms of analysis, which, initially unfamiliar, might burden readers and even increase the risk that they "see" the foragers' plural life as exotic and unique, the opposite of what I intend. I justify my choices by reference to mid-twentieth-century economic anthropologists who questioned studying precapitalist economies in a language that had developed in the capitalist market era. The alternatives they explored eventually turned out to aid economic study of pockets and interstices within capitalist economies.[38] I am convinced that studies of foragers' prenationalist forms of plural life could have similarly broad relevance.

In addressing the ethnonym as a subject of ethnographic inquiry, I have tried to find a way to avoid tagging my study group with a name devised by outsiders—or using locals' we-designation as an ethnonym, which could lead to such absurdities as imagining a government official greeting them as Sonta (Our Own, Relatives). Various aborted attempts to resolve this predicament led me finally to adapt a feature of local praxis: Generally, in each analytical segment (chapter or section), I use the main protagonist's personal name as an anchor (e.g., Bomi) and refer to others in the community as that person's relatives (thus, Bomi and her relatives; I default at times to "Kungan and his relatives" in tribute to Kungan's key position in this study, doing so even when referring to the period after his death). In another adaptation of local praxis (subject to considerations of legibility), I refer to secondary protagonists in terms of their relations to the main one: for example, Bomi's husband, Bomi's sister-in-law, Bomi's older brother, and so on. Using personal names has its downside because Kungan and his relatives predominantly address and refer to each other by kinship terms, as many other forager people do (like ethnonyms, personal names are bestowed on them by outsiders and individualize them in a way they themselves do not; see Downscale 2).[39] My strategy allows me to minimize using personal names that identify foragers as separate individuals when they figure themselves as kin. I primarily refer to life as I observed it in the late 1970s. But because I also want to animate that life and not suggest that what I describe is gone, I use both the present and the past tense, shifting between them for best effect. Local words are spelled not phonetically but as they sound to me. The orthography should be regarded cautiously. A mixture of major Dravidian languages is spoken in this border area— Kannada, Malayalam, and Tamil—and the local dialect changes dynamically from place to place and over time, reflecting ongoing developments and movements of people.[40] Brief translations provided in parentheses are sometimes prefixed by the ~ sign to caution against their being accepted as exact meanings. The translations in these cases serve simply as invitations to explore native senses partly by critically reflecting on culturally particular meanings of certain English terms. In previous publications, I have referred to my study area as the Gir valley (a fictive name). As I generally try in this book to avoid using externally imposed appellations that overshadow local senses, I have discarded that name here. Instead, I use "the Gorge," which gives a better physical sense than "valley" of the landform where Kungan and his relatives live.

Plan of the Book

I have organized the chapters in a way that I hope helps theory and ethnography hunters easily find their way through the book. Each chapter begins with a presentation of the theoretical, topical, or comparative issues illuminated by that chapter's ethnography. The ethnography is organized along an axis that extends from the most local, intimate level to that of the state and imagined communities. For the most part, the ethnography elaborates on everyday life, focusing on the concreteness in which ontologies dwell.

Chapter 1 critically engages the scale-blind extension of the modern "dwelling-in-the-world" perspective into hunter-gatherer studies. Via literature on the formative effect of homes and houses on dwellers' relations and ideas, it ethnographically examines the minuscule forager hamlet as the physical setting and the mind setting of everyday life, paying particular attention to the vernacular architecture of the huts, domestic routines and (dis)order, material possessions, and the semantics of dwelling(s). Chapter 2 expands the viewpoint to the Gorge's five-hamlet community. Questioning insensitivity to local horizons of imagination in anthropological discussions of hunter-gatherers' mobility, nomadism, and travel, it ethnographically trains attention on the inter-hamlet visiting that leads to everyone at one time or another living with everyone else and on full community attendance at any member's birth and death. Chapter 3 questions the dyadic and scalar logic of the idea that sibling-exchange marriage between groups underwrote the development of society and critiques cultural anthropology's general neglect of sibling ties. As it provides ethnography of residential cores of intermarried siblings and their children, the chapter examines the spousal scarcity and marital strategies that generate such interrelated cores, relations between siblings and in-laws, and sib-based forms of communal organizational structures. Chapter 4 highlights scalar blindness underlying discussions of hunter-gatherer gender and child-care practices that inform evolutionary scholarship. Addressing the distortive effect of approaching tiny-scale forager communities of relatives through gendered (men-women) and child-focused (adults-children) analytical categories, it ethnographically explores locals' senses of conjugal and parent-children nexuses through ritual, foraging pursuits, stories of pairing up, and understandings of growing up. Chapter 5 broadens the analytical lens to include nonhuman kin. It critically considers scale-blind depictions of animistic (and perspectivist) ontologies, of indigenous worlds of serialized human and nonhuman persons, relations, societies, and even natures. It reveals another ontological option, a forager's option: a heterogeneous community of being. Through ethnography of locals' "big animistic visit," myth, and interspecies kinship, it delineates being-with instead of being-like as a basis of belonging. Chapter 6 examines the edges of *sonta*. Alluding to scalar issues in discussion of foragers' relations with others, boundaries, and Othering versus

Us-ing, it offers ethnography of out-marriages, relations with migrant neighbors, and migrants' and foragers' respective imaginations of each other. Lastly, chapter 7 considers the effects of scale-blind multiculturalist distributive justice policy in India. Through ethnography of citizens' claims to state recognition as Kattunayaka, it explores the political fallout from not distinguishing between modes of "being many" and it compares pluripresent and imagined community ideals as expressed in locals' we-designation and the state's ethnonymic praxis. Five interludes labeled "Downscales" are interspersed among the chapters; each presents a vignette related to the scalar distortion—or outright scalar concealment—that occurs in different aspects of the translation of an ethnographer's fieldwork experience into text. These interludes serve as reminders of how anthropologists' assumptions about themselves and their practice can lead them to make unwarranted large-scale-biased assumptions about the people they study.

Downscale 1

Maps of Home

A locational map is a standard component of an ethnography. With an arrow pointing to the field site, a map of India provides instant recognition of where on the globe Kungan and his relatives live, recognition dependent on readers' own spatial imaginations and involving colossal scalar distortion of Kungan's world (see map 1). A centimeter on this small-scale map (1:4,400,000) represents forty-four kilometers and marks a distance greater than any Kungan normally traveled to visit relatives (or for any other purpose). Acknowledging such spatial disconnects, ethnographies of tiny forager-cultivator communities routinely include a map of the local region in which the field site is located, with the country reduced to an inset, as in map 2. Even though the perspective is considerably larger (1:126,720), the scalar distortion remains enormous: Kungan's hamlet and those of his relatives, if realistically marked on this map, would appear as closely spaced dots, and the forest between and surrounding them—their world, their *sime* (home area)—would be indiscernible.

Kungan and his relatives' horizons of concern did not extend far beyond their *sime* in the late 1970s (well before significant changes in the 2000s; see chapter 7). This is not to say that these foragers were isolated—a common Western fantasy that endows those beyond the reach of modern explorations and knowledge with an untouched pristineness. From time to time, outsiders passed through their *sime* (e.g., forest traders, surveyors, and smugglers), and some even settled there permanently or temporarily (plantation laborers, timber workers, a plantation manager, an ethnographer). Kungan and his relatives engaged with these people, attentive to their presence and conduct (see chapter 6), but where these outsiders came from did not matter to them. Their interest in them was no different from the interest they displayed in any other, more familiar, presence in their

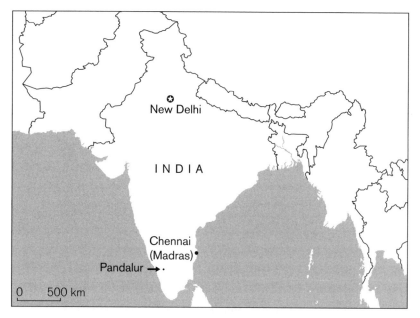

MAP 1. Field site location in India

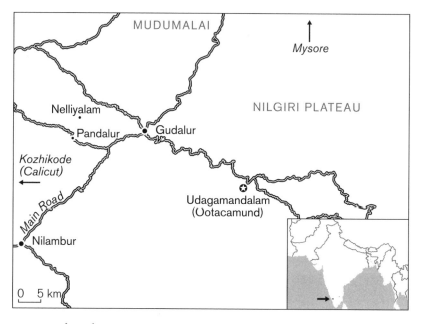

MAP 2. The Nilgiri region

sime. Topographically their *sime* was a steep-sided gorge (this topography provides the name by which I refer to the locality throughout this volume). The Gorge was the hub of Kungan and his kin's everyday lived world, the focus of their daily experience, where they shared the repetitive mundane, leisure and trouble, boredom and excitement with those who were pluripresent with them.

My anthropological project in relation to the Gorge's forager people included amassing maps of differing scales and levels of detail required by their makers for their own varying purposes. One of my maps was a small-scale road map, which helped me navigate my way through India (and, in fact, all the way to India from Cambridge, as I traveled with my partner to my field site by car, one of the last vehicles to caravan the overland route from Europe to Southeast Asia before troubles broke out in Iran and Afghanistan). In Chennai (Madras), I obtained two larger-scale government maps, one of the Nilgiris district (1:126,720) and the other of the Gudalur taluk (1:63,360), both produced in colonial times (in 1907 and 1919, respectively). The title of the first one, *Nilgiri District Map for the Use of Touring Officers*, leaves no doubt about its original purpose: to help orient colonial administrators foreign to the region during their tour of duty there. The more recent map shows key locations depicted on that earlier map, including the capital of the Nilgiris district, Udhagamandalam (aka Ootacamund or "Ooty"), the road leading from it to the taluk capital of Gudalur (about 50 kilometers away), and the road going on to Calicut through Pandalur (another 20 kilometers or so), one of many market stations that sprang up along that road in colonial times. What it does not and cannot show is the narrow, steep "white" route, hardly noticeable to drivers, that diverges from this road to wind through a tea plantation and then through a primeval forest down the side of one of the gorges running eastward to the Kerala Plains. This is the road that leads to the out-of-the-way rubber-and-coffee plantation in whose vicinity Kungan and his relatives live. In a small municipal archive in Ooty, I chanced to find a rare series of large-scale land-use maps (nine large sheets, undated, 1:7,920) that marked state-recognized boundaries between forest and plantation estates in the Nilgiri-Wynaad area. One of those sheets actually showed the "white" route, yet even this large-scale map failed to depict the steep footpath that branched off from it and by which one reached the cluster of half a dozen huts that constituted Kungan's home—and my home during fieldwork. (Their *sime* went completely unmarked on that map.)

That hamlet was the center of Kungan's everyday world; for the most part, he lived there and in other hamlets in the Gorge throughout his life.

He sometimes walked up to Pandalur; once he visited Gudalur; he had never been to Ooty. Pandalur lay within his everyday vivid imagination, Gudalur perhaps figured occasionally at the horizons of his concerns, and Ooty did not exist for him. He lived his rich life within the walking horizons of his hamlet, his home base periodically shifting somewhat but remaining within the same general area of the Gorge. He visited and stayed with relatives in even tinier clusters of huts than his own, a few of them living just up the hillside from him, a few across the Gorge on the facing hillside, and a few farther down the valley as it narrowed and descended to the Kerala Plains. The proximate horizons of these hamlets and the expanse between them constituted his and his relatives' *sime.*

Ethnographers are expected to provide the audiences for their work with detailed maps of their field sites, so toward the end of my fieldwork, I employed Mr. Mohandes, a surveyor from a little township near Gudalur, to help me with this requirement. Mr. Mohandes walked the steep, narrow footpath through the forest down to Kungan's hamlet and, with me and Kungan at his side, paced off the dimensions of the huts and the distances between them and roughly estimated the locations of and the distances to the other hamlets. Back in his hometown, in his shabby one-room office, Mohandes drew sketches of the five hamlets and a rough map showing their locations in the forest, translating the distances he had paced off into metric data that he recorded on a conventional modern representation of the area.

Kungan did not have nor did he need a map of this area, either on paper or as a mental template. He was unable to specify his location abstractly, in terms of any independent system of coordinates. He focused, in Tim Ingold's words, on places that "do not have locations but histories" (2000: 219). I found that, while I lived with him and his people, I did not need maps either, as I moved with them through their *sime,* eventually growing intimately familiar with it myself. The maps that I had collected remained unused and stored away during my fieldwork, and only on my return to university in England did I hang some of them on the wall facing my desk (including Mohandes's sketches on which map 3 and map 4 are based). Most of my fellow students did the same in those pre–Google Earth days, the maps guiding our recollections and imaginations of the areas we thought of daily as we wrote our theses. Today's digital maps and air photographs allow us to zoom in and out of almost any area, shifting up and down scales and back and forth between views, yet still prioritizing the outsider's standpoint according to present-day representational conventions, oblivious to the local subjective engaged viewpoint.

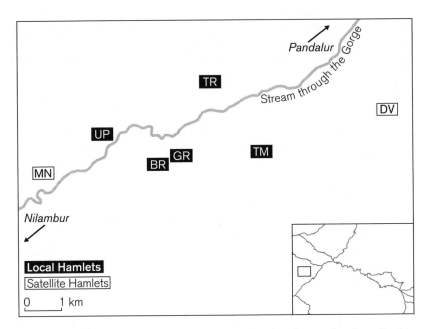

MAP 3. The Gorge's hamlets and satellite hamlets (based on Mohandes's sketch)

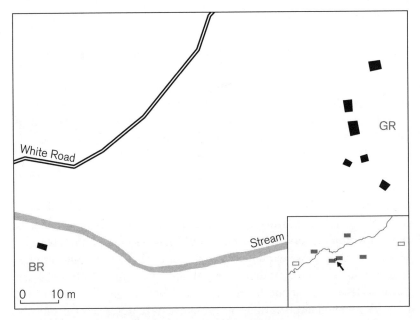

MAP 4. GR and BR huts (based on Mohandes's sketch)

All the representational renderings demarcate spaces, territories, and locations that Kungan and his relatives would be described as living in: *in* India, *in* Tamil Nadu, *in* the Nilgiris, *in* the Gorge, *in* the forest, *in* a hamlet. The seemingly innocent preposition *in* is a tricky Trojan horse that sneaks into Kungan's world a sense of space and society, and of nature too, as abstract containers *in* which individuals live (and which allow them to be imagined from afar). Kungan and his relatives' cultural energies, I argue, were invested not so much in *where* they lived as in those *with whom* they lived (which partly explains the scale of their horizons). Beginning their study by "locating" their huts on small-scale national and regional maps, or even on huge-scale home-produced ones, subjects these foragers to perspectives on the world that are embodied by such means, and it can inhibit understanding their lifeworld as they experienced it. In this ethnography, I set aside modern cartographic conventions and focus first on Kungan's hamlet, the hub of his *sime.*

Two of GR hamlet's six huts. Photographed by the author (1978–79).

1. At Home

Setting and Mind Setting

Kungan awakens every day in the small forest clearing that overlooks the gorge, his eyes opening to the soft morning sunlight. The six closely spaced huts (which Mohandes has measured by pacing them off and then drawn to scale; see Downscale 1) surround him, standing on three small terraces extending down the hillside, the green of the forest stretching all around them. The huts are made of bamboo and grass. On their walls hang small sections of bamboo containing honey hives. Back carriers made of bamboo hang from the roof beams. Kungan is an early riser, and other people are still asleep, lying on the ground beside dying hearth fires, two, three, four, sometimes even five bodies cuddling together on mats made of forest grass or rough jute sack. Bamboo containers and carrying baskets and metal axes and pots are scattered around them. Dogs laze beside them. Kungan arises from the mat he shares with his wife and two younger children. Then they too rise, followed by all the others, to start another day.

This description could be taken as what in some ethnographies is called the "setting" or "background." It could be seen as a literary device to convey a sense of the research site, a static backdrop for the presumably more meaningful theoretical concerns to come. Although, for readers this scene may seem to merely set the analytical stage, for the hamlet's dwellers, who wake to it day after day, it is at once a physical setting and a *mind* setting. It is the focal site of what Tim Ingold (2000) would describe as their dwelling-in-the-world, even as he largely dwells on the world at large, that is, the environment. In this chapter, I delve into and exploit this scene to provide a sense of the local experience of plural life and its scalar context. I probe it for local dimensions of being-*with* others in a tiny hamlet.

. . .

Hunter-gatherer dwellings have previously drawn little interest from cultural anthropologists, with a few tangential exceptions.[1] Their dwellings have hardly been seen as buildings: in popular views and in certain scholarly traditions, hunter-gatherers are distinctive precisely because they do *not* interfere with their environment and do *not* transform it into a "built" one. Peter Wilson (1988) went so far as to suggest that the significant turning point in human social evolution was when people began to live in houses. In doing so, he distinguished, in effect, between hunter-gatherers, who do not have architecture, and other societies, who do. Early twentieth-century descriptions, and even some today, help to perpetuate this impression, if only inadvertently, through the terms used to describe hunter-gatherer dwellings. For example, *shelter* (sometimes in specific combinations, such as *leaf shelter, rock shelter,* etc.) is a broad term that is also sometimes used in conjunction with animals, and *hut* and *camp* are words commonly associated today with outdoor recreation and the military, taking their meaning from the opposition between the interior of the house and the outdoors. This language obscures the fact that these dwellings are *home* for their dwellers and that, even though a structure is temporary, it embodies a permanent way of dwelling for those who occupy it.

Martin Heidegger's (1971) position on the relation between "dwelling" and "building" is helpful here. Building and *then* dwelling in a structure is a common practical experience. Broadly approaching dwelling as a way of being-in-the-world, Heidegger reverses that order (notably, shifting scales) and suggests that "we do not dwell because we build, but we build and have built because we are dwellers. . . . *Only if we are capable of dwelling, only then can we build*" (146, 148). In a widely read essay, Ingold (2000: 172–88) applied this perspective to hunter-gatherer huts, working from a general ecological-anthropological approach and focusing on an archetypal hut as the object of reflection. With Ingold, I pay attention in my ethnographic analysis to Kungan and his relatives' forms of building as arising "within the current of their involved activity, in the specific relational contexts of their practical engagement with their surroundings" (186). I move on from Ingold by shifting the analytical gaze to the forager community and an actual hamlet comprising several huts. With Jean-Luc Nancy (2000: 3), I maintain that being cannot be anything but being-with, and so dwelling cannot be anything but dwelling-with others. For the foragers I know well, those others are close relatives with whom they share a hamlet. The title of Ingold's influential essay, "Building, Dwelling, Living: How Animals and People Make Themselves at Home in the World," expresses a common focus on "people" (in a generalized, large-scaled sense) as they make themselves at home in the *world* (again, generalized and large-scaled), and his analytical focus is the (generic, singularized) hunter-gatherer "hut." Downscaling Ingold's agenda, and opening it to plurirelational everyday life, in this chapter, I zoom in on the huts of a tiny hunter-gatherer community of relatives and look at, in Ingold's words, "building . . . circumscribed within dwelling . . . [rather than] dwelling circumscribed within building" (2000: 185).

My ethnographic study joins other studies that exploit the rich analytical potential of dwellings (though heretofore not of foragers' dwellings).[2] Pierre Bourdieu's oft-cited study (1973 [1971], based on his 1960s work in Algeria) showing that the Kabyle house concretizes symbolic schemata and cultural values is a foundational example of this focus. In his later work, Bourdieu (1977) pointed to the house as part of the objective reality within which its dwellers grow up and acquire their taken-for-granted and often unconscious habits of acting in the world and thinking about it. This idea was amplified by, among others, Janet Carsten and Stephen Hugh-Jones, who suggested that "house, body, and mind are in continuous interaction, the physical structure, furnishings, social conventions and mental images of the house at once enabling, moulding, informing and constraining the activities and ideas which unfold within its bounds" (1995: 2).

Valentine Daniel (1984: chapter 3) conducted a detailed study of the construction of houses in rural Tamil Nadu villages as part of his ethnographic exploration of the Tamil sense of personhood. His study provides an instructive comparative case for my ethnography, which concerns foragers living at the forested edges of Tamil Nadu. The village Daniel worked in had a population of over two thousand persons (56) and so was nearly a hundred times the size of Kungan's hamlet, a relevant scalar disparity to bear in mind. The Tamil village house, he shows, is regarded as a person and, like a person, is perceived to be composed of various substances. Its construction involves a great deal of ritual and divination, the goal of which is to achieve the best fit between the house and its owner. A priest accompanies and supervises the building of a house in all its details. Horoscopes are consulted to ensure that key stages take place on auspicious days. Houses are conceived and born, and their formative years determine their *kunam* (quality, disposition). They have good and bad times. They are self-aware. They have feelings, for example, fearing to be alone. The Tamil house and person, Daniel argues, are in a metonymic relation. The house is not just metaphorically depicted as a person but tangibly presents the Tamil sense of person, not as individual but as dividual (in McKim Marriott's [1976] sense, elaborated by Marilyn Strathern [1988]). Kungan and his relatives' senses of dwelling(s), I show, stand in stark contrast to rural Tamil house culture, expressing the fundamental importance, for them, of pluripresent relatives living together.

In this chapter, I extend this general perspective to hunter-gatherer dwellings, not least to the huts glimpsed above, which Kungan and his relatives prefer, even though they have the know-how and skills to build more solid structures. The issue came into sharp focus for me in 2001, when I visited a school for tribal children in the region run by an internationally supported local development organization. A teacher proudly showed me a display that the children had made, a miniature model of huts built of twigs and grass, each with an outside fireplace marked by small stones. I assumed the display illustrated a traditional hamlet, like the one I had called home in 1978–79, but I was corrected by a sixth grader who, prompted by the teacher, explained to me in simple English that "this is how early man lived." Development organizations had, by then, demolished some of the bamboo and grass huts in the Gorge's hamlets and, in their stead, constructed brick and mortar "permanent" houses for the foragers (see Lavi and Bird-David 2014). The "permanent" houses, however, turned out to be temporary. They were unsuited to the weather and to local needs. Within a short time, some of them were abandoned, annexes made of traditional materials were added to others, and new huts were being built in the old style (see Bird-David 2009; Lavi and Bird-David 2014). Why did Kungan and his relatives continue to build their traditional huts? What did these dwellings reflect about their dwellers' senses of themselves and their world?

At the same time, can one say anything meaningful about dwellings that are small and simple? Huts that can be built in less than a day? Dwellings with no inner divisions, fixtures, or decorations? Huts that continually change? These questions invite further attention to taken-for-granted everyday activities such as sleeping (which, as Carol Worthman and Melissa Melby [2002] have noted, accounts for a third of a person's life and has remained largely overlooked by ethnographers, not least those who study hunter-gatherers). In this chapter, I examine dwelling(s) as process and architectural form. I examine a range of everyday activities and arrangements among Kungan and his relatives as they unfold and are manifested in and around their dwellings, including how huts are constructed, their lack of solidity and inner partitions, their constantly changing layout, where and how belongings are stored and the significance attributed to them, and above all, where, how, and, especially *with whom* Kungan and his relatives sleep, sit, eat, and share other quotidian activities in the home place. I turn, then, to the hamlet in which Kungan awakens. . . .

One of TR hamlet's two huts. Photographed by the author (1978–79).

DWELLING WITH

They lived in a small hamlet of bamboo and grass huts (Take 1)

In the modern evolutionary script, small-scale societies are associated with homogeneity, while diversity and complexity are linked with growing scale (Strathern 1992a: 22). However, the *diversity* of the huts in Kungan's hamlet was striking, as it was in other hamlets I visited.

One could observe huts with roofs extending beyond the walls, creating large shaded spaces, and huts with grass and palm leaves thrown on a simple frame. Some huts were walled on all sides, others were partly walled lean-tos, and still others had no walls but only a thatched roof. One could discern huts erected on mud-beaten raised platforms, others directly on the ground, and still others on rocks. Diversity expressed itself not only in the overall structure but also in the tiny details. For instance, the bamboo used for walls could be split into thin strips or cut open and flattened, creating cracked sheets. In one hut, strips might be laid horizontally, and in another (right next to the first), sheets might be laid vertically. I looked for common patterns in the early days of my fieldwork, and whenever I thought I had identified one, I shared the thought with Kungan or someone else. I was inevitably told that whatever I was pointing to could be or was done in other ways. Often, my interlocutor would then conclude our conversation with words I hoped not to hear yet did time and again: *Bere, bere* (different, different). Once, exasperated, I provocatively asked whether incest was forbidden, and I was told, "It does not happen here but maybe it happens in other places." Kungan and his relatives, I gradually realized, assertively recognized diversity as given.

The huts' diversity, a concrete illustration of this, was apparent in both plan and construction and stood out *because* the structures were so few, thus vividly presenting to attention their idiosyncrasies. The conspicuousness of their diversity was reinforced for me when I learned that, in the late 1960s, Kungan and some of his relatives had built several solid houses, all to a standard plan, for plantation workers who engaged them to do so, using forest materials to the settlers' specifications (a dozen or so of the workers then moved into those houses, which were outside the plantation area in the forest). Had they wanted, then, Kungan and his relatives could have built similar houses for themselves. They did not do so because they did not *build* their huts. From Ingold's perspective, their huts evolved and changed form as part of the foragers' dwelling or, more correctly, dwelling *together*.

The huts in Kungan's hamlet, and in each of the other hamlets in the Gorge, were located close to one another, although there was sufficient space to accommodate far greater distances between them.[3] One could argue that their proximity provided security. However, roaming elephants were the chief danger in this area, and such elephants are better left a clear path between huts, lest they trample one or another down on their passage through a hamlet. The proximity of the huts afforded the dwellers pluripresence and pluriparticipation in each other's lives. The small number of huts (six in Kungan's hamlet, including my own, one to three in the others) and their propinquity (five to ten meters between huts) allowed each dweller to remain in continuous contact with *all* of a hamlet's other dwellers. Kungan and his wife, for example, did not need to make any effort to see and hear what others in the hamlet were doing and saying as they pursued their own affairs. All the other hamlet's dwellers were continuously present within the couple's bodily zone of attention. They were vividly visible and audible to the couple, as they lived both close by and in huts that were often not walled or only partly so.

Huts were rebuilt (in the 1970s) every year to eighteen months, at a very leisurely pace. Sometimes, it took several months to build what could have been achieved within a few days. The wood frame was constructed, and thatch was placed on the roof; walls could remain unbuilt for months, if, indeed, they were ever added. In some cases, only one or two walls were built. In other cases, a lean-to with one or two walls was built resting on a rock face or as an extension to a hut. Four-walled huts had no doors closing their entries, and the walls constructed of split bamboo strips were porous and far from soundproof. The most solidly built huts had open verandas (the solid structure carried the extended roof creating the veranda), and their dwellers used the verandas both during the daytime and at night.

A hut constructed considerably farther away than easy speaking distance (e.g., the hut south of the stream in map 4, separated from the cluster of GR huts by about half a kilometer) counted as a different place. A single hut clearly could constitute a recognized settlement, as was the case for both BR and UP hamlets. The local issue was not that a hut feared to be alone, as Daniel (1984: 110) described for the Tamil house. Rather, the proximity of huts in Kungan's hamlet, and the flimsy partitions, spoke to the extent and importance of relatives' participation in each other's lives.

Much domestic life was carried on *outside* the huts, except during the monsoon periods, when heavy rains poured down relentlessly and the heavily trafficked area around the structures turned to squelchy mud. Relatives cooked, ate, bathed babies, idled, manufactured items, and frequently slept outside the huts, a few meters from one another, within easy communicative reach. To say, as Wilson (1988) does, that life in hunter-gatherer societies typically goes on outside the hut rather than in it is to take insufficient account of scale. When a *few* huts are built close to one another, *outside* a hut, in fact, means *in between* huts, effectively increasing pluripresence. The modern idea of the house as one's sovereign and secure castle is far removed from the local dwelling ideal. To the contrary, for Kungan and his relatives, withdrawal into a hut signified physical or social indisposition and could be contentious. Even ill persons spent as much time as they could lying on mats outside the huts. Kungan and his relatives did not look for privacy in the hamlet; if they desired it, they left the tiny cluster of huts and went into the forest. Though this behavior might seem peculiar to a middle-class homeowner with a master bedroom equipped with lock and key, it recurs in many ethnographic settings, among hunter-gatherers and others, as a response to the pervasive presence of relatives.

People who stayed inside a hut could be accused of being stingy. When Kungan, for instance, complained to me one day about how "bad things have become" and how "nobody helps anymore," he embellished his complaint by relating how, when so-and-so died, he alone had buried the man. Even the deceased's *chikappa* ("little" father; his father's younger brother) had not helped but had hidden in his hut and pretended not to be home. Partly walled dwellings, clearly, had a strategic value, in that one staying inside such a hut was still accessible and could not be accused of being stingy. This helps explain the popularity of such dwellings, or at least their tolerance, and why the huts were built at great leisure. The hamlet's architecture perpetuated the dwellers' pluriparticipation in each other's lives but also changed with it, as I show by focusing on shared compound huts.

DWELLING CYCLES

They lived in a small hamlet of bamboo and grass huts (Take 2)

Kungan's parents dwelled in an elongated hut, which they shared with two other families. Each family had its own "room" (in the sense of a space for living rather than a partitioned-off area). These rooms were arranged in a row, each with a separate entryway from the outside. At the same time, they were barely separated from one another internally. Only flimsy twigs stuck in the ground and reaching to knee height marked off the different rooms (in other cases, a strip of bamboo was laid on the ground, constituting a low "wall"). I once asked Kungan's father why these partitions were so flimsy. He puzzled over my question, especially when I shared with him my recollections of having grown up in a modest household in Israel. In our home, my parents had had a brick wall built to subdivide the one small children's bedroom they could afford and, thus, provided their two growing children with privacy. What I perceived as crude partitions, I began to understand, Kungan's father seemed to perceive as interfaces, markers of separate but adjoined rooms. Occupants of such a compound hut did not step over the low "wall" into another room, yet at the same time, they did not pretend that they did not see and hear their relatives in the other rooms. To the contrary, exploiting the visibility and audibility such flimsy partitions afforded, they talked with one another. But—and this is a salient point—they did not address or expect a response from anyone in particular. They began or continued a generalized conversation that anybody present could join. This form of communication—by no means unique to tiny societies—can be called pluralogue (as opposed to dialogue), and it was especially striking at night, when people lay down to sleep, and in the dark, one could hear the murmur of such conversations going on, linking rooms and outside mats, until everyone nodded off.

A compound hut with multiple rooms (I never saw one with more than three) developed gradually, responding to constant coming and going of visiting relatives and changing relationships. A hut started as a single-spaced structure. Only some dwellings ended up comprising two or three rooms. The process, it cannot be stressed enough, did not involve dividing one hut into separate rooms but was additive, joining rooms together. When the need arose, a lean-to was added to an existing hut. Later, other walls could be added to the lean-to, possibly reusing bamboo from the hut wall it adjoined. The new lean-to was added on the basis of need, for example, for a family who came for a short-term visit and lingered on, a widowed person who had vacated his or her previous dwelling, or a child who started living with a partner. The builders of the annex could be the ones who needed it, the occupants of the original hut, or both. Notably, a room or a lean-to was only added to a structure if no other room was vacant in the hamlet. Often, spaces *were* available, as their occupants had left them, going to visit or live in another place. A game of musical chairs played out over time and resulting in no exclusions provides a helpful analogy for the process. Its result was that, at any given moment, the number and occupation of huts in any hamlet reflected the comings and goings of relatives between hamlets. The huts' forms and occupants at various points provided a series of snapshots, as it were, of the ongoing process of joining and separating from relatives, reflecting chance sequences of loves and deaths, visits and work opportunities, friendships and tensions.

My own living accommodation started a musical chairs cycle of its own, with a novel twist. When you closely share everyday life with those you are studying, fieldwork is an unfolding stream of mutual misunderstandings and adjustments, taking you by surprise, especially on matters that seem to be a part of "what goes without saying." The hybrid situation created by the ethnographer and her hosts is a theater of the mundane, in which necessary improvisations on implicit cultural scripts expose their respective underlying assumptions. After a few months of short visits to the hamlet, I moved with my partner into a two-roomed hut built for us—as I thought then—by Kungan and his wife, whom I paid the same amount they had been paid to build houses for the plantation workers. Kungan obviously thought otherwise: first, his young daughter and a friend started to sleep in the second room. Two weeks later, my partner had to return to his work in England, and when he left, Kungan, his wife, and their youngest son also moved into the second room. Kungan perceived the situation as involving the addition of a room for me in the hut he and his family were building for themselves and the money I provided as something I shared with them. When I left at the end of my fieldwork, their oldest son, a timid thirty-year-old whose wife had left him a few years earlier, moved into the room I vacated.

That no one normally slept alone added to the musical chair movement within and between these tiny hamlets. Sleeping alone was irregular and undesired. When it happened, it expressed tension and conflict resolved by the solitary sleeper's relocation to another hamlet. For example, half-senile and difficult to be with, Kungan's brother's wife's mother at first slept with her granddaughter, then she slept alone, and finally she moved to another hamlet where she slept with a nephew's daughter. A couple always slept together (failing to do so was a sign of tension and imminent separation), and their young children commonly slept with them. Adolescents and unmarried youths shared mats with age-mates and, as need arose, occasionally with widowed persons and visitors. Daniel (1984: 110) described "slumber parties" in which young Tamil boys, young men, and even older men sleep in a row on mats outside their houses or in a group on a neighbor's veranda, rather than retire to the privacy of their houses; women, although remaining indoors, invite neighbors and kinswomen to sleep with them. Plurisleeping practices in Kungan's hamlet went far beyond these Tamil conventions, often involving mixed-age and mixed-gender sharing of mats and covers by more than conjugal couples and parents and children. Mixed-age and mixed-gender cosleeping was preferable to leaving someone to sleep alone and was sometimes the only possible alternative in such a tiny hamlet. Cosleeping and, often, plurisleeping in the open provided warmth; it obviated the need for more substantial bedding, which in turn contributed to perpetuating these practices. As George Foster vividly described for Tzintzuntzan (Mexico), here too, "what seems impossible crowding by the standard of people who sleep one, or at most two, in a bed, is a source of comfort" (1988 [1967]: 105).

Given mixed-gender and mixed-age cosleeping, an unlikely couple in terms of their ages could sleep together without drawing public attention until they began to spend time together during the day (at which point they begin to be viewed as a couple). Of a new couple who seemed to strategize within these conventions to keep other parties away and maintain intimacy, it was said that they "separately, separately, sleep together." This phrase wonderfully sums up the local perspective that the salient point was not the uniting of two single sleepers, a shift from one to two, but rather their separation from others *and* their joining together, that is, a shift from one plurality to another. Rather than see sleeping alone as the natural state of affairs until one physically matures and sexually unites with another— that is, rather than see it and sexual sleeping together as dichotomously opposed states between which a body alternates during its lifetime— Kungan and his relatives experienced the ease, flow, and indeterminacy of joining with and separating from others. They experienced sleeping in a series of shifting pluralities, unfolding one from the other. The same serial pluralism characterized their occupancy of dwellings.

Focusing on a single house, hearth, or body to describe a broader type, following the common singularizing mode expressed, say, in the anthropology of *the body,* of *the house,* and of *the self,* conceals the shifting pluralities I have described. The fluid, flexible nature of dwelling with others in the tiny hunter-gatherer hamlet can only be gauged by examining the *plurality* of huts, hearths, and bodies. And their plurality can be kept vividly in focus, in this case, *because* there were few of them, because they were few-many.

BELONGING(S) WITH

They lived in a small hamlet of bamboo and grass huts (Take 3)

Kungan and his relatives' dwelling experiences are further illuminated by training the analytical lens on the things that lie in and between their huts—their belongings—and by considering them from the perspective of "belongings with." I purposely use *belongings* in preference to *possessions, objects, goods,* and so on, capitalizing on that term's early English synonymy with *relatives* and on the fact that, as Jeanette Edwards and Marilyn Strathern (2000: 159) note, "belonging" today encompasses all forms of human-nonhuman association and appropriations. Scholars have long regarded absence of storage as a defining attribute of hunter-gatherers' mode of subsistence (e.g., see Woodburn 1980; Testart 1982; Ingold 1983). Below, I examine that standard as I use everyday storage praxis as a prism on hunter-gatherers' senses of themselves and their worlds.

I was struck initially by the apparent disorder of household objects (in fact, "hearthhold objects," but I retain the conventional term), jumbled together in corners of huts, hung on ropes, or simply scattered on the ground. On my side of the hut I shared with Kungan and his family, I kept the few things I had brought with me in five plastic storage boxes, stacked one on top of another, one each for kitchenware, food, clothes, hygiene and medical supplies, and professional equipment. My tiny corner of the hut reflected the habitus and logic of a bourgeois household with its functionally differentiated rooms, its cupboards, drawers, shelves, hangers, and other means of storing objects by kind and specific use. The scene in and around Kungan's family's side of the hut could not have been more different: cooking pots left beside the hearth contained leftover food, plates lay on the ground next to pots holding water brought from the river, other plates were piled at the edge of the veranda alongside small open parcels of salt, chilies, and rice. Clothes were thrown together over a rope hanging between the hut's poles. On the same rope were hung blankets, backpack baskets, and traps made of bamboo, all jumbled with the clothing. The family's belongings were not separated and assigned to particular places by class and function, as mine were, and for this reason they struck outside observers as being in disarray.

In *Steps to an Ecology of Mind*, Gregory Bateson (1987 [1972]) offers a starting point for a fresh exploration of the local senses of what I initially perceived, ethnocentrically, as disorganized storage praxis. Through a delightful narration of a bedtime conversation between a father and a daughter who asks him, "Why do things get in a muddle?" Bateson (13–18) develops the argument that "tidiness" references particular habituated locations. And so, what is "tidy" to one person is not to another. In the example he uses, his daughter's paint box is not "in a muddle" only when it stands upright on the left end of a certain shelf, its habitual place (14). In this example, Bateson assumes a bourgeois household with multiple rooms, partitions, fixtures, and furniture, a house that presents a rich grid for defining a tidy state. He could have further defined the right place for the paint box as the daughter's bedroom, not her brother's or her parents', not the kitchen or the bathroom. To give another example (my own), the father might have instructed the daughter to place a dinner plate in the middle drawer of the lower cupboard next to the refrigerator, above the drawer where the cups are kept. The sense of order this instruction expresses hinges on additionally compartmentalizing things by logic of sameness according to kind, purpose, and status. This logic is consistent with a world in which goods are mass-produced for specific uses.

Could the few seemingly muddled belongings lying here and there in Kungan's hamlet express another sense and logic of order? I argue that this is the case and that that logic is underwritten by the idea of things belonging *with* people and *with* other things rather than *in* places. One should not forget that the hut and hamlet architecture afforded only a rudimentary grid, if any, for assigning belongings to their "tidy" places. The hamlet's dwellings did not offer an elaborate storage environment. Huts (and rooms in compound huts) had no fixtures or furniture, no inner partitions, and sometimes no outer walls. Moreover, as I describe above, they dynamically changed in response to circumstances. When Kungan brought home small amounts of rice, chilies, and salt he obtained at a tea shack on the edge of the plantation, he did not have a kitchen, a special cupboard, or a specific shelf on which to store them. The shopkeeper wrapped each of these provisions separately in a plantain leaf and then placed all three packets together in a larger leaf or a piece of newspaper. Back home, Kungan untied the bundles to allow access to the contents, leaving everything together on the leaves until consumed. The foodstuffs belonged together, he explained to me, when I asked why he did not at least separate out the small bundles; they all came to the hamlet together and for the most part would be used together.

Retrospectively, a household survey I carried out throws more light on belongings. I undertook it with little enthusiasm, seeing it as an expected component of fieldwork at the time. An ethnographer, in those days, was supposed to go from family to family and record what kinds of things and how "many" instances of those things each had. I integrated this obligatory task into my informal conversations, regarding the "survey" as occasioning, involving, and taking place within a social process. I simply asked people what they had and jotted down their responses as close to verbatim as I could, as I did for all my other conversations. Having so few people in the study group, and living with them on a daily basis, I felt comfortable lapsing into such informal data collection rather than filling out prepared forms in formal, dedicated sessions at appointed times. Later, I abstracted the information from my running notes. Among other things, I distinguished between objects of forest and market origin (see table 1) and compared the household belongings of an old couple (in their seventies), their married child and his wife (late forties), and their married granddaughter and her husband (early twenties; see table 2). The paucity and simplicity of material belongings clearly stand out in these tables, which represent the household objects in Kungan's world in their entirety, by essential kind, quantity, and owners. Surplus accumulation hardly seemed to have taken root among members of the younger generation, although they had a few novel items, like the two cloth bags, the "cushion," and the stool enumerated in table 2.

TABLE 1. Inventory of belongings by type

Forest origin	Backpacks, fishing traps and traps for wildfowl (all made of strips of bamboo woven or tied with strips of bark), bamboo vessels, bamboo poles (for shaking high-growing fruits and pods), digging sticks and arrows (with iron heads), mats (woven of grass), and ladles (made of halved coconuts).
Market origin	Metal cooking pots, plates, knives, cups, and axes; plastic containers and glass bottles; a torch; matches.

TABLE 2. Inventory of belongings by generation

Grandparents	One billhook knife, one ax, two bamboo carrying baskets, one bamboo container, one grass mat, one medium-size clay pot, two metal pots, one metal plate, one tiffin carrier, three metal cups, one glass bottle, two small metal tins.
Parents	One billhook knife, one metal ax, one bamboo carrying basket, two traps for wildfowl, four bamboo containers, one grass mat, one metal digging stick, three metal pots, one plastic jerrican, one torch, three glass bottles.
Grandchildren	One billhook knife, one pruning knife, two bamboo containers, one grass mat, four metal plates, one metal cup, one glass bottle, two cloth bags, one "cushion" (cotton stuffed in a plastic bag), one small wooden stool.

The tables provide, at a quick glance, a useful perspective on local belongings but reveal nothing about the dwellers' own perspectives.

What did Kungan and his relatives actually say in response to my questions about belongings? For each item, they detailed *who* had delivered it into their world, for example, mentioning the "sickle knife given by the plantation's supervisor," the "grass mat made by an aunt," the "cooking pot given by a cousin," and so on. More than half of the items mentioned were described as having been procured by a particular relative. The remainder were described as made, found, or bought by someone's spouse (these three modes were secondary distinctions). Kungan's wife surprised me when mentioning a plastic jerrican her husband bought with money I gave him, extending the genealogy of the jerrican to include me "with" it as the money giver. Every item, including market-purchased objects in daily use, was connected with a relative who procured it.

The ontological premises underscoring this relational system of belongings can be sketched using the example of a knife. In local terms, as I now understand them, there was no specific singular knife in the world that one could access and make one's own, any more than, say, a brother was a free-for-the-claiming entity in the world. Just as a brother was, ipso facto, prerelated to someone—actually, someones, as "brother" entailed other relations—so a knife was prerelated to someone(s). Someone(s) had made it, bought it, or brought it; it did not appear on its own; someone(s) had delivered it into locals' midst, into their lived world. Its origin in an unknown faraway place was blurred in this register. Attention predominantly focused on it here and now, after the item had become relationally present through a relative, after it had become "relatable with." The knife, then, was perceived relationally, *with* a (familiar) relative in mind but no more exclusively than a brother was, who was related, by definition, to a number of people. The gift in the Maussian sense embodies interpersonal relation, whereas the knife, when passed on to and used by others, embodied the plural togetherness of the relatives among whom it circulated (cf. Bird-David 1990).

In this community, "my knife" was not a statement of ownership. Rather, it registered my constant use of that knife and my being-with it. It was a statement of belonging as a performed relation, corresponding with the way a relative continued to be a relative only as long as he or she remained an actively engaged member of the community (Barbara Bodenhorn [2000] aptly titled a discussion of a similar Inupiat pattern "He Used to Be My Relative"). For this reason, the same knife could be (and was) regarded by Kungan's wife as hers, his, and both of theirs. She referred to it in all these ways, shifting between attributions and confusing me, so I asked her what she meant. She patiently explained that the tool was Kungan's because he had found it and then used it. It was hers because she also used it. And it was theirs because both of them used it. In describing it as *nama* (~ ours), she did not mean that the knife was "with" her and her husband as a unit, as one paired entity. It was not their unity, their two-as-oneness, to which the knife belonged. Rather, it belonged to each of them and to both of them in what I describe as an additive, or a joined, sense: it was with him and with her. The intensity of its co-use was made possible by and sustained their staying together and also reflected that togetherness.

During its constant use, the same knife was employed creatively in multiple contexts and for diverse purposes. Unlike the bourgeois household dinner plate, dedicated to a particular use and stored in a particular place when not in use, here, one and the same knife was plurally and unrestrictedly used. It was used, among other tasks, for digging; hunting; fishing; collecting honey; building huts; making bamboo containers, baskets, and traps; preparing food and eating; preparing forest medicines; grooming and cutting hair; pulling thorns embedded in the skin; even sharpening bamboos for cutting the umbilical cord at birth. The perceived "affordance" of the knife (to use James J. Gibson's [1979] term) was not a priori limited either in terms of its logical categorization (say, a "hunting knife") or its users (e.g., women). The same knife could be used one day by a man hunting, the next day by a child cutting firewood, and the third day by a woman making birth preparations. Often, husbands and wives had *one* knife, which they both carried and used interchangeably. Only couples who casually worked on the plantation sometimes had two knives, given to them by their employers.

Creative multiple uses of one knife rested on one's skill or, in Claude Lévi-Strauss's sense, on a *bricoleur* kind of mind; conversely, such skillful use precluded the need for multiple knives of different kinds and, thus, the need for storage facilities to house them separately and safely when not in use. The idea that a thing should be used constantly in turn placed limits on how many items of the same kind one could keep, and it helped perpetuate nonaggrandizement. The value and even the thingness of something depended on its constant use. In the absence of storage facilities and concern with storage, anything that was not actually used could be taken by others. If it lay where it fell or was dropped, it could be trampled on, get covered by vegetation, and deteriorate. A knife did not commonly go through this trajectory. It is a versatile tool, and if, for some reason, one was left lying around, someone would pick it up. Plates and other metalware, by contrast, could lie unused for a long while, such that petty traders periodically climbed down to the foragers' forest hamlets to themselves "forage" for scattered metalware, offering a rupee or two for each piece they collected. For this reason, increased involvement in wage-paying work and in market consumption did not rapidly lead to self-aggrandizement and accumulation of belongings but rather to increased distribution of objects among relatives. Notably, when relatives moved to another hamlet, they sometimes left belongings behind that others could pick up and use, just as they left their rooms for others to move into. Lest the foregoing discussion imply a world without conflict over things, I hasten to add that conflicts did break out in the interstices of this particular regime. They revolved around belongings that, left lying around, were assumed to be abandoned and so were picked up and used without permission. When sought, permission was always granted, but asking for it was considered proper conduct. For example, in a case I describe elsewhere (Bird-David 1990), a couple departed for another hamlet, leaving an ax behind. Someone used it without requesting their permission. The couple came back earlier than anticipated and an argument broke out over this unauthorized use.

Huts did not substantially vary from other belongings; rather, they were the largest "stuff" of all (as Daniel Miller [2010] regards houses). If no one moved into and occupied a vacant hut, it slowly fell into disuse. As it was built of organic materials, its existence was hard to discern after a few years. The exuberant forest vegetation soon covered it. For example, after Kungan's younger brother and his wife moved to a new hut that they built on a terrace above the other huts, no one moved into their old place. Within a short time, thin veins of bare earth, pathways, appeared between the new hut and the ones below, while vegetation started growing around the hut the couple had abandoned. A few months later, one could hardly see the remains of the old hut, and the hut that had been added up the hill no longer looked new. The hamlet—its huts and the network of footpaths connecting them—seemed to have shifted position. Relocation of one hut in a large village would hardly change the village contours, but the relocation of one hut in a tiny hamlet does! Had Mohandes surveyed the hamlet after the couple moved, he would have drawn a different map.

A Tamil man from a small township in the region, Mohandes registered the huts as constituting a village, albeit tiny, a bounded entity comprising the huts he had individually measured. Did Kungan and his relatives share his view? Did they register the closely spaced few huts in and between which they lived as a single hamlet, *a* camp? I pursue this question in the final section of this chapter, which introduces readers to the local sense of dwelling(s), to a perception of setting, and to a mind-set focused especially on "one and many."

SIME (~ HOME)

They lived in a small hamlet of bamboo and grass huts (Take 4)

Beginning to think about this book, I realized I did not know a local word for the aggregate of huts (equivalent to *hamlet, camp,* or *village*) in and around which Kungan and his relatives pursued many of their daily routines. On my visit in 2001, I asked Kungan's nephew, "What do you call all the huts here?" I trusted the counsel of this young man, whom I had known since he was seven. He thought long and finally answered, "Aparemane." Literally, *aparemane* means "many buildings." *Mane* (building, structure) is regionally used, for instance, by Badaga and Kannada speakers, for "house." *Apare* (many) is more intriguing; it belongs to the kind of unquantifiable "many" that is part of the "one, two, many" counting systems found cross-culturally among tiny hunter-gatherer-cultivator communities (Pinker 2007: 138).[4] Similar counting systems have been debated by cognitive linguists concerned with the existence of numeracy without words.[5] Addressing the issue, Steven Pinker related that he was baffled by these systems until Napoleon Chagnon told him that the Yanomamo "don't need exact numbers because they keep track of things as individuals, one by one" (138). A Yanomamo hunter, for example, recognizes each of his arrows and knows whether one is missing without having to count them. The same habit of mind, Pinker suggests, "would make most of us pause if someone asked us how many first cousins we have, or how many appliances in our kitchen, or how many orifices in our head" (138). The point itself is weak (in these systems, there are words for the first few numbers, which are, in this thesis, the least needed).[6] But the general direction is welcome. The remark prompts me to ask what senses of pluralness are expressed by *apare*, as one of these concepts of "many," before I continue to explore what Kungan's nephew's answer meant, what he was conveying by referring to the tiny cluster of huts not as a camp or village but as "many huts."

The huts in Kungan's hamlet can be added up only if they are serialized; unless they are perceived to be what I shorthand as "same and separate" entities, they cannot be perceived as "six" huts. To be able to say "six huts," one must first perceive them as six distinct entities and, furthermore, as six serialized, same-and-separate units—that is, six times *hut*. As I discuss above, the heterogeneity of the dwellings was striking. Their diversity was cognized as the salient feature, verbalized in the insistence that they were—as so much else was—*bere, bere* (different, different).

Furthermore, before we add the huts up, we must also decide what counts as a "hut" and as part of the group, that is, what should and should not be included in the accounting. Do huts on the other side of the river count? Do two-walled structures count or only four-walled ones? Does a lean-to count or only a full structure? Do dilapidated huts count? Does a compound structure (e.g., a room and lean-to annex) count as one hut or two? If we go by whether one or two families occupy it, we then have to define *family* . . . and so on. Using *apare* preempts such definitional quibbles and the need to standardize. As Kungan's nephew used it, the term, I argue, emphasized the huts' contiguity and pluripresence. In the local register, the huts were what I shorthand as "diverse and pluripresent," adjoined and different rather than same and separate.

My count of six huts is tenuous. Separating and standardizing a fuzzy world is the murky side of any survey. However, in large-scale contexts, the "law of large numbers" minimizes the distortion. Failing to count a hundred dilapidated houses cannot seriously affect a survey carried out in a town with ten thousand houses. By contrast, in the tiny hunter-gatherer hamlet, even a few divergent instances can affect the results. The scalar effect is also two-sided: Kungan and his relatives could perceive the heterogeneity of all their huts and track them as "individuals, one by one," *because* the huts were few. To perceive ten thousand dwellings in this way would be a cognitive feat. Even when a hamlet consisted of more than a handful of huts—that is, had "many" huts—the "many" were still what I call a "few-many." The scale of their manyness allowed registering their vivid diversity and cognizing it.

On the one hand, then, the term *aparemane* reflected the local register of the diversity of huts in the hamlet. Using *apare* precluded setting boundaries and agreeing on criteria of inclusion and exclusion. On the other hand, and this should not be missed, Kungan's nephew's choice expressed absent alternatives, words that assembled, singularized, and reified all the huts as a collective. The lack of alternatives was also generally expressed in the absence of fixed place-names for the hamlets. Kungan and his relatives used topographical features (e.g., "up the hill"), the locations of relatives (e.g., "uncle's place"), or simply a gesture of the hand to indicate where they were going or the place they were referring to. In talking with others (and sometimes among themselves), they used the names of the plantations nearest their huts as place-names. The acronyms I use for the hamlets derive from these place-names.

Their use of *aparemane* for the hamlet, then, reflected resistance not only to itemizing the huts as separate and same entities but also to collectivizing and regarding them as a singular mega-actor. The huts, in this local register, did not constitute parts of the hamlet as a whole; they were not seen through the lens of what Strathern (1992a, referring to the modern view of individuals as components of society) calls the logic of "parts and wholes." In the local register, what I designate "a hamlet" was an irreducible plurality of diverse dwellings where people lived with their relatives. Likewise, when someone asks us, in our large-scale, parts-and-whole world, how many first cousins we have or how many orifices there are in our head, we do not pause because, as Pinker suggests, we know them as "individuals, one by one" but because we know these entities as plurally belonging with one another, each inseparable from all the others, though each is distinctive; we pause because we know them, in other words, as diverse and pluripresent rather than same and separate. We pause to estrange, decontextualize, separate, abstract, standardize, and serialize them to be able to count them. Perhaps, to generalize from this ethnographic instance, hunter-gatherer concepts of "many" are not premised on the understanding of "individuals, one by one" but rather of "individuals, one *with* one," that is, few-many pluripresent individuals each related to all the others but who do not constitute a One.

Kungan's huts stood at the core of the *sime*, another word in wide regional use but one that Kungan and his relatives used distinctively. In their sense, *sime* is best translated as "home." The word *home* carries profound ontological senses and cultural antecedents to native English speakers (far deeper than *many* does).[7] It has been argued that *home* cannot be easily translated into other languages (Rykwert 1991: 51; Hollander 1991: 42) but neither, conversely, can terms from other languages simply be translated as "home." My strategy here is to explore *sime* through its departures from *home*, aided later by comparative reference to *ur*, the Tamil equivalent of *home*.

Sime does not refer to a physical structure, a building (for which the term *mane* is used), and in this way it resembles *home*, which is also distinguished from the English *house*, a building.[8] From this common starting point, however, the meanings of *sime* and *home* diverge. *Home* is closely associated with *family*. In Europe, it has come to be associated with the nuclear family as, in recent centuries, the occupants of a house have in many cases dwindled to include only nuclear family members, excluding other relatives, servants, employees, and so on (see Hareven 1991). Mary Douglas (1991) went as far as to suggest that the idea of "home" frames the house's dwellers as an "embryonic community." By contrast, *sime* is never used for a single hut in a hamlet and rarely for a hamlet consisting of only one hut. *Sime* is inherently associated with a plurality of relatives who live together in a hamlet of several huts.

In Kannada and Badaga, the regional languages closest to Kungan's dialect, *sime* means a bounded territory, a space demarcated by boundaries.[9] For Kungan and his relatives, *sime* spatially connoted the plural huts *and* the arterial of paths spreading between and outward from them. Constant going and coming took place on these paths: down to the stream to draw water, bathe, urinate, or defecate; farther outward in other directions to collect firewood, relieve boredom, stretch one's legs, enjoy privacy; and still farther to forage and visit relatives in other hamlets. *Sime* stretched outward to the horizons of everyday immediate experience. An outside hearth open to its surroundings is a better image than a house for appreciating the spatiality of *sime*. *Sime* refers to an area expanding outward from a shared focus and fading away at the horizons of perception.

Nama sime (~ our home; *sime* commonly is prefixed by a first person plural possessive term) connotes the space where relatives relate with one another, each with all the others. And in doing so, they perform their *sime* into being; the we-centric *nama sime* is not a pregiven space *in which* they live. *Sime*, in this sense, is contingent on the same continuous ongoing work of being-with that I have described as governing personal belongings. One might rightly ask, what happens when several hamlets exist whose dwellers keep in close touch with one another, as was the case for the local group I studied? If, spatially, *sime* refers to an area expanding outward from a focus, fading away at the horizons, what happens when there are several focuses? The image of several hearths provides for more tangible visualization in this case; even better is the image of ripples spreading out from several stones thrown into the water at the same time, at first marking where each stone hits, then spreading and merging together. The inhabitants of each hamlet regarded their hamlet and its surroundings as their *sime*, a domain that extended to the rest of the Gorge and included the other hamlets they constantly visited. The same additive logic, then, that underlies possession of a knife infuses the idea of *sime*.[10]

In his study of the rural Tamil Nadu village, Daniel likens *ur* to *home* and argues that *ur*, like *home*, is a person-centric definition of space. (He distinguishes *ur* from *tecam* and *kiramam*, the last two referring to the nation, country, and village as fixed geographic and administrative units appearing on maps and taught at school.) Daniel introduces the Tamil notion of *ur* in the following words:

> When a Tamil asks the question of a stranger, "What is your ur?" he is really asking "Where is your home?" As in the case of the English word *home*, the contextually determined speech act will determine the response. Thus, if a Tamil is asked this question when he is in Sri Lanka, he will reply that his ur is India. If he is in Kerala, he will reply, "Tamil Nadu," and if in some part of Tamil Nadu itself, he will refer to the district, neighboring town, or to his particular village. (1984: 67)

As is clear from this exposition, Daniel takes for granted that a stranger asks about one's home and, similarly, about one's *ur* and that the question is asked of one who is away from home. In fact, one normally is asked, "Where is your home" when one *is* away from home. The questioner is normally someone who does not share one's home. And the question presupposes a "you" not included among "us." Were one to be asked, "Where is *our* home?" one might suspect the question to be philosophical or symptomatic of some sort of pathology in the questioner. *Ur* and *home*, then, are both bound up in a series of inclusive and exclusive abstractions, premised on a world that is partly unknown (and imagined to be so; i.e., larger than one can personally know). In such a world, one explains to strangers where one's home is versus other homes in the village, versus other villages in the county, and so on.[11] These senses of *home* and *ur* are almost incomprehensible in Kungan's world. As an utterance, *nama sime* (~ our home) is not intended to explain to a stranger where one lives. Rather, it asserts that "we, all of us here" share a home together. This "we" applies to all of the dwellers who reside in the Gorge's hamlets, one of whom would never ask another, "Where is your home?" Each of these dwellers not only knows where the others live but also now and then lives with them, shifting his or her residence between hamlets. Thus, unlike *home* and *ur*, *sime* is bound up with a series of inclusionary circles expanding to the horizons of experience. *Sime* is a home that cannot be imagined from afar; it is the spatial concomitant of dwelling *with* others and, as I show in subsequent chapters, not just with fellow humans.

English dictionaries often define the metaphorical concept of *home* in terms of a single person (e.g., a place *one* belongs to, the center of *one's* affections, where *one's* ancestors dwelled).[12] *Home* is peculiarly associated with a single person, although it involves dwelling with a few others in most cases. This same singular bias underscores Daniel's notion of *home* and *ur* as person-centric definitions of space and descriptions of *home* as a place in the world that, in Joseph Rykwert's words, "does not require any building, even if a house always does. You can make a home, everywhere" (1991: 54). I simply cannot overemphasize, in concluding this chapter, that *sime* is, and can only be, a we-centric definition of space. It is a space pluri-irelationally performed. Perhaps one can make a *home* everywhere, but only "few-many" dwelling together can make a *sime*.

This discussion of dwelling(s) has established Kungan and his relatives' experiential setting and has provided ethnographic grounding for some of the analytical terms through which I approach it: being-with versus being; pluripresent and diverse versus same and separate; expanding ripples versus boundaries; the irreducible few-many versus the infinite many abstracted as a macro-actor, a One. I turn now to varying modes of living with particular relatives who constitute the local pluripresent community in the Gorge.

Census of Relatives

Ethnographers commonly provide some sort of demographic breakdown of their study groups when introducing them to readers. Often they enumerate, either in the text or in a table, the numbers of men, women, and children their groups comprise. Some go an additional step and provide a breakdown by place of residence, age, ethnicity, or other criteria, as relevant to the study's main concerns. I could have followed precedent here and demographically presented my study group in table 3 (reproduced from Bird 1983a: 41) without additional comment. Instead, I want to pause and reflect on the table's methodological and ontological basis, and how the information it relates compromises the study of those it purports to describe.

Tables like mine transform indigenous nanocommunities of relatives into so many generalized, serialized, same-and-separate men, women, and children. The actual numbers in such tables may be minuscule, yet the format of their presentation exerts a large-scale multiplicative alchemy and, in doing so, obscures the nanoness of the study group. The format emulates censuses, which generally are devices used by states and other powers to govern large populations, to represent them and make them known and knowable in particular ways. The census serves a kind of knowing that is superfluous to tiny indigenous communities, whose sense of themselves accrues from their members' years of intimate familiarity with one another. Without denying the effectiveness of the census or the duty of the student to provide demographic information, I narrate how I produced table 3 as a way to reflect on the large-scale-biased "Trojan horse" effect of using this mode of presenting a forager study-community. That is, I present the back-stage of conforming to scale-blind ethnographic standards.

The professional kit with which I arrived in the Gorge included a stack of index cards in addition to notebooks, a tape recorder, and a camera. As the

TABLE 3. The core study group

Hamlet	Male	Female	Children
TR	4	6	3
TM	6	6	5
GR	8	6	12
UP	1	2	3
BR	3	4	—
Total	22	24	23

SOURCE: Adjusted from Bird 1983a: 41, per middle of fieldwork time.

practical precursor to setting up individual computer files, the neophyte ethnographer in those days was advised to carry a plentiful supply of such cards into the field, to be used to record personal information on individual members of the study group. The cards could then be used for easy retrieval of information also contained in the field diary but less accessible there, given its rapidly cumulating masses of data of all sorts. In preparing my cards before leaving university, I had jotted various headings on the top line of each one according to standard survey parameters I had thought were essential for an individual's identification and easy to "measure." Besides an identifying card number, those headings included name, sex, spouse's name, number and names of children, father's name, age, and place of residence. As obvious as those parameters had seemed to me in Cambridge, recording the relevant information in the field turned out to be fraught with problems and the process tale telling.

My problems began with my attempt to record people's names. Personal names are popularly presumed to be universal, a view shared by some scholars (e.g., Alford 1988). Yet Kungan and his relatives, like many hunter-gatherer (and other tiny) indigenous communities, usually referred to and addressed each other by kinship terms. Questioning them about individual names produced thought-provoking vignettes rather than the desired information. "What is the name of this man?" I asked Kungan in reference to a just-arrived visitor I had not previously met. Kungan turned to the man and asked him, "Bava(n)' [brother-in-law], what are you called nowadays?" Then, turning back to me, he replied, "He is called Mathen nowadays on the plantation." "What are the names of your children?" I asked Kungan early on in my fieldwork. "Madi, Motane, and Inneri," he replied, referring to the oldest three. "And this boy?" I asked, pointing to the youngest. "I forget," he said; "we do not remember names." Names and naming have received scholarly attention in recent years because of the way colonial administrations imposed them on entire populations for purposes of governance (see, among others, Alia 1994, 2007; Widlok 2000; Scott 1998; Bodenhorn and Vom Bruck 2006). But they are also important to consider in microsituations like the ethnographic field site. Naming Kungan and his relatives ontologically refigured them as a set of individuals, single essential entities, pregiven in advance of their kinship relations (e.g., "This is Kungan" and "This is Madi" and "Kungan is the father of Madi").

In contrast to the forest foragers themselves, outsiders who engaged with them needed to use fixed personal names for them: the plantation accountant to register their casual attendance at work, the petty shopkeeper to record their custom on credit, and the ethnographer to keep legible records. They commonly used tribal names popular in the region (and increasingly, mainstream Indian names for the younger generation; see Bird 1982). Since the stock of names in use was small, the same name could designate multiple individuals, and since different outsiders compiled their own sets of names, the same individual could be known by various names. Since I already knew a few "Mathens," Kungan's "brother-in-law" entered my notes as BR Mathen (i.e., Mathen from BR hamlet); other outsiders resolved the confusion generated by multiple Mathens by numbering them: "Mathen 1," "Mathen 2," and so on.

Outsiders, however, were inevitably drawn back into the local plural contexts when we tried to communicate about those we so individualized, as became especially apparent to me during my repeated visits. When, ten years after my initial fieldwork, I returned for a visit, I asked what had happened to BR Mathen, and this question started a lengthy process of negotiating contextual knowledge of plural relations. I explained that I meant the "Mathen" who had been married to "Chati," was the son of "Karriyen," had lived in that place next to the river, and so on. I learned by way of response that "Chati" had died, that that place next to the river had been abandoned, that "Chati's" widower had since married so-and-so, and, yes, my perspective and my interlocutors' finally converged: the man I had known as "BR Mathen" was now called "Kalan." This conversation, and others like it, evoked a plurality of related people and what had happened to them all, in a way that surely is familiar to readers, although most of us live a large-scale life regulated by use of personal names and surnames, right down to our most intimate relations. In their intimate community, by contrast, Kungan and his relatives used kinship terms and left personal names at the margins, reserved mostly for use at the interface with outsiders.

When they used them, they deployed personal names relationally, as they did kinship terms or, to coin a term, as *interpersonal* names.

Ticking off the next parameter on my cards, sex, was simple, but the one after that, age, was problematic, again reflecting the tug-of-war between individualizing and relationalizing forces. Kungan and his relatives were concerned with the *relative* order of birth that was known to everybody and embodied in some kinship terms (e.g., separate terms for older brother and younger brother). They could not, however, tell an individual's age. "How old are you?" can be easily answered in large-scale bureaucratic societies that, since the nineteenth century, have incorporated age criteria into their developing complex institutions, practices, and ideas (Chudacoff 1992). In such societies, age is a major regulative criterion. Moreover, you anticipate who one "is"—what he or she likes, understands, does, thinks—according to the person's age, and you do so reasonably well given a society in which shops, food, clothes, media, school classes, hospital wings, books, laws, and more are tailored to specific age groups. Coming from such large-scale contexts, anthropologists have developed methods for assessing local ages: normally, they transform the local relative register into an absolute chronology by identifying events that can be independently dated. For example, if BR Mathen was born just after coffee joined rubber as an important crop on the nearby plantation, and I establish that the coffee was planted in the mid-1950s, then, BR Mathen was in his late twenties circa 1978–79. The coincidence (birth when coffee was planted) and the objective fact (coffee was planted in the mid-1950s) *relationally* produced the "objective" end result (BR Mathen was in his late twenties). The local relational register tied people together. Ages I recorded on my cards detached them from one another, transforming them into individuals ready to be sorted by and assembled into age-based classes, even though they do not understand themselves to be classifiable in this way, and even though in such tiny intimate communities age classes can barely be constructed as there are so few people to fit into each imagined class.

"Residence" was problematic partly because Kungan and his relatives were seminomadic people who moved a lot but also because of the way they referenced locations. As described in chapter 1, hamlets were referred to relationally (e.g., "my sister's place") or topographically (e.g., "up the hill"). This system worked effectively in this tiny community, where places and the people at those places were known to everyone and people were constantly coming and going between hamlets. Among nonlocals and in the satellite hamlets outside the Gorge, various outsider-imposed place names were used. For example, Kungan's hamlet, where I lived, was referred to by the name of the plantation I fictionalize as GR; by the name of a temporary seasonal forest laborers' camp, Koop; and according to the personal name others gave to one or another of its residents (e.g., "Kungan's place"). Even if one selects a specific criterion for assigning people to places in such a fluid society (e.g., residence on a given day, length of residence, primary place of ritual attendance), such assignment in and of itself—although helpful for taking legible notes and writing and reading ethnography—wrongly suggests that they are divided into small local groups and undermines the cultural effort they invest in constantly visiting and living with one another, each with all the others, as I amplify in the next chapter.

Even identifying "parents," "spouse," and "children," apparently simple information to fill in for people who constantly elaborate on their relations, was problematic. In some cases, views diverged as to whether a couple was married, and when asked about his or her children, a respondent might list only those present at the time the question was posed. Ambiguities inhere in real life everywhere. However, in modern bureaucracies people are accustomed to forcing their life situations into preset parameters, and the ambiguities have little residual effect at the macro level, "the law of large numbers" smoothing over and compensating for them. In a tiny community, by contrast, each ambivalent case bears on the aggregate demographic picture.

Altogether, I filled out eighty-nine of my pre-prepared cards—sixty-nine for Kungan and his relatives in the Gorge, whom I came to know quite well in the course of fieldwork, and twenty for people who turned out to be only short-term visitors, mostly from the satellite hamlets of MR and DV. It is revealing that, except for the headings, the remainder of my index cards remained blank, while my notebooks (fourteen of them, 150–300 pages each, purchased in a market store in Gudalur) steadily filled up with daily observations and unfolding stories concerning those I lived with. As close relatives, their lives were so entangled that one simply could not parcel this or that "bit" of information onto this or that individual's card. The index card technology of knowledge suits life in larger communities with multiple separate domains, where a personal name helps project the constancy of "uncle," "teacher," "New Yorker," and "Saturday football player" as one and the same man. In contrast, in the forager community of relatives, the use of kin terms as means of address and reference relates everyone to everyone else.

My index cards helped me prepare table 3. Like the cards, the table separates and abstracts relatives from the shifting pluralities within which they live. Alas, categorical separations that figure forager communities of relatives in terms of "men" and "women" and "adults" and "children" have shaped many ethnographic analyses. In the next four chapters, I explore Kungan and his relatives' ontological alternatives.

Relaxing together in one of GR hamlet's huts. Photographed by the author (1978–79).

2. Living Plurally

Mobility and Visiting

Late morning. People are still relaxing by their hearths, the closely spaced fires providing warmth and comfort. Kungan's daughter, Madi, is the first to take her leave, carrying a sickle knife in one hand and bracing her baby son against her waist with the other. Her husband follows her a moment later, a bamboo basket hanging on his back. Her teenage brother, seeing them leave, rushes after them. Her cross-cousin (a widow visiting the hamlet) hesitates briefly, then makes up her mind to follow. Observing this forming party, I hurriedly join in at the rear. We cruise along the path that takes us from the hamlet, keeping a certain distance from one another, each of us enveloped by the forest. My companions are so unhurried and they step so gently that, at times, they seem to be walking in slow motion. They are quiet, communicating by short birdlike cries when they lose sight of each other at sharp turns or when they want to call attention to something. Alert to their surroundings, each listens to the "talk" of the forest: the whoosh of branches moving in the wind, the crunch of dry leaves underfoot, the fluttering of birds taking wing, the cracking of bamboo culms swaying against each other. We stop to collect honey and wild cotton and then continue along the path to visit relatives living in TR.

In this chapter, I expand my focus to the Gorge's five-hamlet community, and I examine the foragers' everyday movements and routine visiting between hamlets. In the canonical *Man the Hunter* symposium, two basic assumptions pertaining to hunter-gatherers were generally accepted: "They live in small groups and . . . they move around a lot" (Lee and DeVore 1968: 11). Both assumptions have been explored largely in relation to subsistence constraints, via the concepts of "nomadism" and "mobility." Here, I shift to "visiting" as a key analytical concept that resonates with locals' perspectives and that, I argue, indexes the plurirelational dimension of locational changes. I explore extensive visiting, common among hunter-gatherers generally, and also look at visits associated with two special events: birthing and burial, for which people gather from all of the Gorge's hamlets. I show that, for this multisited community, visiting engenders closeness with a shifting cast of characters and thus constitutes the cultural means by which each member participates in the lives of all (or most) of the others. Community, as understood by the foragers, comprises plurirelated relatives.

. . .

Observing people walking separately in the forest, one following the other, one might perceive them as individuals. Observing a man, woman, and children relaxing around one of the hamlet's outdoor hearths, one might see a nuclear family. Both of these readings slipped into classic hunter-gatherer studies, stirring debates about the nature of band societies, debates that, nevertheless, failed to fully register the tiny size of these groups. Early in the 1930s, Julian Steward (1936, cf. 1969) associated some hunting and gathering societies with the "family level of social integration," which, he argued, is representative of the earliest stage of human social organization. At this stage, he posited, the nuclear family is the only social unit, and individual families come together and split apart in an annual cycle. Steward's model went unchallenged for close to thirty years; then, Elman Service (1966) attempted to modify it by among other things suggesting that the entire band be seen as *one family*. In the late 1960s, Peter Gardner (1966, cf. 1991, 2000a) argued that the South Indian Paliyan, like many other hunter-gatherers, are a highly "individualistic" society that sets high value on personal autonomy. By the end of the twentieth century, perhaps resonating with heightening attention to the individual in the Western/ized world, *autonomy* and *individualism* had become key terms in sociocultural hunter-gatherer studies (see Ingold 1999 and Bird-David 2015 for reviews). The individualist approach was not universally endorsed, however, and the idea of the "family level of social integration" persisted in some scholarly work (e.g., Johnson 2003).[1] Fred Myers's (1986) study of mid-1970s Australian Aboriginal Pintupi was a sophisticated attempt to address the tension and articulation between autonomy and relatedness. The essence of Pintupi social life, Myers argued, is achieving balance between these two poles: individuals choose their own courses of action (18) and at the same time "complete themselves through identity with others" (178).

Scant attention has been paid in these debates to the tiny size of hunter-gatherer groups. Myers's study, for example, is based on fieldwork undertaken in 1973–75 in and around the outstation of Yayayi, its population then (at its height, after receiving a large government grant) averaging 200–220, with new outstation communities observed in 1979 comprising between a dozen and several dozen people each (ibid., 42–43, 45). The local Paliyan communities visited by Gardner comprised fifteen to sixty people; the group with which he stayed the longest fluctuated in size, made up of twenty-three men and sixteen women at one point. Such figures have a peculiar effect that perhaps can be described as casting a "large-numbers spell": one can hardly comprehend how few the subjects of study are when so quantified. They are *very* few! In my study, I could count the co-dwellers of two hamlets using two hands, three hamlets with an added foot, and a fourth hamlet with no more than both hands and feet. And the small size of my study group does not reflect a lack of effort on my part to reach and "cover" more people. I walked for hours among the five dispersed hamlets in which these people lived. The minute scale of communities like the ones Gardner, Myers, and I studied *is* the reality of their members' lives and experiences. In this chapter, I follow Myers in looking beyond the "individuals/nuclear families" debate in hunter-gatherer studies, and at the same time, I keep in sharp focus the tiny size of the hunter-gatherer band.

"Visiting" is the analytical category framing the following ethnographic analysis. I examine both everyday visits (in which the community of relatives subsists) and visits on special occasions like births and deaths (by which that community is reconstituted). Excursions in the forest, like that of Madi and her relatives, are usually approached by scholars through the analytical prisms of "mobility" and "foraging." Robert Kelly (1995) dedicates a chapter to these concepts in his widely used textbook on hunter-gatherers, a chapter that, for the most part, surveys various ecological models of the relationships among mobility, environment, and individual forays. But even Kelly notes, glossing it as their "cultural ideal," that hunter-gatherers themselves commonly express "a strong desire to move around in order to *visit* friends, to see what is happening elsewhere, or to relieve boredom" (153, emphasis added). In broaching the subject of mobility, Kelly writes, "There is hardly a more romantic image in anthropology than that of a small band of hunter-gatherers setting off through the dunes and scrub, their few belongings on their back" (111). This image starkly expresses the disjuncture between local and scholarly perspectives, and it resonates with the popular image of the hero who, at the end of a Hollywood Western, rides off alone into the sunset, destination unknown, expansive land awaiting him. For hunter-gatherers, I argue, excursions like that of Madi and her company, rather, are integral to continuous intimacy work with dispersed relatives and with nonhuman relatives in the natural surroundings, all within immediately perceived horizons.

In his book *Mobilities*, James Urry (2007) highlights the growing attention in the social sciences to *different* mobility paradigms, attention that has yet to significantly extend to studies of foraging people, with one exception: in her study of a people she calls "Meratus," who negotiate and exploit their marginality to Indonesian society as they continue to subsist mainly on shifting cultivation and foraging, Tsing (1993) proposes "travel" as key to understanding the group's culture and politics and, more generally, as an analytical category for cross-cultural study. Like "mobility," however, in common understanding, "travel" hinges on dichotomous settlement/road, to/from, and in/out perceptions. Traveling connotes transiting from one place to another, going "outside" one place and ultimately going "inside" another, and in between, staying "*out* on the road" in a somewhat liminal state open to danger and without the comforts of home. Like "mobility," "travel" is meaningful in a space with *fixed* places (*from* and *to* which people travel). But do hunting-gathering people live in such spaces? Their settlements hardly constitute a fixed grid. Their world is one in which paths are places of habitation and places are not stationary. On the move, they instantly construct homes in new locations; even if they build and rebuild huts in the same locations, those "base" locations "crawl" across the landscape. Their clusters of huts are so tiny that the regular conduct of everyday life (going to defecate, fetch water, have privacy) involves leaving them. The forager world, I want to show in this chapter, has a fluid quality unlimited by "permanent" houses, villages, and fields; thus, it is not a physical space *in* which its inhabitants move but a social space they constitute in living each with the others.

In contrast to *travel*, the term *visit*—from the Latin *visitare* (go to see or frequent)—combines subjective experience and spatial movement. "If you visit someone," one elementary dictionary explains, "you go to see them and spend time *with* them" (emphasis added).[2] A visit to a place, another dictionary specifies, is "a short or temporary *stay* at a place" (emphasis added).[3] If the concept of "travel" foregrounds movement *between* places, or even just leaving one place and taking to the road, the concept of "visiting" foregrounds engagement at a destination *with* another person or with something at that place. Travel can take you to parts unknown, while a visit takes you to people or places you are familiar with (though travel advertisements may manipulatively confuse the two). Objects as well as subjects travel, but only subjects engage in visits. In considering the pluripresent nature of tiny hunter-gatherer communities, clearly "visiting" is more suitable than "mobility" and "travel" as an analytical category and one, moreover, that expands on hunter-gatherers' own expressed concerns.

My primary objective in this chapter, then, is to bring to analytical life the plurality of (human) relatives—living in small groups and moving around a lot—who refer to themselves as *sonta* (our own, relatives). I ethnographically elaborate on their constant coming and going among the five hamlets in the Gorge, suggesting that their own sense of themselves as pluripresent relatives subsists in everyday and special visits. A point that I explicitly emphasize in this account, because of its overall theoretical implications, is the extent of each community member's plural involvement *with* almost every other member in the local group, not just in a single hamlet. Constant visiting coupled with the smallness of the hamlets potentiate each-with-all unmediated relatedness and, thus, concretely living *with* others rather than *in* an abstracted community. Exploiting this potential, I begin to argue in this chapter, is Madi and her relatives' cultural project and ideal. And appreciating that ideal, I suggest, is crucial for understanding these people's relations, lifeways, and ontologies. I turn, then, to the ethnography, to Madi and her relatives gliding along the forest path. . . .

VISITING: LIVING *WITH* (SHIFTING) RELATIVES

They live in small groups and move around a lot (Take 1)

After a two-hour walk, we reach TR, where no one pays us any attention. Madi's *chikappa* (junior father, i.e., father's younger brother) and his wife continue going about their business as if we were not there, separating tree bark into thin fibers that will later be used for spinning ropes. They do not greet us, nor do we greet them. Even my arrival provokes no overt interest. We stand about for a moment, then sit down and engage in our own activities. A conversation starts among visitors and hamlet residents about half an hour later, touching on a variety of topics (who the rope is being made for, the bees our party saw along the way, who has fallen ill, etc.). Our visit is short, and after a few hours we set out on our way back home. When we leave, we are saluted with the words *hoite bare* (go-and-come), a common expression of farewell in neighboring Dravidian languages and one that Madi and her people use extensively, whether one is leaving the hamlet simply to collect firewood or departing for a stated long-term absence (as I did at the end of fieldwork). *Hoite bare*, a local equivalent of *see you later*, and here the only way to say *good bye*, frames *all* departures as temporary separations, as moments in a continuing process of coming and going.

What does the unmarked nature of arrival in a hamlet mean? An American authority on etiquette, in a book written in 1952 and still referenced today, spells out in minute detail a middle-class urbanite script of what a host should do when guests arrive at a dinner party. Consider, for example, this brief excerpt from her protocol: "A designated member of the family opens the door, takes the guest's coat and hat and leads the way to the living room, stepping back to let him enter. The hostess excuses herself to any guest she may be with, rises, and comes forward to greet the guest, man or woman. The host comes forward, too, and both host and hostess shake hands with the newcomer" (Vanderbilt 1954: 463).

Or consider that Felicity Heal (1990: 9) describes the hospitable ideal for early modern England (1400–1700) as "keep[ing] the doors open" to poor and rich and feeding and entertaining them as a means of asserting one's status, morals, and worth, in the eyes of man and God. Such treatment of visitors is far removed from what happens during our party's visit to TR and in visits generally among Madi and her relatives. A bounded household, with doors to open, strangers to entertain, poor to be generous to, social status to accrue through lavish hospitality, or friends to welcome with an invitation to "make themselves at home" (which, of course, would be scandalous if they really did so)—all these notions must be put aside in scaling down the analysis to the foragers' nanocommunity.

In an analysis closer in scale to and instructive for my case, Signe Howell (1984: 38–41) describes how visitors behave among the Eastern Chewong, a shifting cultivator and hunter-gatherer people of Malaysia: People arriving from other settlements walk briskly up to whichever house they are going to be sleeping in. They put down their blowpipes, and without looking left or right or acknowledging any persons present, they enter the house, hang up their back baskets on a beam, and sit down close together. The occupants of the house then enter, and tobacco and food are exchanged. Other members of the settlement slowly come to see the visitors. Conversation gradually begins, moving from the guests' itinerary to news of illnesses and, then, other topics. This reserved behavior, Howell states, making a case for analyzing the visit as a *rite de passage* in Arnold van Gennep's terms, cannot be accounted for by lack of acquaintance. All Chewong, she tells us, know each other intimately from birth, all having lived with one another at some time. They move frequently throughout their lives; individuals and whole families go on visits for months on end (39). We thus learn, almost incidentally, how major and sweeping the phenomenon of visiting is among Eastern Chewong, who, when Howell stayed with them, numbered only 131 persons dispersed in six settlements

(18, 15). This scalar context does not enter into Howell's analysis of Chewong arrival etiquette; her rite of passage perspective is equally applicable to the hospitality protocol of mid-twentieth-century American society. Yet the substantial scale difference requires addressing the two cases differently. I shudder to think what Amy Vanderbilt would have said of dinner guests who stay for months on end or of unrestricted visiting that involves everyone in a society.

The network of narrow forest paths connecting the dispersed hamlets in the Gorge attests to the intensive traffic related to local visiting. The fast-growing vegetation means that only routes repeatedly taken remain open. Created by people's feet during everyday activities, these routes reflect habitual movement and social connections. The experience of following these narrow and twisting paths is one of stillness and surrender to the environment, of staying with what lies on the way, at least momentarily. It certainly contrasts sharply with the experience of racing along a "fast" built road. The paths are minutely responsive to topographic features and even to changes from one day to the next: A piece of wood falls onto a path. The first to encounter it goes around it, others follow, and in time the jog in the path is used by everyone, as if it had always been part of the route. Covered by vegetation, the old path is hardly discernible anymore. It is remarkable how fast "slow" paths can be in terms of how quickly they change in relation to circumstance and appear or disappear, whereas "fast" roads are slow to change; they become lasting fixtures, whether used or not.

Setting off from the hamlet on a visit, on one of the several paths that spread outward from it in all directions, Madi and her people usually referred in general terms to the relatives they were going to see and stay with—if they made any statement at all. They would say that they were going to be with *sonta*, or they would specify a particular relative (e.g., parents). They could also simply set out to forage in the forest or work on the rubber and coffee plantation located at the bottom of the Gorge, stopping on the way at one of their relatives' hamlets and staying there for a time. Even with a visit in mind, they left their own hamlet with no idea of how long they would be away. Temporally unbounded, such visits, as among the Chewong, could go on for days, weeks, or months; some visits, in retrospect, turned out to be changes of residence altogether (especially if conjugal relations developed between a visitor and one of the hosts). Resonating with what Howell describes, arrival at another hamlet is strikingly unmarked by greetings or any other overt expression of joy, just as leave-taking is underplayed in saying *hoite bare* (go-and-come). Expressing joy at meeting, notably, would foreground the separation that has just ended and perhaps the separation to come. Arriving relatives simply enter the open area within a hamlet, where residents usually go about their everyday business and leisure. The visitors sit down or stand unceremoniously, making themselves present. If they stand closer to their special host than to others, that proximity is hardly perceptible given the small size of the camp and the lack of partitioned space. Slowly, conversation starts and news is exchanged, as among the Chewong. Everyone is involved, not just visitors and hosts. A visit can hardly exclude anyone in such tiny hamlets.

There are many possible scripts for what happens next, the most formal of which involves visitors being fed by the specific relatives they have come to see, but only on the evening of the first day or, perhaps, for a few days. If the hosts do not have enough food—and this can happen given that visits are ad hoc, unregulated by invitations—the hamlet's co-dwellers, who are the hosts' relatives, contribute food, albeit grudgingly. "What can I do, he is my brother, and he does not work," Madi's father's brother, an industrious and introverted man, often moaned to me when he had to give food yet again to his gregarious, popular sibling to help feed his many visitors.

All visitors staying for more than a day or two take care of their own needs and join in the rhythm of everyday life in the hosts' hamlet; an outside observer would hardly be able to distinguish between visitors and residents by their everyday conduct. Everyone continues the routines of foraging or casually working on the plantation, collecting firewood, cooking, and so on, visitors behaving just as they would in their own hamlets. The hosts do not conspicuously outnumber the visitors in these tiny hamlets, as might be the case in a large village. Visitors' arrivals reconstitute the hamlet's composition. Visits, in this respect, are not liminal times off from everyday life. They do not long remain visits to particular residents of a hamlet, if they even begin that way, but are visits to all residents.

Visits are diversely, and manipulatively, read, as is apparent from local commentary about them. They are motivated by many reasons, such as relocating nearer to a seasonal foraging or employment site; joining relatives to look for a spouse or seek companionship, perhaps after being widowed; or simply for pleasure and a desire to keep in touch (not to mention special social events like birthing and burial). But visits are also triggered by social tensions and, in turn, engender divergent perspectives on relatives' plural staying together. Consider this case: Madi and her husband live in a hut next to that of her parents. One day they go to visit the husband's parents, who live in another hamlet. They say they go there to be closer to the forest site where they collect *sikai* (the pods of the tropical forest creeper *Sapindus trifoliatus*, which are sold to local traders). But Madi's

Relaxing together in GR hamlet. Photographed by the author (1978–79).

father tells me that he overheard them talking in the night, when they thought he was asleep, about how often they have to give him food; this, he says, is why they have left. He is hurt and angry, complaining that they do not care for him, saying that *he* often gives them food and is happy that they are gone. When I consult another relative about what has happened, he responds only, "Who can know what is in their hearts?" Three days later, the couple return and settle back into their quarters, amicably engaging with the no-longer-grumpy father. Some people express their displeasure with their coresidents by threatening to go visit and live with other relatives who will better care for them. In like vein, one old woman I knew repeatedly told me about visits she made to relatives in other hamlets, visits that she could not possibly have made but only fantasized, given her fragile health. This was her idiomatic way of talking about her troubles at home and of the existence of relatives in other hamlets who cared for her. The constant traffic of visiting is used and talked about in relation to the ebb and flow of plurally living together in the hamlet.

Visits are connected to one another, although not simply in reciprocal dyads, that is, one visit prompting a return visit. Rather, each visit triggers a cascade of other visits: Outgoing visitors pave the way for incoming visitors by vacating rooms and taking a few things with them. Incoming visitors move into the vacant spaces and use the things left there, making room, in turn, for incoming visitors to the hamlet they themselves have left. Consider the following sequence of events, a segment of an ongoing multi-sited process: Madi's uncle and his wife live close to the wife's mother, in adjoining rooms. The mother is old and half-senile. She fetches her own water from the river, using a rattling, rusty tin she carries with her everywhere. Her daughter and her daughter's husband give her food, but the mother complains to anyone passing by that they give her nothing, shaming the pair. Exhausted, the couple go to visit the wife's sister, who lives in another hamlet. The old woman, now really unsupported, goes to visit and stay with her granddaughter, who lives in a third hamlet. The daughter and her husband return from their visit a week later, accompanied by a sixteen-year-old niece, who has seized the opportunity to make the journey back with them. She settles into the room the old lady has vacated. A thirty-year-old widowed second cousin, who now and then passes through this hamlet on his way to work on the plantation, begins to stop there and stay overnight—to be closer to work, he says at first, but eventually he moves in with the young girl in what had been the old lady's room. And so the ripples from visits spread from hamlet to hamlet. Social tensions, loves, deaths, the seasonality of forest resources, fluctuations in supplementary casual labor opportunities, and other factors all intertwine and complicate visits in this small and densely interconnected multisited community of relatives.

Foraging, in particular, is closely entwined with these visits, which normally involve walking for several hours through the forest. The two most distant hamlets in the Gorge are separated by about a six-hour walk. People do not simply walk purposefully toward their destination, but, as the opening scene in this chapter reveals, they use the journey as an opportunity to forage and to "visit" and engage with diverse forest beings.

The cumulative consequence of visiting—the shuffling and reshuffling of the relatives one lives with in the intimate hamlet setting—should not be overlooked. While visits do not involve taking time off from everyday routines (either for the guests or for the hosts), what they do involve is a change of *those with whom* one shares these routines, that is, a change of neighbors. Through the ripple effect—and because these people "live in small groups" *and* "move around a lot"—most people end up living in close proximity with most others at one time or another. The frequency of hunter-gatherer visits and the degree to which, as a result, each person stays with (almost) everyone else are suggested indirectly by Howell's discussion of the Chewong arrival code of behavior. It can also be gauged from James Woodburn's (1968a: 104–5) diachronic survey of the Eastern Hadza of Tanzania. Woodburn recorded those with whom one old Hadza widow, quite conservative in local terms, lived on twenty-five separate occasions over roughly three years. His main purpose was to show the extent to which Hadza moved around and the related changes in camp size, both of which are clear from his findings: the old woman stayed with between three and thirty-seven adults on the occasions he recorded. But Woodburn (49) also remarked, and this, I think, is a point worth emphasizing, that during those three years, she lived with *more than a quarter* of the entire Eastern Hadza population (estimated at four hundred when Woodburn studied them). This figure reflects an extraordinarily high degree of direct personal contact between the woman and those she considered to be her people. One can assume that it would have been higher had the study continued through her lifetime. The equivalent, in a university of 18,000 students like my own, would be for a single student to share a dorm room with 4,500 other students during three years of study. And we should remember, the interaction between the old Hadza widow and those with whom she lived was more than fleeting and intermittent. She did not simply meet these others now and then, or just in the evening when they all returned from their respective pursuits. In small hunter-gatherer hamlets, residents' participation in one another's lives is intense, multifaceted, and continuous, and for most, it lasts throughout life, from birth to death.

The very small-scale order of the overall population, together with the intensive visiting and the tiny size of local hamlets, potentiates a high degree of unmediated presence, each in all others' lives. It potentiates participating in relatives' lives to the extent that, as I argue elsewhere (Bird-David 1994a), one's relatives *are* those that one lives with. Those one only knows *of* rapidly fade from conscious awareness. Visits are one means of extending the distance at which relatives can live and remain relatives. They offset the "tyranny of distance"; they involve relation-work or, rather, relatives-work.

BORN SOCIAL

They move around a lot and live in small groups (Take 2)

A large number of relatives visit the same hamlet all at once, arriving from all the surrounding hamlets, when a birth occurs. Births are relatively rare events in such a tiny community, only now and then punctuating the repetitive everyday. During my 1978–79 fieldwork, only one baby was born in GR, where I lived, not too surprising given that only three women of childbearing age then lived in this hamlet, the largest in the Gorge. Luckily, I was present when this birth occurred and could witness it in its entirety. In my description of this event below, I dwell on the experiences of we-ness and the senses of communality the birth engendered and expressed.

Madi's cousin Kalliyani was about twenty years old when she gave birth to a son, her firstborn, some months after I had moved into the hamlet. A shy, soft-spoken girl, she was far more attached to her parents, especially her quiet but resolute mother, than other girls I knew of her age. Her husband was about thirty years old and had a child form a previous marriage. On the day his son was born, he was on his way to sell *sikai* in Pandalur. His heavily pregnant wife had not wanted to climb with him up the steep path leading to Pandalur, and as it turned out, it was good that she stayed behind. Her labor started in midmorning, after some of her relatives had already left the hamlet for diverse purposes, most going to collect *sikai*. This forest creeper attaches itself to large trees that reach great heights (twelve to eighteen meters). Its dark red pods are used in the preparation of commercial detergents and produce a soapy mixture good for cleaning delicate jewelry. The pods are produced biannually and have a short harvesting season; they can be sold for good prices to the plantation and at market stalls in Pandalur. No one able to collect them wanted to miss even a day of doing so. All the same, messages about the approaching birth were immediately sent to the relatives who had left the hamlet, and almost all who received them returned for what was evidently considered more important than a day of lucrative foraging. The news of Kalliyani's labor spread fast throughout the Gorge, and as the hours wore on, other relatives arrived in GR from hamlets farther away, some walking for hours to get there. A Mappila woman, one of the migrants who had begun settling in the Gorge in the mid-1950s, arrived too, explaining to me that she was a friend of the family and was following what she construed as the "Nayaka custom" that friends and relatives be present at a birth. The following account draws directly from field notes I took at the time. . . .

Kalliyani is inside the section of the compound hut in which she ordinarily lives with her husband, in the dwelling they share with her parents (essentially a "room" with an open entryway). A thin cloth is hung for the occasion at the doorway, only half-covering it; arriving visitors approach the doorway and fling the cloth aside to see Kalliyani and let her see them, all with no greeting, before seating themselves outside the hut. A few steps away from the hut, a fire is burning in an open hearth, and people casually arrange themselves around it. Some women and children (including myself) crowd onto the raised mud platform just outside the hut's doorway, only a step removed from Kalliyani. Kalliyani squats on the floor inside, pulling on the ends of a cloth thrown over the timber beam supporting the thatched roof. She tries to hold herself upright and take her mind off her pain. Women come and go in and out of the room, making their way through those sitting close to the entry; while inside, they sit with Kalliyani, at times patting her. Her aunt prepares a special drink for her, to give her strength and endurance. Her mother, her mother's sister, and her father's brother's wife are her principal attendants. Yet they occasionally leave the room too and join their husbands, who are gathered with others around the hearth outside the hut.

Throughout the six-hour ordeal, the visitors relax as they wait, passing the time in various ways. Four girls sit in a circle picking lice from each other's hair. A man seated by the hearth weaves a fishing basket. Next to him, another man lies on a mat and rests. A teenage girl feeds a young forest squirrel, found abandoned several days before and brought to the hamlet to be cared for. I write my observations in my field diary.

Relatives casually chat, breaking into laughter now and then. Adults occasionally share betel nuts with one another, chewing them and then spitting out the red fluid on the ground by the hearth. The waves of sharing do not stop at the hut's doorway. Stepping over to the doorway of the hut, someone passes betel nuts to the women sitting inside with Kalliyani. We can hear Kalliyani's heavy breathing and hushed grunts and moans. She is less than two meters away from those of us gathered on the hut's platform. Hours pass. Kalliyani's father and, later, her teenage cousin go to the tea shack at the plantation border, each time returning after half an hour or so with a glass bottle filled with tea. At the doorway to the hut, the bottle is handed to Kalliyani's mother, and she later passes it back. Even the conversation, rising and falling, does not halt at the doorway but links Kalliyani and her attendants together with all those seated outside on the platform or by the hearth. When Kalliyani's father wants to speak with his wife directly, he has only to take a few steps and stand next to the wall of the hut. His wife stands on the other side, and they talk through the flimsy barrier separating them. Someone seated outside the doorway occasionally peeps into the hut and hands food to or talks with Kalliyani's attendants, checking on progress. New visitors continue to arrive. The area just outside the doorway is completely full by now, so new arrivals find spots around the hearth, where there is still plenty of room.

Six hours after going into labor, Kalliyani sobs and breathes heavily in pain as the baby arrives. The cloth is fully drawn across the doorway while the baby emerges and Kalliyani's body is exposed, but as soon as he is born and she is decently clothed again, it is flung back. Everyone draws closer to the hut or turns attention in that direction. The newborn enters the world, as it were, in the midst of a plurality of relatives socializing and sharing with each other, all around him.

Immediately afterward, visitors are wished *hoite bare* (go-and-come) and leave. Kalliyani's mother and her aunt, who have stayed with her through most of her labor, take care of what clearly is not regarded as the main purpose of the relatives' visit. Kalliyani's mother gently washes the baby's head and puts a drop of water in his mouth; then, very slowly, she stretches his limbs, checking that he is physically sound. Kalliyani's young cousin brings in a piece of bamboo that Kalliyani's aunt sharpens with her all-purpose sickle knife and then uses to cut the umbilical cord, tying it with a string. All is done matter-of-factly, even placing a drop of blood on the baby's mouth and on the foreheads of the baby and the mother. "This is how we do it" is the only explanation I receive to my repeated questions about what it means. Kalliyani's mother then washes the baby, and the aunt helps Kalliyani wash herself. The aunt's husband, I am surprised to see, later helps his wife wash her hands, holding the pot of water and pouring for her.

Kalliyani's husband returned later in the evening. As night fell, he, his wife, and their baby slept together—on the same grass mat the couple had been using before the birth and covering themselves with the same old thin cloth. Next morning, they sat with their baby son beside their outdoor hearth, falling into the everyday rhythm of plural life in the hamlet.

The birth of a first child is more widely attended than the births of siblings, I was told. Kalliyani's father's younger sister had been the last before Kalliyani to give birth to a child in this hamlet, a few months before I began living there. It was her sixth live birth, and she complained to me that no one had helped her; she had delivered the baby, she said, "all by herself in the forest." Some suggested to me that she exaggerated. I could not ascertain reliably what had really happened, but we can learn from her complaint that birthing among relatives and in the hamlet is deemed important. The idea resonates with the local view that dying alone in the forest has dangerous consequences. One should not be born separately from others but among them, not away from and then brought into the hamlet but in the midst of it. What, indeed, was striking about the birth I witnessed— especially if viewed in comparison with biomedical hospital birth, with its physically, temporally, and socially complex system of separations and hierarchies (presented as a rite of passage in Davis-Floyd 1992)—was the way separations were kept to a minimum. Kalliyani was hardly separated during labor from her everyday relatives and neighbors. Moreover, an event that might have been expected to involve strict gender segregation drew in both men and women. Couples and children came to be with Kalliyani, and the curtain was only drawn across the doorway at the moment of birth to preserve her decency. The same knife used in everyday tasks was used to cut the umbilical cord. Sharing and talking connected those gathered together throughout the six-hour ordeal.

Yet the sociality on display during Kalliyani's ordeal was not as effortless as it seemed but rather was a part of what was considered proper conduct on such occasions. The potential danger to both mother and baby during birthing was only too painfully known—precisely because birth was not a secluded event. And among the relatives gathered together during Kalliyani's labor were those who had been present for births with tragic complications. Just a few years earlier, for instance, one of Kalliyani's cousins had died giving birth to a stillborn. The case was described to me as a gruesome event, unique in recent memory, the dead child remaining stuck half in and half out of the mother, until she too died in agony. Socializing the way they did for six hours—not as one body, a collective, directed to do this or that but rather relaxing together, engaging with one another flexibly—reinforced their community as relatives, diversely related to one another and together.

Tragic birthing was ascribed to disruptions in living together rather than to violations of certain rules, no different than other instances of *batha*, a category of illnesses and misfortunes that have no obvious external cause and no cure within the local terms of knowledge (see Bird-David 2004b). Susan Sontag (1978) has shown how the discourse surrounding tuberculosis in nineteenth- and early twentieth-century Europe reflected the emergence of the modern concept of individuality, for example, popularizing the idea that the cause and the cure of illness lie within the self. By contrast, Vieda Skultans (1987) has shown in his work on the management of mental illness among Maharashtrian families that the patient who is diagnosed and cured is the entire family, not just the afflicted individual. For Madi and her relatives, *batha* is not the result of individual or familial transgressions or shortcomings but instead reflects a problem within the entire community of relatives. It is within this community that the cause and the cure are sought. No effort is made to establish specific culpability or responsibility. Rather, divination and other means are employed to determine whether fractured relations with the spirits, triggered by faulty relations within the community, are at the root of the problem. If such is found to be the case, a corrective is sought in promises exchanged with the spirits to henceforth share with and care for all within the community of human and nonhuman relatives (for a full discussion, see Bird-David 2004b; see also Demmer 2001, which examines similar community-based rhetoric and performance among a Jenu Kurumba group in the Mudumali area of the Nilgiri Hills). The seemingly casual staying together of relatives at a birth—passing the time, relaxing, chatting, drinking tea, and engaging in mundane activities— is a ritual of sorts to keep plural life flowing despite the tensions of the event, a safeguard against misfortune.

A Hebrew saying asserts that a man is born alone and dies alone. At least as it pertains to birth, the saying belies biological reality—the one certainty about birth is that it always involves at least two beings, a mother and a newborn (and, often, more relatives, even if not immediately present). The idea of a solitary new life is a fantastical one, as a newborn *cannot* exist alone, without others and their care. It attests to the power of culture and to the idea of multiple ontologies; more specifically, it speaks to the assumption in some modern cultural frames that birth produces "new individuals" (Strathern 1992a). This idea is intertwined with multiple technologies and metaphors (e.g., ultrasound and antenatal surgery, which promote the image of a separate baby in its mother's womb and of the mother as a facilitating container, with the umbilical cord as support system). This idea is intertwined as well with giving the baby an identity-card number and possibly a name immediately after birth. So strong may be our modern sense of a baby as a new individual, or at most a new son/daughter/sibling in the family, that a case needs to be made for the equally obvious proposition that a baby is born as a new relative to a plurality of others. To each of them, a different relative is born: son to one, grandson to another, nephew to yet a third, cousin to a fourth, and so on. In a tiny-scale community, the newborn simultaneously relates in one way or another to everyone. To the relatives who came to be present at the birth I witnessed, it was not a new individual that was born or a son to Kalliyani and her husband. A new relative was born to each and every one of them.

DIE SOCIAL

They move around a lot and live in small groups (Take 3)

Like birth, death occurs infrequently in this small, multisited community, and it occasions visits by relatives from all of the Gorge's hamlets. As Woodburn (1982: 202) points out, death is "relatively invisible" among hunter-gatherers compared with its salience in larger communities and denser populations. During the four years he lived with the Hadza, Woodburn was only once in a camp when someone died, a baby who survived for two days after his birth (ibid., 188). One of the few scholars to have done so, Woodburn compared dimensions of death among hunter-gatherer groups, drawing primarily on informants' statements in the four cases he considered (the Hadza of Tanzania, the Mbuti Pygmies of Zaire, the Baka Pygmies of Cameroon, and the !Kung Bushmen of Botswana and Namibia).[4] With this in mind, readers should understand why it is not trivial that I was able to witness the immediate aftermath of a death. I arrived in the hamlet where Benu had been living only two days after his death and was able to observe the end of the ritual marking his passing and to talk with people about what had happened while the event was still fresh in their memory. The analysis below offers a synthesis of what I saw and what I heard various people say in relation to his death. Twenty-five years later, Daniel Naveh was present in the hamlet of a separate Nayaka local group, substantially more than a single day's walk from GR, when a husband and wife there died within two days of one another. My synthesis draws on his observations in addition to my own.[5]

Benu, a man in his early thirties, died in BR, a ten-minute walk from GR, where I lived. At the time, he lived there with his sister (a homely girl in her early twenties, who, unlike her peers, was still single), his father's older sister (a semisenile widow), his father's older sister's granddaughter and her husband (the husband twenty years older than this second wife), and that husband's daughter from his first marriage and her husband. He had been ill for the five months I knew him, probably suffering from tuberculosis. In the last weeks of his life, he still managed to spend most days lying on a mat outside the hut, engaging as best he could with his relatives. He had been unable to work or forage for some time, and his hamlet-mates largely shouldered the responsibility of looking after him. He died before dawn. His death was discovered in the morning, and the news was quickly sent out. (The following account is reconstructed from my investigative conversations with those who arrived soon after the death, and I retain their vivid narratives by using the present tense).

The body is not removed or covered while those in BR await the arrival of relatives from other hamlets. It is left where death took place, visible, hardly attracting attention except for the gazes of curious children and passersby. No one gathers around the body or laments the death. The sight of the body (and, later, its smell) does not seem to affront or discomfort anybody. People go on with their normal activities around it: one woman washes the pots from yesterday's meal, a couple goes to bathe in the river and then returns, and so on. (Naveh observed much the same behavior in relation to the two deaths he witnessed.) Slowly arriving from other hamlets, at their own pace, visitors throw a glance at the dead body and seat themselves in the area around the hut he had occupied. The tardiness of those yet to arrive generates the usual complaints, lack of care being read into the delays. The hours pass; noon comes and goes. The body continues to lie where it was found, starting to stink. One relative is particularly awaited, an old man who lives in TR, Madi's granduncle, an experienced medium whom local ancestral spirits possess to communicate with the living. Midafternoon arrives, and he still has not appeared. Losing their patience, four male relatives begin to wash the corpse. (Had the dead person been a woman, women would have washed the body.) Since no new cloth is available, they leave the deceased's old cloth on him, place his corpse on an ad hoc platform made from wood, and carry it to a spot up the hill, a twenty-minute or so walk away. There they dig a pit, about a meter and a half deep, seat the corpse in it, cover the pit first with the mat Benu lay on when he died and then with soil, and return to the hamlet.

These procedures are straightforwardly pragmatic, at odds with the centrality of burial ritual in other societies/cultures, in which it is often marked and elaborated, socially and culturally. The disposal of the body in many contexts is often the starting point of a ceremonial process that can extend over many years, involving primary and then secondary treatment of the remains. Burial is frequently linked with ancestor worship, and graves and tombs often have a prominent role in social life. Permanent and elaborate graves and tombs can serve as symbols of family unity, national unity, and connections to the land. Some migrants in today's global world attach great importance to being buried in their place of origin. Burial in the homeland has been important in the Jewish tradition for two thousand years, and the bodily remains of the wealthy in the Diaspora have often been transported back to Israel for final burial. Even when cremation, rather than burial, is the norm, as in Buddhist and Hindu traditions (to liberate the soul from its fleshy entrapments), the place and manner in which the body is cremated and in which the ashes are disposed are at the center of attention (ritual, social, emotional, and spiritual). Mourning and other codes for after-death behavior are commonplace, in some cases remaining in effect throughout survivors' lives; in some traditional Hindu practices, they cost a widow her life.

Against this background, the burial procedures for Benu are startlingly simple; in this respect, they resemble the procedures for treatment and disposal of the body in the four African hunter-gatherer groups Woodburn (1982) compared. In all these cases, people do little more than attend to the "practical requirements for getting rid of a rotting corpse" (202). They rarely prepare the corpse; they dig a shallow grave, place the body in it, and cover it, or they leave the corpse in a hut, which they cause to collapse over it. All deaths are treated in more or less the same manner, with those of young persons handled in an even more banal and matter-of-fact way than adult deaths. In all of these cases, no specialists are involved in the burial. There is no one whose task it is to administer or control death rituals. Beyond men being expected to do the manual work of digging and filling the grave and women to do more lamenting than men, no particular responsibilities are allotted to particular persons, kin or other. In all four cases Woodburn reviews, no one expresses serious concern that a death may be supernaturally caused: causes are not sought by means of divination or attributed to witchcraft that needs to be identified and redressed. "The cause," as Woodburn puts it, "at most is a matter of speculation not for action or decision" (ibid., 203). In all four cases, neither mourning nor other codes of specific behavior are expected: directly after the disposal of the body, ordinary life goes on, without any required mourning period or any outward signs that a death has occurred. Immediate remarriage of a widowed person, for example, is not objectionable. A burial place is rarely visited, and if it is, it is not for social or ceremonial functions but only to ascertain that the body has not been dug up by animals. Lastly, in all four cases, human death is not discursively associated with a belief in an afterworld or with ideas about fertility or regeneration of life in this world. For the Hadza, in particular, Woodburn notes (ibid., 188), taboos and prohibitions on sexuality are associated with hunting (i.e., the death of animals) but not with the death of humans.

Woodburn (1980) offers a structural-functional explanation for these recurring patterns among the four hunter-gatherer cases he examines. All of the groups he canvasses belong to the immediate-return hunter-gatherer type, one characteristic of which is orientation to the present. Given little local concern with the future, Woodburn argues (1982: 206–7), no questions of succession and inheritance arise, there is no need to socially replace the deceased, and there is no concern about continuity of social positions. Factually, in all the respects Woodburn notes, Madi and her relatives are not very different from his four cases, and as I have shown in previous work, they also belong to the immediate-return type (Bird 1983b, Bird-David 1992b, 2004a). I depart, however, from Woodburn's explanation, shifting from dwelling on individual offices and persons to dwelling on communities. Social continuity, I submit, is a matter of great concern for Madi and her relatives. However, it does not focus on continuity of the deceased individual or his or her possessions, office, or even relations but rather on *the continuity of the assembly of relatives living plurally.* Furthermore, what may be regarded by outsiders as inaction and disrespect for the dead is perceived differently in this particular hunter-gatherer setting. No disrespect was shown to Benu's dead body, left lying outside, visible, until burial. As discussed in chapter 1, domestic life usually takes place in the open. Withdrawal into a hut is considered asocial and a sign of stinginess; sick people go to a lot of trouble and endure discomfort in an effort to stay outside a hut for as long as they possibly can. Likewise, to place the corpse in a hut, to separate and conceal it from others, would be a show of disrespect. Equally, to build a grave or a tomb in which to inter the corpse would be incongruent with the general open and shared residential mode of the living, in flimsy huts lacking solid exterior walls and interior divisions. To wail and mourn the deceased's departure by the graveside would be generally inconsistent with the avoidance of rites of departure and arrival. What happened after Benu's burial reveals the local concerns with the continuity of plural life. . . .

By the time the men return from disposing of the body, there are more than two dozen relatives in the hamlet, including Madi's long-awaited granduncle. Rice is cooking on an outside hearth not far from where Benu died. The food, when ready, is shared, eaten by people seated here and there in the area around the hearth. Then, the first of two rites begins. A small pit is dug in the ground, and its bottom and sides are tamped down (sometimes, I am told, it is lined with leaves). Grass stalks are stuck in the ground around the rim of the pit (sometimes, the tops of the stalks are tied together). Madi's granduncle pours water into the pit, filling it. He pours a little oil on the grass stalks, which then drips down into the water. Everyone watches intently as the drops of oil float to the surface. When some of the drops coalesce, the first to observe it declares, "Olle" (Good). This amalgamation is a sign of togetherness, intimating that Benu's soul will join the plurality of invisible other-than-human relatives living in the area.[6] This oil rite is less about the deceased's change from one status (alive) to another (dead) than about moving from one plurality (the living) to another (the dead).

The second rite, involving the giving of a ring, further supports this reading.[7] When everyone is still gathered by the pit, Benu's cousin gives a ring to his wife (also a cousin of Benu), who wears it in Benu's memory. This rite always involves *at least three people:* the giver of the ring, the receiver-cum-wearer, and the deceased party. Sometimes, more than one ring is given, involving more than one triad. The ring changes hands between relatives of the same generation rather than being passed down to a child or some other successor. Items used by the deceased, such as pots, bracelets, cups, and knives, are sometimes taken by relatives. Their continued everyday use keeps the deceased in mind as a co-user and/or originator of the items. The "ring" ritual, insofar as it involves at least two living relatives and the deceased, recalls Woodburn's (1982: 190–91) description of what happens in the Hadza *epeme* dance, which routinely takes place every month or so. The person wearing the *epeme* costume dances several times, each time for a different person: for himself, one of his children, another relative, and the deceased. He may also dance for gourds, regarded as surrogate children. The *epeme* dance, like the "ring" and "oil" rituals, is about the web of relations that include and surround the deceased, not just the dyadic relations with others that are severed by his or her death.[8]

The grass stalks around the rim of the pit were left unattended after the ritual, to wilt where they had been stuck. Except that Benu's cousin now wore a ring, life went on as before.[9] Three months after Benu's passing, there was still one more procedure to complete in relation to his death. A certain concern lingered over his demise, although Benu had died in the hamlet amid relatives, which is considered a good death. Had he died alone in the forest, the concern would have been much graver, as the soul of one who dies away from relatives roams the forest and can be harmful.

The final procedure occurred during the "big animistic visit" (or more simply, "big visit"; see chapter 5),[10] a culturally packed event in which local spirits arrive in the hamlet through possession of the living. Several mediums fall into trance, and the spirits come through them; this mediumistic performance continues for twenty-four hours. Most if not all the Gorge's dwellers attend these events, which take place in each of the hamlets with more than one hut. The timing of these events is known in advance (if only by one or two days), and attendance at them is larger than at unpredictable events like birth and death. Key events for Madi and her relatives, they offer the ethnographer insights into many aspects of life in the Gorge (see Bird-David 1996, 1999a, 2004a, 2004b), including treatment of the recently deceased. I participated in the first "big visit" to occur in GR after Benu died. Drawing on my field notes, below I describe the aspects of the event relevant to his death....

The ring worn for the past three months by Benu's cousin is placed where Benu died. One of the mediumistic performers carefully and reverently picks it up, wraps it in cloth, and carries it to the hub of the celebration, the hut specially built each year for the other-than-human visitors. He is accompanied by people who walk all around him, some of whom play drums and flutes. He places the ring next to the personal items of those who predeceased Benu, all laid at the front of the special hut; the dead associated with these items are presented with offerings and, at the meal concluding the rite, receive their shares of cooked food, as do the living participants. Not all of these predecessors are clearly identified or known to everyone; as the years go by, from one "big visit" to the next, some of them merge with other invisible and dead local beings and their vivid idiosyncratic characters fade. The transfer of the ring from the place of dying to the predecessors' hut is the only occasion during the entire "big visit" to provoke controversy over my presence and tape-recording. Up to this point, I have been recording and photographing continuously throughout the twenty-four hours of the spirit-possession performances, and nobody has shown any concern at all. The ring's transfer from one plural context (that of the giver, the wearer, and the deceased and of the place where the deceased had lived with others) to another (the hut of the invisible other-than-human beings whom the deceased joins) stirs especially strong emotions among those participating in the ritual. At this stage, the deceased is alone, in between pluralities, for which reason, I think, there is, atypically, much tension in the air.

The quick return to everyday life and the absence of institutionalized expressions of grief, sadness, and sorrow after a death should not be taken for emotional indifference. One of Benu's relatives, for instance, stopped working on the plantation because his son, a talented young man, had worked there before he died. Working on the plantation, the bereaved father said, was a painful reminder of the boy, and so he no longer went there. I witnessed people's intense emotional responses—and learned something important in the process—when I revisited GR in 1989. I brought along photographs I had taken ten years earlier, including pictures of people who had died in the interim. Completely unprepared for their reactions, I was shocked when relatives looking at photos of the dead (especially those showing them as lone figures) broke into tears and sobbing.[11] In retrospect, I now realize that what the photos might have done was to suddenly disassociate the deceased from the plurality of other-than-human beings with whom they had, by then, merged.[12] The photographs suddenly brought the dead into attention as particular(ized) single beings. The oil and ring rituals and the trance gatherings delivered the dead from a state of being-with one unindividuated plurality of relatives, the living, to being-with another, the dead. The photographs suddenly reindividualized the dead, bringing losses sharply into memory as well as evoking deep concern about "socially naked" relatives, now seen as lone figures. Like my photos, elaborate burial, in a sense, involves individuation of the one who has died, separating him or her from others. For this reason, among others, burial is not something that the foragers of the Gorge elaborate on publicly and culturally. The oil and ring rituals pursue an opposite effect, repositioning the dead within another plurality. They are given cultural attention because they celebrate plural life.

· · ·

Sonta as a community of relatives is a significant ontological entity in locals' experience and imagination. Within the horizons of *sonta*, both everyday life and special we-cycle events take place. From the ethnography presented in this chapter, one begins to intuit that *sonta* is not about a simple assemblage of discrete entities, whether individuals, relations, or nuclear families. One begins to suspect that it cannot be understood as a collectivity, a singularized and hypostatized social unit. Neither assemblage nor collective is foremost in locals' sense of themselves; instead, their existential touchstone is their plurality as relatives. *Sonta* appears to be about a pregiven and irreducible plurality of (shifting) relatives living together. In the next chapter, I begin to examine diverse modes of living-with relatives within the plurality of *sonta*, exploring relatives' distinctions from and articulation and negotiation with one another.

Downscale 3

Tree of Relatives

Small kinship diagrams, prominent features of many anthropological accounts, persist today despite radical changes in kinship studies. Through conventional graphical symbols for males and females and their links via marriage and descent, these diagrams showcase connections between the protagonists in an ethnographic tale to help illustrate an analytical point. They focus on protagonists relevant to that point and exclude others deemed to be irrelevant. Diagram 1, for example, which depicts the sibling and affinal ties linking the core members of the hamlet in which I lived, serves my discussion of sibling-exchange marriage in chapter 3. Anthropologists have long used fragments of family trees in this manner; the practice is rooted in the "genealogical method" that W.H.R. Rivers (1968 [1910]), one of anthropology's own ancestors, developed in the course of working with Toda pastoralists living on the Nilgiri heights, a mere 50 kilometers from Kungan's home. Rivers prescribed sessions with informants in which the ethnographer asks them, one by one, who their relatives are, systematically exhausting all the genealogical options up, down, and sideways (i.e., who the informant's father is, the mother, the father's older and younger siblings, their spouses, their children, the mother's older and younger siblings, etc.). The kinship trees that the ethnographer constructs from this information, Rivers argued (an argument generally endorsed by his peers and in subsequent years), constitutes a map of the society under study, one that is essential for analysis of "small-scale" societies in which locals' actions and institutions are underwritten by kinship relations. The universally assumed genealogical construction of kinship at the base of this method, the English roots of the idea of "pedigree" that inspired Rivers, and even the European origins of the iconography used to represent kin ties have drawn critical attention (e.g., see Schneider 1968,

Strathern 1992a, Bouquet 1993, 1996). My concern lies with the scalar confusion and distortion involved in applying Rivers's method to tiny indigenous communities, and again, I draw on my relevant experiences as a fieldworker.

Madi and her relatives were reluctant to list and map their kinship relations for me, though they ordinarily used kinship terms to refer to and address each other. Even my close associates were less than forthcoming, taking their leave after enduring a few moments of my attempts to pursue the kinds of sessions Rivers had prescribed (they would say that they were going to "collect firewood," a common excuse for disengaging from relatives). They readily mentioned the few relatives currently residing with them, but they had to be persuasively primed to speak of those no longer living—grandparents and others in ascending generations. Exasperated, they would eventually tell me that they "had not lived with them, and so did not know them" (or words to that effect). My field diaries, though, continued to fill up with fragmentary kinship "information" gleaned from everyday observations and conversations. And I succeeded in partly mapping my friends' kinship ties through conversations with several outsiders who had lived in the Gorge for two decades and who knew the foragers extremely well (the plantation's bookkeeper and others discussed in chapter 6). I spent hours with them discussing the foragers' intricate kinship relations, and together we linked our jigsaw pieces of information into small partial diagrams. I completed the process, thousands of kilometers away from the Gorge, in the course of processing my fieldwork data, linking those partial diagrams, and more, into a large kinship tree that turned out to include 147 individuals, practically everyone I personally knew or was told of. What the foragers who "lived" those relations did not (and perhaps could not) tell me, I finally mapped from the vantage point of growing distance and scale. My technique was allegorical as much as it was pragmatic: Using a pair of scissors, I literally extracted all references to kinship ties from my field records, spread those bits of paper on my desk, sorted and resorted, cross-checked, reshuffled, and moved them around, and then, one by one, collated them, eventually arriving at the large kinship tree shown in diagram 2. To the best of my knowledge, most, though not all, of the descent links included in this diagram are genealogically or biographically based, the result of marriage strategies discussed in the next chapter. The gray-shaded areas demarcate each hamlet's prominent co-dwellers during 1978–79.

Rivers extolled his method for providing "more definite and exact knowledge than is possible to a man who has lived for many years among the people" (107), unintentionally pointing at its weakness as a tool for

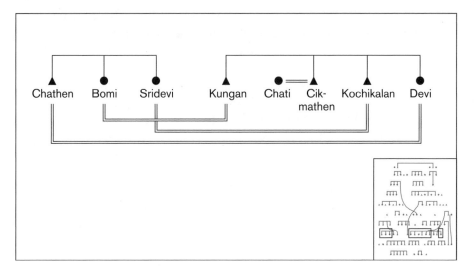

DIAGRAM 1.   Kinship ties among GR's core members.

understanding locals' own praxis and understandings. Just as cartographic maps do, a kinship tree provides an overview of a territory—a relational one—that those who intimately "walk" through do not have or need. In fact, the kinship tree trains attention on dead predecessors more than on coevals. The connection between two, even very close, coevals is inscribed in the family tree via shared predecessors, including some long dead. A simple example illustrates this pattern: to trace the kinship links between ego and his or her second cousin—who, in a tiny forager community of relatives, often live close together in the same hamlet—one would proceed upward on the tree from ego to ego's parent, then farther upward to ego's parent's parent, then laterally to ego's parent's parent's sibling, then downward to ego's parent's parent's sibling's child, and finally, down to ego's parent's parent's sibling's child's child, the cousin with whom ego lives. Certainly a convoluted calculus to describe two people who essentially share lives.

Kinship mapping is effective when kin are dispersed within and constitute only a small part of a larger population, but it constitutes a Trojan horse in ethnographies of miniscule societies in which each member is related, multiply and dynamically, to almost every other member. Large kinship trees like diagram 2 are barely legible because of the multiple ties crisscrossing among *all* members, and conversely, small kinship trees like diagram 1 conceal kinship links that affect protagonists' strategies in a specific situation. In training attention on particular one-to-one kinship ties,

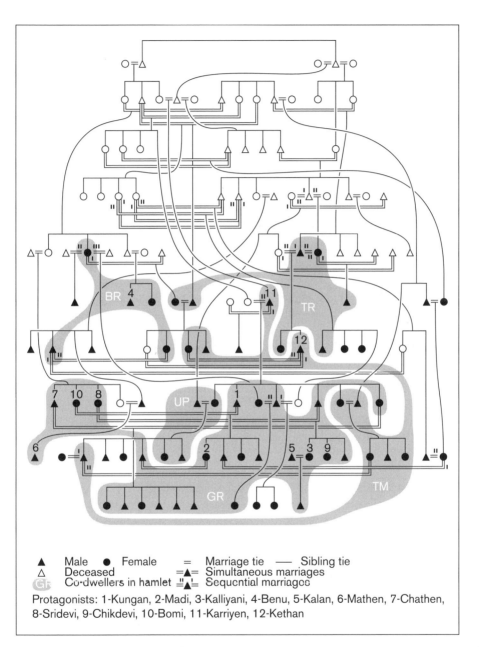

▲ Male ● Female = Marriage tie —— Sibling tie
△ Deceased =▲= Simultaneous marriages
GR Co-dwellers in hamlet ⁼▪▲= Sequential marriages

Protagonists: 1-Kungan, 2-Madi, 3-Kalliyani, 4-Benu, 5-Kalan, 6-Mathen, 7-Chathen, 8-Sridevi, 9-Chikdevi, 10-Bomi, 11-Karriyen, 12-Kethan

DIAGRAM 2. Kinship tree of relatives in the gorge.

both diagrams undermine locals' register of themselves as "[all of] us, relatives" and the space for strategically shifting among multiple optional kinship routes. Both diagrams inscribe relatives ego *knows of*, subverting locals' primary register of relatives as those who continuously constitute and reconstitute themselves as such.

In retrospect, I recognize that mapping kinship connections in the field hinges on identifying individuals by names, a practice that speaks loudly to the grip of anthropology's scale-blind ethos. It does not matter whether the ethnographer asks an informant, "Who is Madi for you?" or, conversely, "Who is your *akka* [older sister]?" to which the informant responds, "Madi." Both strategies yield complicated results in a tiny community whose members either use kinship terms to refer to and address one another or employ multiple inconsistent personal names (see Downscale 2). The complication might appear to be a superficial difficulty, but it expresses a deep ontological matter. Asking either question, the ethnographer premises a set of individual beings (the nodes in the diagram), and she assumes a single kinship link connecting two persons. In retrospect, I also recognize that Madi and her relatives responded to my attempted textbook-style inquiry about kinship matters in accord with their deepest understandings of "being relatives," teaching me far more about those understandings than I could appreciate at the time, understandings that I subsequently even subverted through my "professional success" in producing their kinship tree. They downscale their community to relatives who are pluripresent and multiply connected, and those active relations also shape the contours of the community, especially the sib marriages discussed in the next chapter.

Siblings and cousins cutting firewood. Photographed by the author (1978–79).

3.   The Sib Matrix
Dyadic and Sequential Logic

Kalliyani and her husband relax at their hearth with their young baby, and I sit with them; around us are small clusters of relatives, seated in semicircles around their own hearths, positioned to avoid the fires' smoke. A group of youngsters, siblings and cousins, are preoccupied with cutting firewood. Vibrating waves of laughter reach us from one of these semicircles, soft murmuring from another. "These are all," Kalliyani tells me, gesturing with her hand to include everyone around, "sonta kudumba,"[1] *and when I ask her to elaborate she adds, "Our older and younger brothers and sisters, their spouses, and their children." Night falls; as we continue to enjoy laughter and comfortable silences, Kalliyani's cousin, a young unmarried man, materializes out of the darkness to join us. Drawing him into our conversation, Kalliyani's husband teasingly asks him if he wants to marry his cousin. The young man blushes, his face as red as the base of our fire, but before my fieldwork ends the two are married. When, ten years later, on a return visit, I learn that the respective siblings of Kalliyani's and her husband's cousins also subsequently married, I retrospectively realize that I have observed an episode in a typical sequence of sibling and cousin intermarriages. The residential core of GR is the veritable embodiment of such a sequence, one that played out more than two decades earlier and resulted in two sets of adult siblings who have three marriages between them, a brother and two sisters in one set married, respectively, to a sister and two brothers in the other set (see diagram 1).*

Claude Lévi-Strauss (1969 [1949]) canonically proposed that sibling-exchange marriage between family groups underwrote the development of society. Lévi-Strauss may have intended his proposal not to be taken literally, as it often is, but rather to highlight the "exchange logic" on which he considered society to be predicated. In this chapter, I ethnographically examine the *process* resulting in residential cores of intermarried siblings and cousins and show that it does not express a Lévi-Straussian "exchange logic" but, instead, what could be called a "sequential logic," one that underscores forager lifeways and ideas more generally. I argue that limited spousal prospects in tiny communities, together with the local praxis of frequent visits, produce *paths* of siblings' and cousins' marriages that, in turn, determine local scales of visiting and horizons of imagining community. In my theoretical preamble, I suggest that the (dyadic) "exchange logic" Lévi-Strauss transposed from modern to "primitive" society and, more generally, the analytical language of "one, two, many-as-One" (discussed in the introduction) have undermined, if not concealed, what is often the framework of forager-cultivator communal life: the sib set. Generally, siblingship has not been much explored in anthropology, and I pursue some of the reasons as they bear on the relative neglect of siblings in the study of forager communities, even though often sib sets are the cores of those communities.

. . .

Lévi-Strauss's monumental *Elementary Structures of Kinship* (1969 [1949]) abstractly models two family groups who directly exchange women and so forge alliances. The prototypical example involves two men exchanging their sisters as wives, a transaction that, when perpetuated in the next generation, becomes bilateral cross-cousin exchange and mobilizes broader societal structures. Leaving aside concerns over the model's male subjects exchanging female objects, here I dwell on its large-scale-biased basis, which Lévi-Strauss himself explicates in no uncertain terms in elaborating on the kind of social experience that inspired his analysis. With great ethnographic finesse, he describes two strangers sitting "less than a yard apart, face to face on both sides of a table in a cheap restaurant (an individual table is a privilege to be paid for, and is not granted below a certain tariff)" (59). Their mutual tension and uncertainty regarding one another are resolved when they exchange wine:

> Wine offered calls for wine returned, cordiality requires cordiality. . . . From now on the relationship can only be cordial or hostile. There is no way of refusing the neighbor's offer of his glass of wine without being insulting. . . . In this way a whole range of trivial social ties is established by a series of alternating oscillations, in which offering gives one a right, and receiving makes one obligated. . . . This apparently futile drama, which perhaps the reader will think has been given a

disproportionate importance, seems on the contrary to offer material for inexhaustible sociological reflection. . . . [T]he respective attitudes of the strangers in the restaurant appear to be an infinitely distant projection scarcely perceptible but nevertheless recognizable, of a fundamental situation, that of individuals of primitive bands coming into contact for the first time or under exceptional situations meeting strangers. . . . Primitive people know only two ways of classifying strangers. They are either "good" or "bad." (59–60)

Drawing "sociological reflection" from this urban experience clearly bases the analysis of "primitive society" on "inexhaustible" large-scale ontological possibilities and truths, among them, that unrelated strangers may intimately eat together at the same table; that groups, collective entities, act as if they are single persons; that, just as these two intimate strangers exchange wine and cordiality for cordiality, groups exchange women; and that the exchanges in these cases are balanced transactions. Lévi-Strauss's basic model assumes *two* siblings as the parties to the exchange of women, and it draws on *two* persons exchanging wine, when an equally (if not more) probable assumption would be that a *few* siblings on each side of the marriage exchange and a *few* friends treat each other to glasses of wine. In later work, in which he developed his concept of "house-based societies" (*sociétés à maison*), Lévi-Strauss (1987) took inspiration from the noble houses of medieval Europe, and perhaps the idea of marriage as a political tool had also influenced his earlier work on sibling-exchange marriage as means of forging alliances between groups. Whatever the case, a large-scale "one, two, One" sociological logic implicitly informs his sibling-exchange marriage model, and that logic is ill suited to tiny forager communities.

Recall Nancy Howell's (1979) study of !Kung demography (discussed in the introduction), which is based on close to one thousand individual records, an exceptionally large database for a hunter-gatherer community. Howell cautioned that, even so, "noise generated by random fluctuations of events . . . continually threatens to drown out the regularities to be observed" (19), and so she ran a computer simulation that "produced" (mathematical) "individuals" over a thousand-year run, determined their sex and life span randomly, and married them according to stochastic demographic availabilities at successive points in time. Without engaging here more broadly with this exercise—think, for instance, about the scope of changes potentially taking place over a thousand-year span!—it is instructive to see what Howell learned from this exercise regarding marriage rules. She notes that "any rigid rules of matching spouses will regularly produce a situation in which a substantial proportion of one or the other sex will be unable to marry due to random fluctuations in the sex ratio at birth and the sex ratio at mortality" (246). Her records of actual (not virtual) individuals include marriages of women to men twenty and even thirty-five years younger than themselves, so great is the diversity practiced and tolerated under this scalar predicament. Her study, if anything, cautions that "noise" *is* the "regularity" to be observed by situated agents living in such tiny populations. And yet, it also invites taking into account the unique demographic features of a tiny community, the proportionally large presence of siblings and cousins and their spouses in one's field of potential mates. I leave computer (mathematical) production of sibling sets, instead of individuals, to other studies. Ethnographers have seldom studied siblingship, and the few exceptions have seldom foregrounded it as a major axis and framework of forager communal lifeways, including myself in previous work.

For over a year I lived in the tiny hamlet of GR with its core of intermarried siblings, yet in more than two dozen earlier publications I have not explored adult siblingship as key issue. In a professional tribunal, had I been charged with this neglect, I would have pleaded that I am no different than many ethnographers of hunter-gatherer and other tiny societies, and I would have referred for supporting evidence to Alan Mason's work with the Brazilian Oronao' in the late 1960s. Three decades after he did that work, Mason (1997) pondered how what he terms their "sibling principle" had previously escaped his attention. It was elusive, he proposes, because the Oronao' have no explicit ideology concerning and do not engage in explicit talk about siblings in residence. The same holds, he suggests, for the (South American) Siriono, Apinaye, and Kalapalo: among all of these groups the "sibling principle" is both cardinal and anthropologically unacknowledged. Though Mason does not pay analytical attention to settlement size, working as most of us have within the conventional bounds of scale-blind anthropology, from the ethnographic background he provides one can learn that the Oronao' numbered only about 120 people when he worked with them and that they lived in nomadic settlements of one to a few dwellings each (353). Does the scalar context partly explain why anthropologists have overlooked the striking salience of siblingship in those communities—even those of us who have lived in them?

Were three married couples from two sets of siblings to reside in an apartment building in a modest-sized town, their pluriconnections would stand out. They would not pass unnoticed; in fact, they might be the talk of the town. In a hamlet as tiny as GR and those Mason studied, where intermarried siblings constitute the core as well as the overwhelming majority of residents, they are passed over in scale-blind ethnography as the hamlet's inhabitants (in my terms, the plural replication of inhabitant). When they are ontologically figured in this way, their sib relations are an optional choice of study rather than the touchstone for understanding their communities. Siblingship is rarely pursued for several reasons. One reason, as Mason suggests, is that those people themselves do not much talk about siblingship, possibly because, for them, it "goes without saying" (cf. Bloch 1992). Yet another reason is that, generally, siblingship has been grossly understudied in anthropology, and much of the blame for this can be attributed to its marginalization in American and English kinship cultures, a positioning that has slipped into ethnographic analysis of tiny communities. Reflecting on these reasons, though briefly for lack of space, helps me open up a conceptual space for "observing" and examining the role of siblings in tiny-scale(d) communities.

In mid-twentieth-century anthropology, when Lévi-Strauss developed his model, descent and alliance defined the discursive space of debates and discussions. If siblings received attention, it was filtered through myriad marriage and parenthood issues: for example, "sister exchange" as a marriage form; the "mother's brother" as a parental role in matrilineal societies; and "sibling care" as a substitute for parental care. In the 1980s, a spate of works showed that siblings have a prominent place in many Amazonian and Southeast Asian groups and in some hunter-gatherer groups elsewhere.[2] Engaging with contemporaneous debates on descent, some students of those societies argued that siblings should be viewed as its originators (marrying and reproducing the next generation of siblings) rather than its byproducts (children of parents—and derivatively, siblings, if those parents have multiple children; Shapiro 1985: 4, cited in Mason 1997: 351). Siblings enjoyed a brief time in the limelight, with studies of the time showing that marriage is often thought of in terms of siblingship (Carsten 1995; T. Gibson 1995); that siblingship and marriage are seen as transformations of each other (McKinley 1981); that lovers and spouses use sibling terms for one another (Kipp 1986); and, among the hunter-gatherer Australian Pintupi, that the sibling set is "a basic unit" in the "kinship model," that relations are traced back to originating siblings, and that people present themselves as co-residing siblings (Myers 1986: 193). This flurry of interest left little mark on the study of those societies in later years and had even less impact on anthropology more broadly.

Siblings, if one were to judge by major late twentieth-century reference works, have not taken their proper place alongside other key kinship categories in anthropology. You would not, for example, find an entry for "siblings" in the *Companion Encyclopedia of Anthropology* (Ingold 1994), the

Encyclopedia of Social and Cultural Anthropology (Barnard and Spencer 1996), or *The Dictionary of Anthropology* (Barfield 1997). You would find "marriage," "parents," and "children," but "siblings," "sisters," and "brothers" do not appear as topical entries or even in indexes. Using "the child" (singular) and "parent–child" (dyad) as figures of speech, some entries, in fact, indirectly conceal siblings as the *plural* children of parents. One recent book (Alber, Coe, and Thelen 2013) has begun to redress the neglect of siblings in anthropology. Again I ask, could the widespread disinterest in siblings, if not their neglect, reflect their ontological status in Western kinship cultures?

Sibling relations are altogether absent in certain English and American bourgeois kinship models, if one goes by David Schneider's classic *American Kinship* (1968) and Marilyn Strathern's (1992a) influential study of English kinship. The words *sibling, brother,* and *sister* are barely mentioned in these works. Their omission could not be more surprising in models that decidedly amplify biological or genetic closeness (if not as exclusively as Schneider originally maintained). After all, full siblings are the *closest* of genetic relatives, closer than a parent and child, as they share the biological imprint of both parents. Their life spans overlap more than do those of husband and wife (who join as adults) and more than those of parents and children (successive generations). The concealment of siblings in the genetic models speaks loudly for their marginalization, a reflection, first, of the tenets of the "nuclear family" script and, second, of the script of leaving home as measure and analogue of independence and self-sufficiency. In the "nuclear family" cultural script, man and woman marry, have a child, and become a family. Sibling relations are viewed as "added on" with the births of further children (cf. Mason 1997: 353). Conjugal and parental relations are the cardinal axes in this family and, as Schneider (1968) and Strathern (1992a) noted, both are associated with "love." Sibling relations are associated with rivalry, quarreling, and dispersal (going back to archetypal biblical siblings, from Abel and Cain to Jacob and Esau, Lea and Rachel, and Joseph and his brothers, and to Shakespearian siblings in *King Lear, The Taming of the Shrew, Richard III,* and *As You Like It*).[3] Even if siblings get along well as they grow up, according to this script, they normally and normatively move away from their parents, potentiating if not causing their dispersal from one another. They are expected to leave the parents as part and proof of becoming adults, each setting out to form his or her own nuclear family. In this key scenario, the social grammar is one of two separate individuals, a man and a woman, who unite and produce a child, constituting them as a family unit. One child suffices for the three to be a family; that family reproduces itself through its multiple children, who disperse and make family units of the same sort.[4] These scripts are now connected with the modern idea of individuality and a world with large-scaled horizons that one can get distant in.

Siblings have secondary, even tertiary, ontological status in Western cultures, and this is reflected, to a surprising extent, in a myriad of institutionalized codes and bureaucratic practices. Consider the following few eclectic observations, beginning with mourning terms and conventions. There is no special term for a surviving sibling as there are for spouse (*widow/er*) and for child (*orphan*).[5] Siblings are not, ipso facto, entitled to compensation, insurance, and welfare upon one another's death, as are spouses and children of deceased persons. A shorter period of mourning was formally prescribed in nineteenth-century England for siblings (six months) than for children (a year) and spouses (two years minimum, though it could be perpetual; Wolfram, cited in Strathern 1992a: 55). Adopted children today are far less inclined to search for birth siblings than they are birth parents, parentage constituting a "fixed point of reference for identity" (Strathern 1992a: 70).[6] One rarely hears the multiple terms of address and endearment used for parents, spouses, and children directed at siblings. Peculiarly—further deemphasizing shared identity in lieu of shared parentage—siblings commonly "privatize" their parents, each referring to them not as "our" but as "my" parents/father/mother (Schneider and Homans 1955: 1203).

At the same time, sibling terms (*brothers* and *sisters*) are appropriated in public space for *unrelated* people who share part-time membership in certain, often same-gender, associations (like college sororities and fraternities). These terms constitute metaphors of solidarity, friendship, harmony, and cooperation (cf. Kipp 1986: 639). These terms foreground equity among siblings and, so, subvert the inherent diversity of siblings in a family, if only in gender, age, and place in the set, the kind of diversity foregrounded by Kalliyani and her relatives through their use of the South Dravidian kinship terms *anna(n)*, *tamma(n)*, *akka*, and *tanga*: older brother, younger brother, older sister, and younger sister, respectively. Kalliyani and her kin have no generalizing, gender-neutral term equivalent to *siblings* or age-neutral equivalents for *brothers* and *sisters*.

Relegating to the background these theoretical reflections on why siblings "disappear" in ethnographic analysis, I return to the fewer than half a dozen dispersed tiny hamlets on the forested slopes of the Gorge, specifically, to their (often sibling) occupants' marriages. . . .

THE GEOGRAPHY OF A "GOOD MARRIAGE"

Siblings, *their spouses, and their children* (Take 1)

Olle mave (a good marriage) is one in which one spouse comes from outside the closely enmeshed and inbred local community yet not from so far away as to preclude constant visits back and forth with his or her natal community. The "good marriage" opens new routes for visits and marriages. It is relational in the sense that it is specific to a particular moment in a dynamic situation that it reconfigures. The "good marriage" breaks away from an existing sequence of marriages and starts a new one. The move can be triggered by a variety of factors, including the personality and whims of heart of a "first" incoming spouse, the unpredictable field of spousal options in a tiny community, and economic changes related to good foraging sites and places of complementary employment. The "good marriage" changes routes of visits and subsequent marriages and, thereby, the contours of the local world.

A "good marriage," which departs from an existing marriage path, is, by definition, unusual, exhibiting agential choice at its clearest. One such marriage was that of Kalliyani to her husband (henceforth Kalan), a man originally from the forest surrounding a plantation I fictionalize as SF. His relatives lived there in three tiny hamlets (together comprising a dozen huts). One of those hamlets was exceptionally isolated: its dwellers (including Kalan's sister) occupied a spacious cave during the rainy season and subsisted almost solely on foraging. To reach this hamlet, one either had to walk down an extremely steep path or—as I did when Kalan took me there, insisting that we go by this roundabout way—travel by bus into Kerala to the foot of the hills, cross a wide river on a raft made of bamboo (which could not be done during the rainy season), and then continue on foot, climbing the final distance.

Kalan had been married in the SF area but had lost his wife and child. His travels had perhaps extended beyond his local world even before he made the visit that turned out to be pivotal in his life and pertinent to my story here: a visit to an "uncle" relation in DV, a small hamlet comprising three huts within easy walking distance of the bustling market village of Devala. Although relatively close to that village, DV was "isolated" in terms of the foragers' geography of intervisiting. It lay along the far rim of the Gorge's world but also at the far rim of the local SF world. It was a "satellite" hamlet started by relatives who moved to be closer to a place of employment. Satellite hamlets like DV played an ironic role in locals' changing circumstances, serving as occasional links between out-of-the-way communities, as happened in this instance. The "uncle" relation whom Kalan visited in DV mentioned his unmarried "niece" relation in GR to Kalan and told Kalan that there were good opportunities for work there. Kalan went to GR, met the niece (Kalliyani), and subsequently settled with her and her people. With one exception—when he took me there—he did not return to visit his relatives in the SF area. It was too far, and he said that he had "forgotten" all about them, that he could only think about "this" girl and "this" place. (He was still living in GR in 2001, with a woman he married after Kalliyani died in the mid-1990s giving birth to their fifth, stillborn, child.)

Kalliyani and her husband's marriage "begot" the marriage of their respective cousins (descent is perhaps as good a metaphor as sequence for these marriages that follow one another, one out of the other). Kalliyani's cousin (henceforth Mathen) was a shy twenty-year-old man, an orphaned single child of Kalliyani's mother's sister. When Kalan teasingly suggested his cousin in DV as a match for Kalliyani's cousin, the young man blushed, and Kalliyani and Kalan laughed, but the idea clearly sank in, not least because Mathen's local marital options looked grim at that time.

The search for food is often emphasized in cultural-ecological studies of hunter-gatherer mobility. The search for a spouse, however, can be a major trigger for movement. Scarcity of spouses is an endemic problem in forager communities. Because of their minute size, the male/female ratio in these communities can easily become unbalanced. Without the evening effect of large numbers, any stillbirth, any run of same-sex births, any death of a child or of an adult (resituating a widowed partner back "on the market"), any divorce or marrying out can affect one's marriage chances. The prospects were often grimmer for men than for women, who occasionally married out of the community (and women died during childbirth more frequently than men did in such risky pursuits as climbing tall trees and steep cliffs to collect honey and *sikai*).

At the time that Kalliyani's husband mentioned his unmarried cousin in DV to Mathen, fourteen women between the ages of ten and thirty were living in the Gorge. Affairs with married women were rare, which excluded seven of these fourteen from consideration as a mate for Mathen. Affairs with prepubescent girls were contentious, excluding another four. Of the remaining three, a sixteen-year-old cousin was already engaged to a man twice her age (the husband of her deceased sister, whom she later married). The remaining two did not suit the young man's personality at all: one, a pretty twenty-two-year-old girl, was too lively for this shy man and, according to rumors, had affairs with timber contractors. The other was a homely, stout, and somber twenty-five-year-old, unusual for still being unmarried at her age. Mathen's widowed father had courted her, but then,

even he had been put off by her taciturn demeanor. Had Mathen waited for
the three female cousins under the age of sixteen to grow up, he would have
found himself competing for them against male cousins who came of age at
the same time. Given these limited prospects, Kalliyani's husband's suggestion had not fallen on deaf ears.

A few weeks later, Kalan and Mathen climbed up the narrow footpath
that wound through the forest and then one of the tea plantations and led
to the main Calicut–Gudalur road. They took a bus from there to Devala,
then walked to the tiny hamlet of DV where the girl lived (to have walked
all the way to her hamlet would have taken them the better part of a day).
Kalan returned to GR the next day, and Mathen stayed on in DV for a few
days. When he returned to GR he told me that he liked the girl, but, he said,
he did not know the people there. His relatives in GR thought that he had
acted hastily in making the trip only with Kalliyani's husband; they told me
he should have taken along his mother's older brother (Chathen), the most
senior person then living in GR, but that uncle showed no enthusiasm for
the trip. On his next visit to DV, Mathen took along another "uncle" relation. The two men returned to GR, accompanied by the girl as well as her
younger sister. Mathen's wife-to-be had just turned sixteen, and she spent
as much time with her younger sister and other children in GR as she did
with Mathen. The two slept together at night, but they went their separate
ways during the day. The girls' parents showed up a few weeks later in GR,
complaining that the couple did not visit them and that Mathen did not
send them any money to give to their relatives in DV. They wanted to take
not only their youngest daughter but also her older sister and Mathen back
with them to DV. Mathen absconded and stayed in the forest for a few days.
The girl's parents approached his "uncle" relation, who convinced them to
stay in GR at least until the approaching ceremonial "big visit." After the
festival, the parents returned to DV, accompanied by their two daughters
and Mathen. The next few months saw Mathen coming and going between
GR and DV, staying in each place for weeks at a time, until he finally settled
in DV. Though DV and GR were quite far apart, Mathen's cousins from GR
occasionally visited him. The result was a third marriage in the GR–DV
sequence, between Mathen's wife's younger sister and Kalliyani's younger
brother. To the best of my knowledge, this marriage route then closed, perhaps because DV was too small and too far away from GR for it to be sustained. At the same time, a lively traffic of visits and marriages with another
satellite settlement, MN, continued.

MN was a relatively large hamlet, reached by traveling down the nar-
rowing forested valley, then through a gap between the steep hillsides into

Kerala. Uninterrupted forest lay between GR and MN; I estimate the distance between them to be about a four- to five-hour walk, two hours beyond UP, the hamlet farthest from GR on the opposite side of the Gorge. Under Kerala's Communist-influenced policies, MN was a "developed" colony and differed in many respects from the scattered hamlets on the Tamil Nadu side of the border. Various tribal people co-resided in that colony at the edge of the forest, which, when I visited in 1989, boasted twenty-five brick-and-mortar houses, each with allotted land that the registered indigenous owners commonly leased to outside agriculturalists. Mathen's father originally had come from MN, and his marriage was *olle* because four further marriages followed in its wake within a decade or so, two between MN and BR and two between MN and UP. More marriages have occurred since 1989, as visits back and forth between these settlements have continued. In fact, had I done my fieldwork in the 2000s, I probably would have regarded MN (then referred to as UP, the original UP, which had been located in the same general area, having disappeared in the interim) not as a satellite community but as part of my study group (as does Noa Lavi, who worked in the Gorge in 2010, 2012, and 2014; see Lavi 2012).

GR'S SEQUENCE OF SIBLING MARRIAGES

Siblings, *their spouses, and their children* (Take 2)

Taking a longer-term view, how did the two sets of adult siblings illustrated in diagram 1 come to intermarry and plurireside in GR? One theme that clearly surfaced in residents' recollections was that in the wake of the first "good marriage," the in-marrying spouse's siblings and cousins visited GR, and in the course of those visits others in the hamlet—siblings of the spouse who had originally resided in GR—met and married the visitors.

Kalliyani's mother was one of four siblings, a brother (Chathen) and three sisters. The four lived in GR in the 1950s. Chathen was in his early twenties, and his sisters were in their late teens. Although he was the first-born, he was the third to marry. His eldest sister was married first, to Kungan, who came from TM and who, in 1978–79, related to me how he and his wife had "gotten together." An open-minded and extroverted man, Kungan had moved around quite a lot before finally settling down with Chathen's sister in GR. He related a story that had all the elements of a common local genre, the "medicine" genre (for more on this genre, see chapter 4). They included his initial resistance to the marriage, followed by his surrender to the magic of a medicine put in his food, after which he only had at heart his wife, her place, and her relatives, and so he took up life with them. His younger brother then came to visit him there.

Kungan's brother (i.e., Kalliyani's father) was an introverted man who did not talk much with his neighbors in the hamlet. His wife (Kalliyani's mother) was even more reserved than he. He told me that after Kungan "got together" with his wife, he frequently visited the couple. He sometimes went to work on the plantation, he said, and stopped in GR on the way. "This girl [his brother's wife's sister] was there; we got to know each other and started living together." In these brief words, he enfolded a social process of sibling visits leading to intersibling marriages, not—and this is important—by arrangement or even through "falling in love" but gradually, through "knowing each other." Siblings grow close to one another as they grow up together in these tiny hamlets. One wants to visit an older sibling who has left the hamlet, and in a tiny-scaled world there are few destinations apart from the homes of kin. Visiting older siblings who have married and moved to another place is common, and "getting together" with a sibling's in-law in these tiny hamlets is a likely eventuality, as the third (unhappy) marriage in this sequence demonstrates.

The third marriage angered everybody because the girl was still very young. The sister of Kungan and his brother, each of whom was married by that time to one of Chathen's sisters, she came from TM to stay with her brothers. Her breasts had hardly developed, one brother told me; she was not yet past her puberty, the other brother said. She helped Kungan and his wife when they had their first child, accompanying them on those days when they went to work on the plantation. One night, Chathen, a sullen man given to moods, who was well into his twenties then and still unmarried, went to her and slept with her. In the morning, when she told what had happened, there was an uproar. Eventually, however, she and Chathen "got together," and she stayed on in GR. Their relationship remained tense, though by 1978 they had had five children together.

Yet another brother joined Kungan, his brother, and his sister in GR more than a decade later. A carefree, buoyant man, he almost always had a broad grin on his face, revealing a dark-red toothless mouth, the result of decades of chewing betel nuts. He had been married three times before. His first wife had died, and his second and third marriages had dissolved because the women in both cases lived beyond the range of easy visits to the Gorge. He was not happy, he told me, living at their places, too far from the relatives he had grown up with to permit frequent visiting, and they were not happy living in his place for the same reason. Chathen's last-born sister (Mathen's mother) was married by then (to a man from

MN), or the last brother to arrive might have married her. He finally married his brothers' wives' parallel cousin, twenty years younger than he, after having been alone in GR for some time. Like Kungan, in telling me how he and that cousin "got together," he wove in the usual "medicine genre" motifs, including his initial disinterest in the girl and resistance to marrying and, then, after consuming medicine, finally bonding with her and the people of GR. This narrative genre reveals much about the local dilemmas and tensions surrounding marriage. In the present context it expresses the difficulty of exercising agential choice in the face of severe demographic constraints, and it highlights the involvement of relatives (often siblings and cousins), who, unbeknownst to the reluctant spouse-to-be, administer the "medicine" causing him or her to stay with them. The "medicine" genre bridges over the complicated nexus of desiring a spouse, limited conjugal options, and the wish to stay close to siblings and cousins one grew up with.

The field of spousal choices is limited by the size and dispersal of hamlets but also by downscaling the horizons of imagination. The youth who sets off from the home hamlet does not head "out into the world" but normally goes to visit and be with married relatives who are living in neighboring hamlets, or with *their* married relatives living in yet other hamlets or, at most, in "satellite" hamlets. If he moves far beyond regular reach of the home hamlet and does not even return for the yearly festivals during which all in the Gorge convene, then he is no longer counted as "our sonta," one of us. Given the extremely small population, the peripatetic youth who remains within the orbit of visits commonly ends up marrying a relative's spouse's relative, often the spouse's sibling or cousin. Yet marriage with an in-law is not idealized as *olle mave* (a good marriage) or seen as an exchange of siblings. As stated, the "good marriage" is one that extends the field of spousal options while still allowing for regular visiting between the spouses' respective hamlets.

HISTORY OF SEQUENTIAL SETTLEMENT AND MARRIAGES

Siblings, their spouses, and their children (Take 3)

Taking an even longer-term view (although not as long as a thousand-year computer simulation would take us), I start with the grandparents of the oldest person I knew in 1978–79 and offer a history of settlement in the Gorge from the piecemeal information I gathered and cross-checked, insofar as possible, against outside sources. This longer-term view further illustrates the recurrence of sibling marriage sequences, including sororal marriages, and also reveals the occasional expansions and contractions of the horizons of regular visits.

The oldest person I knew, about seventy-five years of age, related that his grandparents and the grandfather's brother were the first to settle in the Gorge. They had come from the Bene forests, he told me, and "became familiar with the mountains, the rocks, and the roots" in the Gorge or, in another version, found these "gods" there and so stayed with them. They settled in the bamboo forest on the rocky side where TR stood in 1978–79. The bachelor brother then married a woman who subsequently came to live in TR, and they had three children, two sons and a daughter. One of the sons married two sisters, and the daughter married their brother. All of these couples stayed in TR, building and rebuilding their huts in that locality. (This local story accords with historical accounts: the original trio arrived in the Gorge before the rubber plantation was opened along its lower slopes in 1888. Intensive timber harvesting was taking place in the region surrounding the Gorge during preceding decades, and restrictive measures had been imposed on the activities of tribal inhabitants in some places, among them, so the literature says, the Bene forest and the Mudumalai National Park and Wildlife Sanctuary, about thirty-two kilometers from the Gorge; Francis 1908: 219–20; Grigg 1880: 448.) Few, if any, visits took place thereafter between the Gorge's foragers and the Bene forest people, to my knowledge.[7]

In the 1930s, two couples, one following the other, moved out of the TR area and, in fact, out of the Gorge, settling in forest close to the Rani's elephant stable near the Nelliyalam Palace, about sixteen kilometers away. The Gorge then belonged to the Rani, and one of her employees recruited the foragers to work in the elephant stable. The men helped look after the elephants and foraged with their families in the forest. Visits between TR and that new settlement resulted in the sequential marriages of two brothers from TR to daughters of the Nelliyalam couples. The first brother married one girl, and the second married that girl's two sisters. (Again, this local account tallies with external information: in 2001, I succeeded in locating the ruined abode of the Rani of Nelliyalam, which in 1978–79 was still referred to as a palace, and I interviewed the Rani's grandson's wife and several neighbors, who remembered the foragers working in the elephant stable for a short period; see Bird-David 2004a: 413). Eventually, all but one family returned to the Gorge and settled on the hillside across the valley from TR, where TM stands. The family that remained behind included one old woman who was too frail to travel to the Gorge and visit her relatives there. Her son married and started a new life in the Nelliyalam area.

Meanwhile, in the 1950s, one of the families who had remained in the hilly TR area moved down the hillside, closer to the valley floor and the lower reaches of the rubber plantation, to live in the GR area. GR shifted its location at least nine times over a period of eleven years (1959–69) before being established at the site where I did my first fieldwork. Sometime in the 1960s, the three families living in TM (those who came from TR via Nelliyalam) moved downslope to GR to be closer to the plantation. But then a severe skin disease broke out among them, which was read as a sign that the nonhuman co-dwellers at TM were annoyed at having been abandoned. Those three families returned to TM. Their children married people living in GR, the visits between GR and TM producing the marriages at the core of GR that I describe above. Extensive visits took place among TR, TM, and GR, as well as two one-hut hamlets that split from TR and TM (BR and UP), during 1978–79. TR, TM, and GR were the principal hamlets in the Gorge at that time, with ten, twelve, and fourteen adults respectively dwelling there. Seven adults lived at BR and three at UP. Many of these people were the descendants of generations of sequential marriages between sets of siblings (as can be seen in diagram 2).

SIB DEVELOPMENTAL CYCLE

Siblings, *their spouses, and their children* (Take 4)

For an ethnographic glimpse of growing up as and among siblings, I return to the ethnographic present of 1979 and to the children living in GR. Kalliyani has two younger siblings, a brother and a sister. The two often sleep, eat, take leisure, and forage with their parents, and therefore with each other. They often play with other children who reside in the hamlet, all of them together. Two siblings may constitute a negligible proportion of one's peers in a large community. But here they constitute a significant part of the hamlet's child population, the other children being close cousins, their parents' siblings' children.

Kalliyani's younger brother or sister occasionally visits and stays with relatives living in other hamlets. Child visitors live with their host couple, their children, and other children who may be staying with their hosts at the same time, and they share with hosts and other visitors the same domestic and subsistence activities they engage in with their own parents and siblings. The shifting pluralities forming around conjugal nuclei involve shifting pluralities of young siblings and like-siblings closely sharing all activities. The seeds of both conjoined action and intermittent separation are built into the childhood phase of the sib developmental cycle.

Now and then, Kalliyani's sister helps Kalliyani and her husband; for example, she accompanies them when they occasionally go to the plantation for a day's work, sitting and holding their baby until break time, when the parents take over. She would continue to help them were they to live elsewhere, during visits to them or others in the new hamlet. However, as she sexually matures, her relation with her sister and brother-in-law grows increasingly restrained. She is now a potential partner for her brother-in-law. In this tiny community, which suffers chronically from episodes of spousal scarcity, sororal marriages occur, as do marriages with siblings of deceased spouses. The fact that spouses spend so much time together (see chapter 4) eventually drives a wedge between Kalliyani and her younger sister, even though they co-reside in the same hamlet.

The restraint in their relation is described as *nachika*. *Nachika* can be translated as "shyness," "restraint," "reticence," and "holding back." It should be understood as a relational, transpersonal issue rather than an individual's emotional state. In these tiny hamlets, where domestic life takes place largely in the open and partitions are flimsy and minimal, the dwellers find themselves together in what I have elsewhere called "involuntary intimacy" (Bird 1983a; Bird-David 1987). *Nachika* describes skillful interpersonal avoidance, which is expressed in myriad ways: for instance, avoidance of addressing opposite-sex in-laws, handing them something directly, staying with them alone in a confined space, approaching them on a narrow footpath, or engaging in private, even if only casual, conversation with them. Avoidance should be accomplished as discreetly and subtly as possible, not demonstratively (e.g., by pointedly turning away). The smooth flow of life together in this tiny hamlet, its inhabitants all close relatives and, for the most, familiar with each other from childhood, must not be fractured. The pluripresent nature of this life makes such discreet avoidance far easier than the reader might imagine. For example, within the pluralogues that take place in the hamlet, Kalliyani's younger sister can communicate with her brother-on-law whenever she wants to; she does so indirectly, as other dwellers do who speak without designating a particular addressee. As all spend a great deal of time, day and night, between rather than inside their huts, she can talk with her sister without having to step next to her and her husband or without entering their hut. She can avoid face-to-face encounters with them, exploiting the state of pluripresence. Increasingly, then, as she grows up, Kalliyani's younger sister distances herself from her sister and her husband, but she remains alongside them in the same tiny hamlet, strategically exercising *nachika*. Unmarried older teenagers who visit their married siblings in another hamlet abide by this *nachika* decorum. Certainly, they do not sleep with a sibling and his or her spouse. Instead, they sleep with other hamlet residents, for example, another youth or a widowed person. New marriage relations sometimes start this way.

Kalliyani's younger brother, by contrast, can be more relaxed with his sister and her husband as he grows up. Opposite-sex siblings do not have to be as vigilant in following *nachika* as same-sex siblings do. That Kalliyani's brother is the same sex as his sister's husband preempts sexual tension in this triad. Were an unmarried sibling then to marry an in-law's sibling—giving the appearance of two men exchanging their sisters (although this is not at all what is occurring)—all four could be at ease with one another since one's man's wife is the other's sister, and one's woman's husband is the other's brother. It is only in modern bourgeois society, however, that one finds an idealized family foursome of father, mother, son, and daughter. Siblings commonly occur in multiples of more than two that are unbalanced in terms of sex. The computational complexity that *plural* siblings introduce into lived reality far exceeds simple models assuming brother and sister and (dyadic) brothers-in-law.

Ethnographers of South Asian hunter-gatherers have by and large discussed dyadic same-sex and opposite-sex sibling and in-law relations. Peter Gardner (2000: 113–14) argued that Paliyan brothers-in-law cooperate closely, especially in collecting honey, whereas brothers never do; Gardner further described the brother-sister relationship as particularly friendly, helpful, affectionate, and supportive in times of need. Brian Morris (1982: 183) counterargued that Hill Pandaram brothers cooperate, though less often than brothers-in-law do; and Ulrich Demmer (1997) described brothers-in-law as normatively cooperating in the collection of honey. But what happens when a sib set comprises *several* members? Taking into consideration the real-life context of *pluripresent* siblings co-residing in *tiny* communities, my material shows a more complex situation. In GR—where Kungan resided with two brothers and a sister, who constituted, with his in-laws, the core and *majority* of the hamlet's residents—situationally based cooperation among either brothers or brothers-in-law might have been expected. What was striking was its relative rarity. One usually cooperated with his or her spouse, children and single people joining them, *alongside* siblings and siblings-in-law, and only on exceptional occasions did groupings of three or four men (often including brothers, in-laws, and cousins) cooperate in collecting a particular type of honey (that of the *Apis dorsata* found on very high treetops; see chapter 4). At the same time, siblings expected, demanded, and provided help when necessary, in the manner described in the literature as "demand sharing" (see Peterson 1993; Bird-David 1990).

SIB PLURISTRUCTURES

Siblings, their spouses, and their children (Take 5)

An effective register of lifeways in a tiny forager community is achieved by shifting from a dyadic to a sequential structure: that is, by envisioning community in terms of a sequence of members who follow and join one another. This structure can be visualized by reference to a party of foragers cruising single file on a narrow footpath winding through the forest, one following the other(s), joining together during pauses in their journey and at their destination. Sequential following-and-joining rather than dyadic exchange lies at the core of this form. The logic that informs models of exchange–cooperation between two actors, or two groups as macro-actors, leaves other parties concealed in the background as it theorizes and generalizes from two to society at large, seen in terms of an indefinite number of dyads (see the introduction). Such logic is untenable in tiny communities such as Kalliyani's, where the presence of others is irreducible and unconcealable. The sib group is the perfect instantiation of this structure: brothers and sisters are born one after the other, divergent in gender, age, and positionality, and they join together as they constitute the sib group and family.

The sequential logic is expressed in a bricolage of my fieldwork observations and information, some described in earlier chapters and some in chapters to come. Its clearest explication is embodied in the notion of the *modale* (~ first). Colonial and contemporary Indian officials have commonly misconstrued *modale* to mean "headman," a gloss that serves administrative needs. This reading, in turn, is potentiated by, and perpetuates, a sense of the community as a collective—a "many-as-One"—that the headman speaks for. The head of a corporate body is invested with the right to control others and make decisions on their behalf. The head (taking the metaphor seriously) directs, thinks, listens, and speaks for the community. Such a reading misrepresents Kungan and his relatives' sense of *kudumba* and *modale*. Consistent with their alternative ontological senses of plurality, the *modale* is not the *head* of any sort of body but the one *ahead* in a sequence. The *modale* is the first to arrive or the first to be born in a hamlet. The *modale*'s position is situational; no power of coercion or control inheres in it. This position involves leading by virtue of being first; others follow at their own discretion. Just as people can decide whether to follow someone embarking on a trek through the forest, hamlet dwellers may follow the lead of the *modale* or not, weighing the respective advantages of each option. The responsibilities vested in the *modale* derive from the fact that, as the first comer to the *sime* (home), he has engaged the longest with all the other local dwellers (human and nonhuman) and has the most experience of those beings and that place. (Nothing in this logic prevents a woman from being a *modale*; however, no woman I know or heard of was formally regarded as such.)

Other eclectic expressions of this sequential logic can be cited. As described in previous chapters, a domestic object is always associated with the person who made it or who first obtained or used it, even if this object later circulates and is used by others (see chapter 1). The birth of a first child, that is, the start of a new sib sequence, is culturally elaborated more than subsequent births (see chapter 2). In this chapter, this logic is expressed in sequences of marriages, one following the other, and the idealization of the first in the sequence as *olle* (good). It is also reflected in the relocation of hamlets. A hamlet's residents, though all are close relatives, do not pick up and relocate their living site as one body. Rather, one couple moves and then others follow them, weighing the benefits of joining the first couple against other options. If enough follow the first couple, their separate, cumulative actions are tantamount to the abandonment of the old hamlet and the establishment of a new one. To those examples, one can also add that the first man to see a tree harboring the huge honey hives of the *Apis dorsata* is regarded as the tree's owner, with the right to initiate collecting the honey from it (the honey is then shared; see chapter 4). This logic is also expressed in the "big visit" that is sequentially celebrated in the Gorge's hamlets in the order of their settlement and in the *modale*'s responsibility for initiating building of the special hut serving this occasion. He brings the first pole and puts it in the ground, and others follow him, when moved to do so, adding this or that piece to the gradually growing structure. The *modale* does exercise authority to the extent that where he puts the first pole dictates where the others put their poles, if the hut is to hold together. His action, as the first one, catalyzes and orients the others' actions. He cannot, however, control the others or coordinate their work, nor can they coerce him to perform his role. If the person who happens to be *modale* is unable or unwilling to do what is expected of him, then someone else does it. For instance, when Mathen decided to visit Kungan's cousin in DV, his mother's older brother Chathen, who was *modale*, declined to accompany him, so another uncle went in his stead. Such substitution can happen even during preparations for the "big visit" (see chapter 5).

Do these multiscale overviews ethnographically support Lévi-Strauss's large-scale-inspired sibling-exchange marriage model? To the contrary, they reveal a case involving an emergent assembly of relatives, its contours shaped and reshaped by "paths" of marriages but its overall form perpetuated by siblings and like-siblings who maintain close relations as they grow up. Instead of groups exchanging women, this ethnography shows a sibling-scaled community, a sib matrix, its changing outlines reflecting the ebb and flow of sibling and siblinglike ties. Out-marriages do occur, and I consider them in chapter 6. Sibling and cousin intermarriage, however, is the striking and common form, and its effect, contrary to the norm for siblings in the modern "nuclear family" script, is to militate against sibling dispersal. And contrary to "modern" siblings' tangential secondary, and even tertiary, ontological status, siblings, their spouses, and their children (the *kudumba*) constitute the residential cores of the tiny forager hamlets in the Gorge. Although *kudumba* connotes "family" in various Dravidian languages, for the foragers of the Gorge, as Kalliyani explicated for me, it refers to pluriresiding siblings, their spouses, and their children. Having begun, in this chapter, to throw light on the foragers' *sonta kudumba* (our family) by focusing on its sibling axis, I turn in the next chapter to the spousal and parent-child components.

Family fishing. Photographed by the author (1978–79).

4. Couples and Children

Gender, Caregiving, and Foraging Together

Sridevi and her husband cruise ahead on the footpath that winds through the forest, going back to the hamlet after a successful fishing expedition. Their twelve-year-old daughter (Chikdevi) hurries to catch up with them, while her younger cousin straggles behind and I trail after her. We pause to collect firewood and then continue on, Sridevi balancing her pile of wood on her head and her husband carrying his on his shoulder. The sun begins its descent, shadows grow, and the surroundings start to blur with the approaching twilight. Fires have already been lit in some of the hearths when we reach the hamlet. Back at their hut, Sridevi and her husband sit down to rest, remaining close to one another, their bodies almost touching, their faces turned in the same direction, their eyes taking in the vast greenness all around them. Rested, they walk down to the river, where she washes clothes and he stands beside her, then both bathe. In the hamlet, meanwhile, their daughter collects a hissing piece of charcoal from her aunt's hearth and carries it to her own hearth, a few steps away. She places it in the cold ashes, and her cousin blows on it through a thin bamboo tube, coaxing a tiny flame into flickering life. By the time her parents return from the river and join the girls, the fire is burning brightly. All four sit in a semicircle around the hearth, amid the closely spaced hearths of their relatives, enjoying the warmth in the cool evening and anticipating their meal of roasted fish.

In this chapter, I engage with scale-blind discussions of foragers' gendered division of labor and practice of alloparenting as I continue to explore locals' notion of *sonta kudumba* (our older and younger brothers and sisters, their spouses, and their children). I focus on conjugal nuclei and the children that orbit them, striking sights in an area where gender-segregated groupings are rather commonplace. Conjugal couples in this community ordinarily stay together yet without excluding others; they constitute gravitational cores to which others attach themselves, especially children and occasionally single older relatives. I show that in this forager world, where plurality of social life is pregiven, "two together" rather than classes of "men" and "women" or "parents" and "children" constitute a basic, minimal form of pluralness. Questioning unthinking recourse to serial classes as analytical coordinates in studying tiny communities of relatives, I examine how Sridevi and her relatives ontologically and culturally figure conjugal twoness and parents-children connections and how those relations develop within their sib-based community. Through ethnography that spans ritual, foraging pursuits, narratives of conjugal attachment, child-care practices, and notions of growing up, this chapter reveals the salience of conjugal bipresence in everyday activities and children's circulation among relatives as essential to developing *budi* (~ the skills for living *with* others). And it continues to explore organizational pluristructures in the forager community and the spatiotemporal modes by which its members are present in one another's lives.

· · ·

Foragers are viewed as among the most egalitarian communities, which is one reason their gendered division of labor has drawn so much scholarly and popular attention.[1] This interest, however, is rooted in the (unacknowledged) large-scale ontological basis of "gender" questions that is extended to their ethnographic and comparative discussions. These questions underwrite the catchy titles of early publications, for instance, *Man the Hunter* (Lee and Devore 1968), *Woman the Gatherer* (Dahlberg 1981), and *Woman the Hunter* (Stange 1977).[2] Such titles capture the gendered positions debated, with some scholars redressing the longtime focus on male hunting by stressing women's contribution to daily subsistence and, in some cases, women's engagement in hunting as well. At the same time, they commonly posit "men's activities" and "women's activities" as the basis of discussion. Marilyn Strathern (1988) famously cautioned against assuming the Western notion of gender antinomy as the basis of ethnographic analysis, citing Melanesians as illustrating another possibility: that is, a pregiven male-female *relation* within which gendering unfolds and is made apparent. In the tiny-scale forager community context, I suggest, one also needs to question gendered groupings as pregiven coordinates of analysis. One should critically consider whether, for example, Sridevi and her husband primarily differentiate themselves from one another as a "man" and a "woman," that is, as individual instances of categorical classes: social groups comprising "men" and "women."

In the late 1970s, Sridevi did not imagine a "Nayaka" people far beyond the horizons of the Gorge, beyond the few dozen men and women she personally knew, beyond the half dozen couples she and her husband lived with, all of whom were their close relatives. Is there any reason to assume that she understood her experience with her husband in terms of gendered imagined communities? Whether she did or did not—and I argue that, in general, she did not—is an issue to be explored ethnographically rather than assumed beforehand as an element of the model guiding analysis. A couple cast away on an island, who grew up in a context that presented masses of men and women to their attention and in which "men" and "women" were not abstractions but semiotic-structural categories engendering their public materiality, may continue to perceive and conduct themselves as instantiations of imagined gendered communities even after being marooned. But can we assume this option for Sridevi and her husband, who had lived their entire lives with *sonta kudumba*?

In her study of modern English kinship, Strathern (1992a: 79) explicates the ontological register of married man and woman, another antinomy that could limit exploring the experience of pairs like Sridevi and her husband. Strathern (ibid., citing Wolfram 1987: 16–18) observes that until nineteenth-century reforms in English law, man and woman became, in marriage, "one flesh," with the woman regarded as a "part" of the husband-person. David Schneider (1968) likewise argues that marriage in mid-twentieth-century American kinship meant the *uniting* of a man and a woman through sexual intercourse and in the eyes of the law. In the modern English language generally, even the word *together*, which in Old and Middle English meant "being in each other's company, in contact, in companionship," has assumed the sense of "things or persons who merge into a unity, a whole, a mass, a body."[3] Though less so than *marriage*, even the "softer" phrase *living together* may connote a sense of union to some readers. Over time, though, Strathern suggests, the idea of "the pair united as one person" gave way to that of "pair of one persons (that is, two individual persons)" (1992a: 79). "The English," she observes, can even conceive of "one-parent families," and in "some two-parent families, spouses negotiate with each other as though they were a pair of single parents" (ibid.). The register of the man-woman couple as either "the pair united as one person" *or* "a pair of one persons" (in my shorthand terms, "two-as-One" or "two ones") excludes the bipresence of couples like Sridevi and her husband ("one-with-one") from the center of ethnographic analysis, ignoring what, I argue, matters most to them. We need to consider

how people like them form, transform, and understand their conjugal relations as their lives unfold in the midst of tiny communities of relatives that
coalesce around coresidential cores of intermarried siblings.

Specialists on hunter-gatherer gender relations Karen and Kirk Endicott
(2008) did fieldwork among the Batek—a hunter-gatherer people in
Malaysia who number roughly eight hundred and live in nomadic camps of
twenty to forty persons (10, 12). In their joint ethnography, they disclose
the background of their gendered analysis in remarkable detail and with
great frankness:

> Gender was not a frequent topic of conversation among Batek. . . . They
> did not have beliefs such as menstrual blood is polluting to men (a
> common idea in Melanesia, for example), that required them to pay
> continual attention to the sexes of their companions. Nor did they have
> adolescent initiation rites, as many societies do, that explicitly articulate
> their cultural concepts of the nature of the sexes and the roles they
> should play in society. . . . To Batek, gender was just one of many
> qualities of people—including, personality, position in the kinship
> system, age and ethnic identity—that might be prevalent in particular
> situations. Gender was the focus of *our interest rather than theirs*. . . .
> Notions of differences between men and woman were only minor
> features of their thinking about people in general. (26, my emphasis)

In all of the respects mentioned by the Endicotts, Sridevi and her relatives
are similar to Batek. In hunter-gatherer societies with more pronounced
separation of male and female spheres of activity, locals still clearly express
their preferences for staying with the spouse. The words of Nisa, an exceptionally articulate !Kung woman, whose life and words Marjorie Shostak
(1981) recorded, convey this preference. Referring to her first husband, she
says, "He did not want me to leave him, and we were always together; when
he went to gather food, it was the two of us that went; when we went to get
water, it was the two of us that went. Even to collect firewood, that's the
way we went—together" (162). In her study of the Australian Aboriginal
Warlpiri, surely among the most gender-segregated hunter-gatherers
known, Françoise Dussart (2000), another expert on gender issues, shows
that bridging obligations of care and nurturance exist alongside rigid separation between women and men, drawing them together even though they
may not engage in the same activities. From their opposite ends of the
hunter-gatherer ethnographic continuum, I read these ethnographers as
cautioning against "overgenderizing" hunter-gatherer intimate communities of relatives. Notably, at the close of the 1970s, before gender had
emerged as a major issue, nongendered models of hunter-gatherer and

small-scale agriculturalist societies were proposed that centered attention on married/single and unisexual (male-male)/heterosexual distinctions (Goodale 1980 and Collier and Rosaldo 1981, respectively).

Approaching Sridevi and her husband as "two ones" and as particular instantiations respectively of "men" and "women" sets the grounds for pursuing (and confusing) the gendered questions of "what men and women do in hunter-gatherer societies" and "what married men and women do in the household" (the household here a particular instantiation of the series constituting society). The concept of "labor" itself, notably, abstracts "work" from its social context (cf. Ingold 2000: 323). A cardinal concept in the formal logic of capitalist production, it trains attention on discrete tasks and so allows one to ask, *which* tasks are those of a woman/women and which are those of a man/men in a household/society? The fact that Sridevi and her husband both carry firewood would in this register figure as a "man" and a "woman" doing the same task, and conversely, at the river, when she washes clothes and he stands beside her, as the woman, not the man, doing the washing. Meanwhile, what is prominent in their experience is their companionship and bipresence at those times.

Sridevi and her relatives, I suggest, do not configure "being many" in gendered terms, that is, as two subgroups, one of men and one of women. Rather, their primary coordinates are "parents" and "children," which for them are not separable categories reflecting age distinctions but, instead, existentially pluriconnected entities: "parents of children" and "children of parents" (Bird-David 2005b, 2008). Parents in a sense are born with their children. And in fact, a marriage can be born alongside a child, as I discuss below. Compared with men and women as *two* series of same-kind, separate members (e.g., many instances of "one man" and of "one woman," their numbers, in principle, infinite), the "parents-children" vector as locally perceived involves finite and diverse plurirelated members: father, mother (wife of father), child (of each of the foregoing and of both), second child (of father, mother, and both, and sibling of first child), and so on. The "parents-children" vector is temporal and plurirelational.

Elsewhere, I have argued that "parents-children" is a core cosmological construct for Sridevi's people and other tropical forest hunter-gatherers (Bird-David 1990, 1992a, 1996, 1999a). For its local significance to be fully appreciated, this construct has to be rescued from the clutches of its large-scale-based ontological grounding. Outside the ordinary family context, the English phrase "parents and children" often connotes two temporally stratified series—many instances of "parent" and many of "child" (rather than many instances of "parent–child"). "Children" refers to the replacement generation "further on in time from their parents" (Strathern 1992a: 15). Child-dedicated spaces, institutions, and services exist in Western/ized large-scaled consumer settings, expressing and making real a separate child's world and substantiating the idea of "children" as a distinct sociocultural population. Could children be approached as a subpopulation or a series of persons of the same kind (young, fragile, or otherwise denominated) in a tiny forager community that included—as Sridevi's community did in the late 1970s (see table 3)—about two dozen children of all ages, all (or most) of them siblings and cousins? Could children be so regarded in any intimate domestic setting without recourse to imagined large-scaled classes of children as external categories of reference?

General interest in hunter-gatherer children goes back to the mid- to late twentieth century, largely within evolutionary and child development research (see Hewlett and Lamb 2005b). It intensified when attention in anthropology recently turned to children as a distinct subpopulation (in some views, even an ethnic minority or a subaltern culture) that, some argue, has been scholarly neglected, just as women had been ignored in earlier research (Hirschfeld 2002; cf. Derevenski 1994; Kamp 2001). The early years of childhood (up to about the age of four as a rough measure) have been the main focus in child-focused hunter-gatherer research (Hewlett and Lamb 2005a: 16), much of it comparatively engaging with John Bowlby's (1969) seminal work on attachment and loss, a cornerstone of modern child-care theory and clinical work. Ignoring huge scalar disparity, students of hunter-gatherer children elaborated on the difference between the modern cultural scenario (and often the experience) of a single caregiver and hunter-gatherer *alloparenting,* in which multiple group members act in a parental role.[4] *Allo* (which means "other") lumps together caregivers other than biological parents, leaving room for one to unthinkingly posit the father-mother-baby nuclear family as the minimal, basic module from which to start analysis. For the most part, however, in tiny-scale contexts, such "others" are close relatives. Moreover, they are essentially plurirelated from the outset, and with the birth of a baby, another relative (see chapter 2), they become even more complexly interrelated.

Alloparenting is argued to be a uniquely human phenomenon in the natural world and a critical development in the evolution of our species: for example, it has been invoked to explain the "grandmother hypothesis" (i.e., the evolutionary benefit of women's longevity beyond childbearing years; e.g., Hawkes 2004) and is regarded by some as the evolutionary motor for human mutual understanding, intersubjectivity, and empathy (Hrdy 2009). Given such high stakes, paying close attention to the distortive effect of scale-blind discussions of hunter-gatherer child-care practices is important, and one should especially ask whether distinguishing *alloparents* from *biological parents*, instructive though it may be in large-scale contexts, does not cloud understanding of parents-children relations in a tiny community whose residential core is often a set of intermarried siblings.

Downscaling discussions of men-women and parents-children is more easily said than done because of an inbuilt ambiguity of the plural form that pops up the moment an ethnographer shifts from particular persons (Sridevi and her husband, Chikdevi and her parents) to the ethnographic generalizing mode (men and women, parents and children). Does "men and women hunt" mean that men (plural of man) and women (plural of woman) hunt or, instead, that men and women (plural of man and woman together) hunt? The problem persists even should the careful ethnographer write that a couple, a man and a woman, jointly hunt because the term *jointly* may obscure bipresence. For example, in her classic study of middle-class English families, Elisabeth Bott (1957) distinguished between those with "joint" and those with "segregated" organization, defining the former by reference to activities "carried out by husband and wife together, *or the same activity . . . carried out by either partner at different times*" (53, my emphasis). *Jointly* trains attention in this case on the *same task* being pursued by men and women, regardless when or where; this, rather than on the *man and woman doing it together*. The latter, I argue, matters to Sridevi and her husband far more than the former, which instills within the domestic microcosmos a sense of "meanwhile" (a spatiotemporal concept that, Benedict Anderson 2006 [1983] argued, arose with nationalism; see the introduction). Against the "many ones" and "many as One" grain of my analytical language, in this chapter's ethnography I try to steer a course between received senses of gendered *groups* and conjugal *unions* and received senses of parent and child *generations* and parent-child asymmetric *caregiving* relations (see Bird-David 2008) in exploring foragers' ontological sensibilities of conjugal and parents-children connections. With the cautionary insights gained from this theoretical detour, I return, then, to the few-many relatives I lived with in the Gorge, continuing the exploration of *sonta kudumba*. . . .

CULTURAL FRAMES

*Our siblings, **spouses, and children*** (Take 1)

One day, Sridevi's father-in-law surprised me when he suddenly said, "Right from the beginning, there were many couples living here and there, our grandfathers and grandmothers." I had failed so many times to elicit origin stories from him and others (unusual as it may appear, this forager community had no instituted forums for telling myths and stories; see Bird-David 2004a and chapter 6 of this volume) that, hearing him say this, I snatched up my pen and notebook and waited for more. But he did not elaborate. He had made the point he wanted to make. His one-line story might seem easy to dismiss, but it is nevertheless striking, compared, say, with the Judeo-Christian script of *one* god, who created *one* man, and out of the man's rib *one* woman, who in pain and labor reproduced *many* humans. His story gives expression at once to a sense of a pregiven "many" and to twoness, the husband-wife pair as an elementary form. In some cosmologies, in-laws are pregiven (see Viveiros de Castro 2009); in this story, husband-wife togetherness is depicted as primordial. The husband-wife structure was not elaborated through kinship terminology; for example, I hardly ever heard terms of address for or reference to spouses in the hamlet, unlike the constant stream of terms for siblings, parents, and children.[5] This itself, in Maurice Bloch's sense, was another sign that husband-wife togetherness was a part of "what goes without saying," a part of what "things are really like" (1992: 48).

Again, I preliminarily turn to the "big visits" held in the Gorge (discussed in detail in chapter 5) for the special perspective they offer on the husband-wife twosome. These gatherings include a performance that I have not previously accorded much attention, an episode of playacting that constitutes a reversal ritual of sorts, one that, in inverting all but twoness, communicates the pregiven and irreducible nature of the pair. At the same time, as it involves only two characters, it reverses the normal order of couples who live with few-many relatives. This reversal ritual/playacting takes place in the midst of the "big visit," stirring everybody up and evoking laughter and great commotion. The following account draws directly from field notes I took during one of several such performances I observed. . . .

Two men enter the hamlet, dressed grotesquely as male and female. Their appearance accentuates sexual differences. The upper part of the "male" body is bare. He wears shorts, with a folded dhoti wrapped around them as a belt. A large penis made of grass is tied to this belt and dangles down in front of him. The "female" performer wears a sari that falls to the ankles, leaving the upper part of the body bare except for a necklace. The "male" carries a sack full of dry leaves and thorns on his back and has a heavy stick, which he sometimes leans on but more often waves in the air or carries on his shoulders. The "female" carries a digging stick.

Regarded as evil spirits (*pichachio*), the pair come from the forest. As they approach the hamlet, they are cordially invited to enter (as are all the

Pair of spirit visitors. Photographed by the author (1978–79).

local spirits during the "big visit"). Everybody gathers around the new arrivals, staring (and laughing) at what they do, avoiding them when the two try to initiate interaction. The pair behave outrageously, reversing normal manners and etiquette. They walk one after the other, the "man" first, reversing the usual sequence. Their faces are blackened; the "man's" mouth is distended by a fruit he has stuffed inside it. They are offered a mat to sit on and plantains and rice to eat. They put the food on the ground and then pick it up using only their mouths. They eat the plantains without peeling them, stuffing their mouths full to overflowing. Afterward, they wash themselves with fire ash, smearing it all over their faces. The male figure makes advances toward girls, who run away. He follows them, wiggling his straw penis in the air as he charges after them. Eventually, he returns to the female figure's side. Other than during these brief moments, the two performers remain together throughout their act; they are rarely more than a meter apart. At the same time, they reverse all etiquette of being with others in the hamlet: they address their attendants in shrieking voices, screaming obscene insults. They nag and pester everyone for money, and they do not relent until given some coins. Finally, they leave the hamlet, walking one after the other, and disappear from sight, returning to the forest to roam, away from the hamlet's sociality. Although this performance involves many reversals of everyday ordinary behavior, it does not deviate from the paired mode of being. The *pichachio* are eccentrically recognizable as a male-female twosome; however, they are a couple (in the phenomenological sense of the term) unto themselves.[6]

Other spirits arrive in the hamlet, through spirit possession. They do not arrive in pairs, like the *pichachio*, but one after the other or alongside one another, and they are addressed and referred to in the aggregate as *dodappanuawanu* (~ great parents; literally, great fathers-mothers) or *sattavaru* (~ eldest, first people), and they, in turn, address and refer to the attendants as *makalo* (~ children). These spirits are extremely diverse (including ancestral and animistic spirits, forefathers, recently deceased people, and even deities of neighboring people). They dance, eat, and talk *with* the celebrants. They discuss with their hosts shared concerns and reassure each other of unfaltering future visits and mutual caring. Although the spirits only "materialize" during the "big visits," they are an integral part of the foragers' everyday lives. Even the earlier ancestors, the first people, "are not bygone, over, something that *was* and is never to return, something beyond reach that is no longer here, something about which or whom one can learn only from narratives" (Bird-David 2004a: 416); they are present in everyday life, and relations with them subsist in interacting with them, if only now and then. A sense of parents and children as subsequent generations, one coming after the other, substituting for one another, or as carrying the same substance or property through time, is clearly not the sense of *dodappanuawanu* and *makalo* that the "big visits" foreground. *Dodappanuawanu* and *makalo* connote almost the opposite: continued pluripresence, continued shared plural life (see Bird-David 2004a).

WORKING SEPARATELY TOGETHER

Our siblings, **spouses, and children** (Take 2)

Mundane foraging and domestic pursuits showcase the routineness of conjugal bipresence. Every day I observed individual couples setting out from the hamlet on the narrow footpaths leading into the forest, the wife usually going first and the husband following her. Walking as they did, single file at a distance from one another, they were easy to follow, and children and others often did so (as in the scene opening of chapter 2). I cannot recall ever observing a couple explicitly requesting others not to follow them. I briefly describe below the main types of activities that these groupings pursued, with special emphasis on the extent and the manner in which husband and wife cooperated with each other and with the children and others who joined them.

Fishing

I joined several fishing parties during 1978–79 and jotted down who did what and when and where they engaged in those tasks. I processed my notes as schedules, which, since they did not reveal a gendered division of labor (a hot research topic at the time), I consigned to a drawer. Revisiting them from my current perspective shows a pattern that can be glossed as "working separately together." This pattern is characterized by a lax rhythm of one and many, a fluid division of labor, the task itself mattering less than being together and sharing the experience. The following account of one expedition draws directly from my field notes. . . .

Sridevi's older sister (Bomi) and her husband go fishing. Three of their four children, a divorced son aged thirty, daughter aged twelve, and son aged nine, join them. I am invited to join them too, not just as a "daughter" but also as the owner of a fishing basket, which I am asked to bring along. (Only a few men show interest in making these baskets, and I had asked one of them, Bomi's older brother, to make one for me.) Bomi leaves the hamlet first, and then, one after the other, the rest of us in her party walk after her, in a file, keeping a meter or so apart from one another, on the footpath that runs down one side of the ravine. The plantation stretches along the opposite side of the ravine. A plantation field supervisor and a small party of day laborers are working there, preparing the soil for new coffee plants. This work party includes three of Bomi's relatives who have chosen that day to work on the plantation. Their figures on the hillside are small in the distance, but no doubt they see us just as we see them.

We arrive at the river and begin working. Three hours later, we have changed the landscape dramatically. Where before a stream gushed down a rocky slope, spluttering down a series of small waterfalls, a pool of calm water is now impounded by two weirs. The weirs are built of rocks, mud, and leaves and are about 50 meters apart. The fishing basket is fitted into the lower weir. The river's current now flows through a new diversion, as if this bypass had been its course from primordial time. Preparing the weirs and the diversion requires intensive labor, which is done by all the party members. No one supervises or coordinates the work. Each does what he or she wants, separately within what is clearly a joint project. Bomi and her husband sometimes work next to one another and sometimes a few meters apart. They do the same tasks and, occasionally, complementary ones, in the latter case without any apparent coordination. That is, I do not see them work as "one body" or even communicate about what each does or should do. Rather, alongside one another or apart, they carry out a range of tasks: they haul rocks and set them in place as part of the structure for the weir; they dig and carry soil and press it between the rocks; they further tighten the weir by squashing leaves into the remaining cracks; they deepen and widen the alternative flowage; they cut and crush the poisoning root (*kuibulu*, i.e., *Adenia palmata passiflora-ceae*); they spread the poison in the water and wait for the intoxicated fish to rise up to the surface for oxygen. They either scoop up the fish by hand and twist their heads or slash them in the water with their sickle knives and then pick them up. Some fish eventually drift into the fishing basket, carried by a mild current generated by loosening the upper weir.

The children help in all these tasks but not with the same intensity as the couple, taking time off to play and rest. Even the youngest clears vegetation and mud from the diversion route, carries small stones and leaves for use in tightening the weir, helps to pound the poisoning root and spread it in the water, and takes part in catching the fish and killing them by twisting their heads. Whereas Bomi and her husband place the fish they have caught on nearby rocks, to be collected later, the children place the ones they catch in a fold of their dhoti or bundle them in a spare cloth. Another participant eventually joins the fishing party: one of the three relatives who have been working that day up the hill in the plantation area and saw us pass by earlier. He arrives after the lengthy preparatory work is over, when people begin to pick up the fish. He simply steps into the water and picks up fish alongside the others, making his own pile.

Sikai collection

During the collection of *sikai*, the salable pods of a forest creeper, the forming and reforming of small groupings around conjugal nuclei was particularly vivid. Almost everybody from GR and the other hamlets congregated during the short harvest season in the same restricted area where the creeper grew abundantly. To collect the *sikai*, someone (a man, in the dozens of instances I observed) climbed a tree (to a height of 9–10 meters), from which, using a pole (3–4 meters long), he shook the creeper's vines, making the pods fall to the ground. It took an agile climber ten to thirty minutes to do this job, after which he climbed down and joined the others in collecting the pods from the ground. This second phase lasted, on average, two hours.

The situation would seem to have been ready-made for certain forms of labor organization and division, not least same-sex working groups and strictly defined gendered tasks. But, on-site, work groups comprised a couple and associated children (the couple's own and others'), each group separated from the others by up to a dozen meters or so, sometimes within eyesight and sometimes only within earshot because of the dense vegetation. The gentle hum of laughter and talk within each group intertwined now and then with louder exchanges between relatives in different groups. Some work groups were joined by single young men and once in a while by the couple's married daughter and her spouse. Strong, agile young men were an asset in this activity. Couples and associated children were such a normal sight during these harvests that I recorded the *exceptional* instances of groupings that included more than husband, wife, and children (theirs and others'). Of the thirty total instances I recorded and analyzed (Bird 1983a: 173–80), not one involved cooperation of couples; rather, a single young man generally joined the conjugal pair and children and undertook the climbing.

Honey collecting

Sridevi and her relatives (who were well known for this activity) collected three types of honey. Two types—the "small honey" produced by a small black bee of the genus *Melipona*, which nests in bamboo hollows, and the honey produced by *Apis indica*, a bee that nests on small trees and bushes—were collected during the daytime by foraging parties who came across it. Each party ordinarily comprised a couple and one or more children or single relatives. In the first case, the bamboo was simply cut down when encountered, split open, and the honey extracted. Some bamboo hives were taken back and hung on the roof joints of huts in the hamlet. In the second case, the man climbed up the tree with a burning bunch of twigs or grass and a basket made of bamboo strips. He filled the basket with honey and lowered it to his wife.

Only the "big honey" produced by the *Apis dorsata* was collected by men alone. The nests are huge and hang from the tops of trees reaching 60–70 feet in height or from the tops of high cliffs. Nests occur in clusters, and collecting the honey was a risky job, carried out only during moonless nights. Two to three bamboos, each about 15 feet long, were placed against the tree trunk or the cliff, atop one another; one man climbed up them carrying a burning torch and a long rope. He smoked as many bees as he could out of the hives, and amid the swarm buzzing around him, he pulled up one or more baskets that his mates on the ground tied to the rope, filled them, and lowered them back to the ground. This type of honey was usually sold to forest traders; the first two types were often consumed by the foraging party on-site.

Digging roots

Sridevi and her relatives collected nine types of *Dioscorea* tubers (see table 4, p. 149); some extended deep underground. The ease and flow of the work, and the general lack of rules governing the way spouses cooperated in doing this job, struck me. For example, Sridevi's husband would start digging the

Family collecting honey. Photographed by the author (1978–79).

deep-growing wild yam while Sridevi stood and watched, and after a while, they simply changed places. When the pit grew deep, he climbed into it and continued to dig while she removed the soil. They continued to change places in this way until the root could be removed.

Hunting

Men alone occasionally set out together with their dogs in search of large game (mainly deer, wild pigs, and monitor lizards). Often, acting on the reports of forest travelers, they set out to secure game killed by large forest predators (cf. Raghavan 1929: 59 on Kurumbas). They took their billhook knives and digging sticks with them; they had no especial hunting equipment.[7] As Brian Morris (1975: 128) described for the South Indian forager Hill Pandaram, in fact, they *gathered* animals, family groups opportunistically taking small animals they encountered on their way through the forest. Sridevi and her relatives did not identify themselves as "hunters." Neither did they attribute any special ritual significance to hunting.[8]

Plantation wage work

The foragers' involvement with wage work on the plantation fluctuated a great deal and was most intense from the 1960s through the 1980s, after which the plantation closed down (see Bird-David 1992b). During 1978–79 less than two-thirds of Sridevi's adult relatives who were able to do so (around two dozen) worked on the plantation. Except for Sridevi's brother (Chathen), who had a permanent job as a watchman, the others worked intermittently, on average two and a half days a week, from 7 A.M. to 2 P.M. (Bird 1983b).

Sridevi was one of the more regular wageworkers on the plantation. Following a common pattern, her husband worked on most days she did. On such days, Sridevi would rise, pick up her machete, and start to walk down the path leading to the plantation, followed soon after by her husband. Other couples followed, if they so chose, usually several moments later. Proceeding from the narrow forest path onto the broad "white" route going to the plantation, husband-wife couples filing one after the other created a sharp contrast to the Muslim workers making their way to the plantation, walking in gender-segregated groups up to five persons abreast. The Muslim laborers also worked in gender-segregated groups, the men in rubber tapping and the women in weeding and coffee picking. Sridevi's male relatives resisted working as tappers, although they were constantly entreated to take on this skilled job, which paid better than weeding. They preferred to do weeding work with their wives, alongside the Muslim female laborers, in a mixed-gender gang or in a separate gang; in the latter case, during the shared break time, husbands and wives sat down together to rest. Couples generally succeeded in the late 1970s in working together on the plantation—or in avoiding work there—despite the plantation's attempts to impose its own gender conventions. For example, the plantation supervisor complained to me that when "Nayaka men" were occasionally assigned building and carrying jobs, away from their womenfolk, they did not report to work. By contrast, when the task they were given called for gender cooperation—for example, regulating shade on young coffee plants by cutting down the branches of trees overhanging them—they reported enthusiastically. Couples worked on this task as teams, the husband climbing the tree and cutting down the foliage, then joining his wife in clearing the debris away. Two couples even succeeded in negotiating a job-sharing arrangement with the manager of a nearby forest estate, working together to patrol the estate as watchman and woman, as needed. Couples often brought their young babies to work, an older child coming with them to hold the baby while the parents were occupied with their duties, then relinquishing the child to one or the other parent during breaks. This routine provided a striking contrast to that of migrant mothers, who rushed home at break times to breast-feed their babies.

Sridevi and the other workers approached working on the plantation as a sort of gathering of wages, which, from their viewpoint, allowed them, on the way home at the end of a shift, to collect foodstuffs on credit from the small tea shacks at the plantation's border. The vendors collected the money due them on paydays; eventually, for everyone's convenience, they began billing the plantation accountant directly. As I described it elsewhere, Sridevi and her relatives were part-time "wage-gatherers" when they engaged in casual work on the plantation (see more in Bird 1983b; Bird-David 1992b).

Domestic chores

Given the foragers' propensity to dwell on diversity and personal differences, I found that my direct questions about male and female tasks at best produced descriptions of the migrant neighbors' gendered division of labor and even exaggerations of their conventions to the point of caricature. For example, early on in my fieldwork, I asked Sridevi's older brother-in-law (her husband's older sister's husband) to describe to me what his wife did. We were sitting quietly together, and to break the silence, I asked this gendered question, taking care to phrase it specifically. I asked him to tell me what *his wife* did. The gist of what he related (detailing afternoon activities only) follows:

> She leaves the estate at 2:30. On the way home she gathers firewood. At home she cleans first inside the hut and outside, then, afterward, she

cooks the rice. She cleans the rice. She puts the pot on the fire, when it is cooked she tastes it with her finger, then she turns it over so the water drains. After cooking the rice, she cooks curry. When both are ready, she will first serve me and the children and she will sit till we eat. Only after we finish our food does she eat.

The brother-in-law was completely serious when he embarked on this account, and I wrote down every word he said until I realized that what he was relating was completely alien to what he and others in his *sime* did and, indeed, was at odds with his own personal circumstances: his wife did not work on the plantation, and the two of them did not have children. He was depicting his Muslim neighbors' ways, exaggerating their standards and conventions. This old man, I think, was not toying with me but was earnestly trying to please me, generalizing in the only way he could, by reference to his Muslim neighbors (cf. Gardner 1985 on Paliyan claiming to follow Tamil kinship practices). My other close associates whom I questioned about gender-specific activities responded, "*Bere, bere* [different, different]," to emphasize that each couple devised their own idiosyncratic domestic arrangements. Notwithstanding, my observations suggest that each of the tasks women did men did as well, if often to a lesser extent, including cooking, washing clothes and pots, carrying babies, dressing children, and lighting the hearth. Whatever the case, partners were often bipresent when one or the other did these tasks.

CONJUGAL ATTACHMENT

Our siblings, **spouses, and children** (Take 3)

Bowlby's absorbing interest in the conditions of maternal abandonment and attachment has little purchase, emotionally or practically, in the tiny-scale(d) forager context, where newborns are prefigured as relatives to *all* in the community and they literally come into the world surrounded by relatives (see chapter 2). Bowlby's concern was triggered by problems he encountered in hospitals, institutional settings within large-scale cultural contexts in which newborns are figured as "new individuals," a perspective that can complicate adult-infant bonding. A paramount concern among Sridevi and her relatives, by contrast, was bonding with a conjugal partner. The development of conjugal attachment is a serious issue in a minuscule society faced with chronic spousal scarcity and where the formation of a couple, especially in a "good marriage," involves a dramatic transformation for at least one of the parties involved, as that person must begin to identify primarily not only with his or her spouse but also with the spouse's relatives, disengaging from the close relatives of his or her own childhood and adolescence. This challenge faces any bride or bridegroom anywhere who moves into an unfamiliar household or group; given the intensity of pluripresence in a tiny hamlet, though, it can be overwhelming.

Usually poor storytellers, Sridevi and her relatives were fond of telling me in great detail how they ended up living together with their spouses. The actual cases I observed were varied (demographic factors, fancies of heart, and quirks of personality all playing their part), but in narratives of conjugal pairing, a particular theme recurred (see also chapter 3). Sridevi's husband's older brother, for example, related the following account:

> I was independent from childhood and wandered a great deal from place to place, managing everywhere I went. Then I came to GR, where my mother's sister lived. There was this girl here who was ready to marry. Her people talked with me about her, but I was not interested. Her people pressed, and I consented. But in the night, I got a fear and a shiver. I left her and slept the rest of the night separately. In the morning, I escaped back to my people in TM. I stayed there for several months, and all this time the people from GR kept urging me to come back. Finally I did, and they put some medicine in my food. After eating it, I stayed in GR with that girl. Only she, these relatives, and this *sime*, were in my mind.

Sridevi's husband's second brother—whose first wife died and whose second and third relationships with women from distant places did not work out—narrated his fourth conjugal attachment in the following way: "I was alone for some time, and then my brother and father found the girl for me. I was not interested at first; for weeks I neither slept nor talked with her. She would go on her way and I on mine, and people wondered about it. Then, something was put in my tea, and since then I did not want to leave the place or the girl."

Women as well as men related variants of this story. An incoming spouse was entangled in all of these accounts with a place (*sime*) and with the close relatives (our *kudumba*) in that place, all of whom the person was described as marrying. The end of the story was always the same, a dramatic, total physical-cum-emotional shift of attachment, against one's wish, effected by ingesting "medicine." Expert in preparing and using natural medicines of all kinds, which they were willing and even eager to show me, my interlocutors burst out laughing when I asked to see this particular "medicine." Stories of its use were usually told with chuckles and laughing eyes, and yet they addressed a serious matter. Given the chronic scarcity of spouses, this narrative of resistance to marrying an available spouse was telling. The salient point of the story, I now reckon, is not the medicine itself but *who* administers it: the *relatives* of the spouse-to-be, who thus appear to play a decisive part in forming the conjugal attachment. These narratives depict a shift in status from "being many" in one place to being so in another, moreover, a shift of focus from being a single person joining other conjugal nuclei to becoming part of a conjugal nucleus that others would join.

Indeed, conjugal bonding assumes general significance in this tiny community not only because it directly affects everyone but also because a new couple constitutes a new nucleus that others can join. The local usage of *mave* ("marriage," a Kannada term) clearly illustrates the point, as the following case shows. Sridevi's nephew, a skillful honey collector, was widowed at the age of thirty. His first wife had died during childbirth, and several months later, he started staying overnight in GR on his way to and from work on the plantation. His deceased wife's youngest sister, a sixteen-year-old girl, was also then staying in GR. He often slept with her, but at first no one paid special attention to the arrangement. Firstly, the age difference between the two cast doubt over whether they were having an affair. Secondly, the deaths of the first wife and child during labor were read by some people, including the girl's parents and the widower himself, as a warning against his entering into another marriage with the sister. Thirdly, and more importantly, during the day, the girl often spent a lot of time with other children and relatives. The couple's being together was thus intermittent, ebbing and flowing, and accordingly, their relation was variably perceived. Some people used *mave* and others did not when referring to it. Some people changed their view from day to day. After about four months, the two were no longer separating from one another during the daytime, at which point they were unanimously regarded as "married." (They were still living together more than twenty years later, when I revisited them in 2001.)

Even on the odd occasion when a marriage was ceremonially marked, people did not consistently refer to it as *mave* until the couple were seen to routinely spend time together, both at night and during the day. I return to the case I first described in chapter 3 involving another of Sridevi's nephews, a twenty-year-old man from GR (Mathen) who married a sixteen-year-old girl from the "satellite" settlement of DV. Mathen was a single child who had received some money from the plantation when his mother, a longtime worker there, died. Because he had money to spend, because the marriage involved a partner from a settlement beyond the horizons of ordinary visits, and because Hindu influence was greater in that settlement, just outside Devala, than in the Gorge, his marriage was marked by a modest wedding celebration held in DV. It included a meal during which the bride and bridegroom demonstratively fed each other, Hindu style. The two then moved to GR, and as I described in chapter 3, although they slept together, initially during the day when the man went to work, the girl played with the other children. Moreover, when she stayed with him in his place, she missed her relatives, and when he stayed with her in her place, he missed his. For several months, the two oscillated between living together and separately, in GR and in DV, and although they had been ceremonially "married," the term *mave* was applied to them in the same inconsistent, fluid sense as in the above-described case. For me, these discursive practices made for a confusing state of affairs—and neighboring people read lack of morals into them—until I realized that, in the local view, a ceremony did not change the fact that two people only constitute a pair when they constantly stay together. The conjugal attachment often becomes an irrefutable fact when a couple have their first baby, the first child relative who joins them.

GROWING UP

*Our siblings, **spouses, and children*** (Take 4)

Barry Hewlett et al. (2000) compared (in the conventional scale-blind terms I discuss in the introduction) the daily experiences of three- to four-month-old infants among Aka foragers and Nagandu farmers in central Africa with those of upper-middle-class Americans in the Washington, DC, area They found that Aka people held infants 94 percent of the time when the infants slept and 98 percent of the time when they were awake, whereas the American infants were held 22 percent of the time while sleeping and 44 percent of the time while awake (290). These African hunter-gatherer infant-care assessments are consistent with those reported for hunter-gatherer peoples elsewhere.[9] Notably, Ayako Hirasawa (2005) reports that, even forty years after they gave up foraging for a more sedentary life, the central African Baka continued to hold infants as much as possible, demonstrating how deeply ingrained this practice is for them. My observations in the Gorge are consistent with the general tenet that babies in hunter-gatherer communities "are held, touched, or kept near others constantly" (Hewlett and Lamb 2005a: 15). Yet, here, I want to shift away from ethnographic analysis in scale-blinding terms—which, no less than scale-insensitive comparisons, I maintain, limit understanding of child care and maturation—as I follow how children grow up among Sridevi and her relatives.

Sridevi's infant grandson was always with his parents or other relatives. He slept with both his parents from the night he was born; he was constantly carried by one of them or occasionally by another relative (e.g., his grandmother, his grandfather, his mother's younger brother, or other children living in the hamlet). I never saw him lying alone on the ground. I would see him nestled on one parent's lap when both were crouching together by their hearth, even when one of them was cooking, riding on one parent's waist when they set off to forage, or nestled on his mother's younger sister's lap next to his parents when they were working on the plantation. One strong memory I carry is of his father matter-of-factly stretching his arm out and holding him away from his body while the child urinated.

Even though he was always carried by relatives, I cannot recall ever seeing anyone directly address Sridevi's grandson, coo at him, or try to engage him in face-to-face interaction. In fact, I never recorded and cannot recall anyone initiating any sort of play dialogue with babies (before they could talk), responding to their imagined questions or asking them questions that the infants were imagined to answer or even playing with them in a nonverbal way aimed at triggering an interactive response. In her acclaimed study of Inuit childhood, Jean Briggs (1998) closely examined dialogues between Chubby Matta and her relatives. But Chubby Matta was a three-year-old able to converse with, approach, and walk away from her relatives. When Sridevi's grandson developed these capabilities, people would directly address and approach him. Until then, he was simply *with* his parents or other relatives, and the way they carried him illustrates one aspect of his manifold experience. Consider child-carrying devices that one can now buy in stores: they suspend the baby from the carrier's back, facing into it, or from the front, facing either toward or away from the carrier's chest. These devices leave the *carrier's* hands free for various tasks, and they control and limit the *baby's* field of vision. Sridevi's grandson (like all other babies in the Gorge) straddled his carrier's waist, braced by the person's arm. He moved *alongside* that person, *the carrier* constrained (not a small matter for foragers) while the infant was able from his situated position to independently see his surroundings, taking in a panoramic view with a slight turn of the head. When his mother carried him, he could breastfeed at will as she went about her daily activities. The baby was *with* his relatives while growing up to be *one of* them. When he was no longer perceived as an infant, he joined the ranks of the *makalo* (~ children).

Makalo refers to those able to talk with, respond to, walk toward, and avoid relatives (children roughly from the age of three or four; younger toddlers are referred to as *kusu*, "babies"). These capacities matter not as diagnostic of development stages per se but for their affective potential, as they mark children who can independently initiate interaction with others. Sridevi's teenage daughter was still considered one of the *makalo*; in fact, in many contexts she would be regarded as such until she became a parent herself, and even then, with all her relatives, she would continue to be a child vis-à-vis the *appanuawanu* (the spirit senior parents). Primarily a relational category, *makalo* most often implies plural sons and daughters rather than persons of young age (see Bird-David 2005b).

Children among some hunter-gatherer peoples forage on their own, providing a significant part of their own subsistence.[10] But in the hamlet where I lived, parties of children seldom fished or collected fruit by themselves, away from the hamlet and from the presence of adults. Their play took place in the hamlet, which, given its size, meant in the midst of adult relatives.[11] If they foraged by themselves, they did so in the hamlet's close vicinity. There were no youth-only dwellings or areas in the Gorge, unlike youth dormitories instituted among some tribal peoples in North and Northeast India (e.g., see Kirk et al. 1962; Fürer-Haimendorf 1950). Thus, Sridevi's daughter spent a great deal of time alongside adults, her parents or other relatives—sleeping, eating, and taking leisure with them by the side of their hearth, setting out with them to forage, and so on.

At the same time, Sridevi's daughter occasionally left her parents and visited or stayed with relatives. She began separating from her parents at the age of four or so, to stay with other relatives in her hamlet. But as she grew up, her visits gradually took her farther away to relatives in the Gorge's other hamlets. Children took advantage of the traffic of adults' visits between hamlets to make their trips, joining parties moving from one hamlet to another during the course of their own visiting circuits (discussed in chapter 2). By the time Sridevi's daughter reached her late teens, her visits could last weeks and even months at a time.

Forager children's separation from their parents from a young age drew the attention of Peter Gardner (1966), who observed this phenomenon among the South Indian Paliyan. In the same vein, Morris (1982) described how, by the age of five or six, a child among the South Indian forager Hill Pandaram begins to leave the parents. Morris further observed that the child "acts almost as if he were an independent person, though economically he is far from being so" and almost as if he (or she) "has ceased to have close emotional ties with his parents, though there may be still affection between them" (147). Gardner (1966, 1991a) noted the widespread recurrence of children's separation from their parents from a young age among hunter-gatherer groups in other parts of the world, and he associated it with hunter-gatherers' values of individual autonomy and independence.[12]

To appreciate this forager course of maturation, we have to distance ourselves from the modern association of growing up with disengagement of children from parents, evidence, in this view, of their maturity and self-sufficiency. Disengagement of children from parents was common in England as early as the medieval period, expressing, Alan Macfarlane (1986) contends, English individualism even then. In the early modern period, Strathern maintains, concurring with Macfarlane, physical distance had become both a measure of and an analogue for independence and self-sufficiency. Individualism was to be found "in the literal capacity of a person to move away from the society of others" (1992a: 13). "Physical removal could stand for an exercise of independence" (ibid.). In this cultural—and one should add, large-scale—context, the child becomes a person by "setting him or herself off from proximity to and relationships with others, [personhood] thus created in being separated from the constraints of relationship itself" (Strathern 1992a: 13). These ideas seem to seep into and underscore the argument that in leaving their parents, hunter-gatherer children prove their maturity and self-sufficiency, reinforcing hunter-gatherers' putatively individualist ideals.

English children who leave their parents clearly do not remain alone. They join other people. However, their separation from their parents is what attracts cultural attention, partly because this shift is imagined as one from the family as known, intimate context to the larger world as anonymous setting and from child as parents' responsibility to independent adult subject responsible for his or her own well-being and fate.

If we take the tiny scale of hunter-gatherer society into account, we must ask: when a child like Sridevi's daughter leaves her parents, where does that child go? Or rather, *to whom* does the child go? As children in the Gorge left their parents, they did not "go out into the world"; rather, they visited and stayed with other relatives. Their circulation involved living intermittently with parents and with other relatives. When she left her parents, Sridevi's daughter joined other relatives, adult couples and their children, such that a casual observer could easily have mistaken her for one of the hosts' children. The inclusion of a visiting child within a host family is elucidated by one unexpected, and therefore instructive, response to an episode in which I played an active role. Neighboring plantation workers proudly displayed family photos in their homes, having gone to great expense and effort to obtain them from a small photography shop in Pandalur. During my visit in 1989, I was asked to take similar family photos of Sridevi and her relatives. They posed serenely for the photos, standing erect and motionless, just as their neighbors did for the commercial photographer. Like their neighbors, each couple posed for the camera; however, unlike their neighbors, they were joined by all the children who were then with them, their own and others.

During their visits with relatives, rather than depend on them, children actively aided them. The older the children were, in fact, the more they actually helped their hosts (e.g., lighting fires, fetching water from the river, holding a young baby). Such visits, in general, were described in terms of a child having gone to be-with such and such relatives and to help them. The focus was not on the children's departure from their parents but rather on their visits with relatives. Helping and caring for kin were read into their visits, rather than proof of self-sufficiency.

Growing up and separating from parents to visit other relatives were associated less with growing independence and individual autonomy, then, than with developing *budi* (~ social intelligence).[13] *Budi* is a difficult notion to translate and explain. Perhaps it can be conceived of as social skill, tact, or even, in contemporary jargon, social savviness. *Budi*, though, is not an inherent ability. It is learned during and, at the same time, is what enables and inheres in living with multiple others. *Budi* cannot be taught because it is not about rules for proper behavior, a set of procedures, an expected etiquette and decorum. Rather, *budi* is about the art and skill of reading a particular social situation, gauging vivid idiosyncratic others, and behaving appropriately toward them in that situation, avoiding antagonizing them and fracturing relations with them. *Budi*, in other words, is the sense of convivially living with particular pluripresent others,[14] a sense that arises from familiarity with one's peers and dictates how to conduct oneself with them in a way that does not affront their specific personalities and circumstances. *Budi* describes skillful interpersonal engagement with others, whereas *nachika* describes skillful interpersonal avoidance (see chapter 3).

The meaning of *budi* can be brought into further relief by comparing it with the large-scale notion of "etiquette," which also supports being-with others. Etiquette is intended to regulate behavior toward present but unfamiliar persons, whereas *budi* helps one to respond wisely to intimately known relatives with whom one lives continuously. The first case involves normative conventions of behavior toward certain types of persons, and the second, responsive attentiveness to vivid related others. *Budi* is, thus, effective within the zone of communal intimacy, among personally known and intimately knowable cosubjects. It is hardly generalizable beyond this zone. Youngsters' circulatory visits among relatives—relatives they will continue to live with in their plural nanoworld—are crucial to their development of *budi*. But *budi* continues to develop throughout life and even after death; ancestral and forefathers' spirits have more *budi* than the living, and adults have more than children.

SPATIOTEMPORAL PLURAL STRUCTURES

Our siblings, ***spouses, and children*** *(Take 5)*

In his ethnography of a small Amazonian community of people known as Urarina, who call themselves *cacha* (real people or true humans), Harry Walker (2013) offers the concept of "accompanied life." He beautifully shows how the child's sense of self emerges through involvement with a series of others, beginning in the womb, where the placenta is the first companion, and continuing after birth with the baby's hammock as a second companion, then the mother as a third, and so on, until the child eventually establishes a relation with a nonhuman soul mate. Urarina people live in scattered small hamlets, each comprising eight to ten houses, unwalled and open to one another (in my terms, a pluripresent mode).[15] "Accompanied life" captures the critical local sense of being-with others, even as Walker only examines the *dyadic* company of a *series* of others through which the child's sense of self emerges. My scale-sensitized analysis and recognition of pluripresence directs me to consider the *multiple* relatives who *simultaneously* participate in a child's life in the Gorge's community of relatives. From the foregoing ethnographic analysis, I think, a picture clearly emerges of the spatiotemporal plural structures within which children in the Gorge grow up and acquire a sense not so much of self as of being *one of* few-many plural relatives, or (in a more concrete reading of Jean-Luc Nancy [2000] discussed in the introduction) "being singular plural."

Beyond establishing the Gorge's forager community as a pluripresent one (as are most tiny forager-cultivator communities—but others as well), it is productive to distinguish among several modes of achieving pluripresence. In other words, it is useful to read the above ethnographic discussions with a view to the expressed modes, degrees, and cycles of spatiality within a pluripresent regime. Three modes are illustrated by but not limited to the conjugal, parents-children, and sibling substructures of the *kudumba*. Conjugality subsists principally in constant staying-together and sharing, parents-children togetherness in intermittent staying-together and sharing, and (adult) siblingship in parallel, proximate coexistence and an ever present potential mutuality. Here I further illustrate these modes with examples that reveal how they articulate and are interwoven in everyday practice.

Sridevi was ill, and feeling weak, she stayed close to home for a few days. Although her sister lived close by, it was Sridevi's husband who stayed with and cared for her, forgoing work. He complained to me about his relatives' lack of caring during this time, singling out for mention their reluctance to provide him with food and so make it easier for him to stay with Sridevi (not, as one might expect, their reluctance to stay with his wife so that he could go to work). Time and again, I was told that one's spouse is one's best friend, with whom one can talk about everything without restraint, and that one's spouse helps one when one is ill. Only with the spouse does one not have *nachika* (avoidance, restraint).

A withdrawn man with one eye blinded by a years-old injury, Sridevi's brother worked every day on the plantation as a watchman, and his wife stayed at home, looking after their unusually large family of five children, the oldest twelve years of age and the three youngest under five. The spouses' regular separation on a daily basis was exceptional in this community in the late 1970s. Exceptional too was their constant quarreling, their voices reaching everyone in the tiny hamlet. The wife repeatedly complained to me about this or that incident; for example, that her husband had pushed her away while she was combing her daughter's hair. She moaned (and again, what she singled out for attention was revealing) that her husband fed her and her children but "did not talk with her for days." With this complaint, she emphasized lack of companionship, traceable in large part to his permanent plantation job, which kept the couple apart much of the time. In this case, even had they both wanted her to, she could not have joined him at work with their three young children. By the same token, their relationship would not have survived such daily separation had the husband regularly gone to forage by himself or with other companions. One or the other would have left to visit and stay with relatives, and the relationship would have dissolved. As *mave* (~ marriage) was tantamount to staying together, staying apart was normally tantamount to its dissolution. The conjugal relation was by and large produced and reproduced, and known and made known, through day-by-day companionship, and staying apart led to its demise.

One day, when Sridevi's sister-in-law complained to me about her previous night's quarrel with her husband, I asked her brother, who lived in the same hamlet, why he did not intervene. He replied that his sister and her husband were together and nothing could change that, but then, taking a remarkable step that expressed his deep concern for his sister, he turned to the plantation bookkeeper in the hope that he might be able to reason with her husband. He could not himself intervene in his sister's marital affairs. If the normal spousal mode of togetherness can be characterized by a lack of tolerance for corporeal distance, the married sib mode involved parallel proximity and need-based cooperation and help—but not when it interfered with the spousal relation.

Lastly, game was always shared among everyone present in the hamlet, and as the following instance illustrates (discussed also in Bird-David

2005a), it dramatizes the articulation of all three pluripresent modes.[16] A relative arrives from MN reporting that on his way he spotted forest dogs who had caught a deer and were eating the flesh. Two of Sridevi's brothers-in-law and another young man (their parallel cousin) go to the site. It is pitch dark when they return with the meat; dogs bark in the distance, announcing their imminent arrival. Children leave their respective hearths and rush to the edge of the terrace in anticipation. Meanwhile, although sharing large game is a relatively rare and much appreciated event, adults remain seated around their separate yet closely spaced hearths, betraying no sign of excitement. The children bring containers—a metal pot, a plate, or simply a large plantain leaf—and place them around the carcass, to be used to carry meat back to each hearth. As one of the hunters begins to butcher the meat, the children help him: here holding up a torch to provide better light, there pulling on one of the animal's limbs to ease its separation from the carcass, and occasionally playfully intervening in how the butcher divides the chunks of meat between the containers (urging the man to place the chunk on this plate ... no, another child suggests, in that pot ... etc.). When the meat is all divided, the children carry portions to their waiting parents or hosts, who cook their allotments and share among those seated with them at their hearth. The children, in a sense, "give" the game to parent-couples, commonly siblings and cousins themselves, who cook and consume the meat separately while still in the midst of community.

Generally, the parents-children mode of togetherness somewhat extends the limits of pluripresence by affording rotational rather than constant presence. It extends strict conjugal bipresence temporally, whereas the sibling mode extends it spatially. None of the three modes of belonging to our "our *kudumba*" and, more generally, to the local community of relatives, human and transhuman, involves togetherness in the modern sense of "persons who merge into a unity, a whole, a mass, a body." To the contrary, to adapt Jean-Luc Nancy's words (1991: 1), they show us three modes of "existence *with*," in the absence of which nothing exists.

Downscale 4

Taxonomy of Nonhuman Relatives

Lists of locally important plants and animals are standard in ethnographies of forager-cultivator peoples, ecologically and culturally focused studies alike providing species' names in the vernacular and in the Latin classificatory standard (e.g., Lee 1979: 99–102; Descola 1994: 88; Viveiros de Castro 1992 [1986]: 327–31). I dutifully produced such a listing (see table 4, p. 149), and now, in retrospect, thinking about the process involved, I recognize a tale worth the telling.

I had asked a dozen or so residents of the Gorge's hamlets to list the local plants they used, and they all mentioned the names of the same half-dozen plants. Individuals then went on to mention other names that no one else repeated. Names I heard from one person and repeated to another went unrecognized by the second person. Ethnographers of other Asian hunter-gatherers report similar experiences (e.g., Howell 1984; Kirk Endicott 1979; Wazir-Jahan 1981; Ellen 2006). Working with the South Indian hunter-gatherer Hill Pandaram, Brian Morris (1976: 552) suggested that they have systems of classification that "are employed idiosyncratically" by individuals. Notwithstanding the challenges it posed, assembling a list of the natural taxa that figured prominently in the lives of Kungan and his relatives was a professional expectation I had to meet. So, one day, I finally asked Kungan and his relatives to help me by bringing me actual plants they used. They spread out in the forest and collected any seasonally available plant part (root, bark, pod, fruit, etc.) of species they used throughout the year. They brought back dozens of specimens, which I put in separate bags, noting down vernacular names and local uses mentioned by the collectors. The next day, I traveled with my box full of specimens to the local branch of the Botanical Survey of India (BSI) in Coimbatore and asked botanists working there to identify them for me. They immediately recognized some of the specimens, and for the others, they turned to reference books and to a comparative collection of preserved specimens on their office shelves. Three of the specimens excited them: *Dioscorea* species previously not known to grow in the Nilgiri-Wynaad. They added those to their comparative collection and threw the rest of the specimens into the garbage after identifying them.

One could cast the contrast between the botanists and the forest people in terms of scholarly learning versus practical experience. Doing so, however, misses a critical difference in actors' scale/ing projects and horizons. The BSI was set up by the British in 1890 to survey the plant resources of the Indian colony, and it continued to operate after independence under the Indian Ministry of Environment and Forests. The botanists working in the tatty offices in Coimbatore had extensive field experience. In their excursions to collect specimens, these botanists sometimes employed forest people to help them. But, simultaneously, these botanists saw each specimen they collected as standing for an entire class that had to be fitted into large-scale regional and national schemes and into a globally recognized hierarchy of taxonomic ranks. Their project was to map all the floral species growing in the Nilgiri-Wynaad, thus contributing to the scientific project of mapping all the species growing in Tamil Nadu, in South India, and ultimately, in the world. They were excited by the three previously undocumented specimens I brought them as furthering this project, as new additions to a list assumed, in a sense, to be infinite—for there are always more specimens to discover and add to it.

Table 4 presents the list I ultimately compiled. One column shows what Kungan and his relatives *brought home:* plants that grow and thrive in their home area, which they variably named, consistent with their plural and shifting person-names, place-names, and kin terms, according to a system that was effective in their tiny-scale, intimately shared, and familiar world. The other column presents the same plants by their Latin names so as to be recognizable to members of the global scientific community wherever they happen to be. Resonating with the maps, tables, and kinship diagrams I have discussed in previous Downscale interludes, and like them, this table draws attention to ontological spillage from the large-scale project of anthropology into the local nanoscale world. My list, then, is a native-scientific coproduction illustrating the commonality, divergence, and negotiation between two distinct communities, both of which were intimately familiar and concerned with the flora of the Nilgiri-Wynaad but only one of which further engaged with large-scale national and global (imagined) communities of botanists and bureaucrats. Whereas one community, the botanists, framed the specimens collected in the forest as members of ever-growing sets, within unlimited horizons of exploration, the other, the foragers, engaged with plants as they did with other nonhuman beings (hills, animals, stones, and many other natural entities) within their immediate horizons. They regarded all of these entities as "our own," our relatives, family, beings living with us, together. In the next chapter, I explore Kungan and his relatives' engagement with the nonhuman beings who lived with them in their nanoworld and were pluripresent in their lives.

TABLE 4. Plants gathered for food and medicine

Nayaka name	Latin name	Common name	Use
		I. Plants used for food	
		Roots	
Aaleganazu	—	—	Occasionally used as staple food, boiled or roasted
Annaarasu	*Curcuma angustifolia* Roxb. (Zingberaceae)	East Indian arrowroot	Ground and made into porridge
Ana aracina	*C. pseudomontana* J. Graham (Zingberaceae)	Hill turmeric	Ground to make arrowroot powder; also used medicinally
Benuganazu	*Dioscrea hamiltonii* Hook. f. (Dioscoreaceae)	—	Staple food, boiled or roasted
Cavaleganazu	*D. oppositifolia* L.	—	"
Collekganazu	—	—	"
Coreganazu	—	—	Occasionally used as staple food, boiled or roasted
Kauleganazu	—	—	"
Koraneganazu	*D. pentaphylla* var. *linnaei* Prain & Burkill	—	Staple food, boiled or roasted
Mayaluganazu	*D. alata* L.	Asiatic yam	"
Nadichiganazu	*D. bulbifera* L.	Air potato	"
Nureganazu	*D. hisʒida* Dennst. and *D. pentaphylla* L.	Asiatic bitter yam, Fiji yam	"
Nopanuganazu	*D. tomentosa* J. Koenig ex Spreng.	—	"
Sodeganazu	—	—	Occasionally used as staple food, boiled or roasted
Yekuganazu	*D. waʒlichii* Hook. f.	—	Staple food, boiled or roasted

(continued)

TABLE 4. (continued)

		Spices	
Aracina	*Curcuma longa* L.	Turmeric	Used as a spice and medicine
Arimanasu	*Capsicum* spp.	Wild chili	Mixed with other foods
Kiramanasu	*Capsicum* spp.	"	"
Undamanasu	*Capsicum* spp.	"	"

		Fruits and berries	
Alcankai	*Artocarpus heterophyllus* Lam. (Moraceae)	Jackfruit	Boiled and used as substitute for staple food
Indekai	*Cycas circinalis* L. (Cycadaceae)	Queen sago	Nut is leached with fresh water to remove toxins, then ground into flour and mixed with water
Ingo	—	Variety of fig	Dried, ground, and made into porridge
Kaduagale	—	Variety of fig	Used for curry
Kadupawaka	*Adenia wightiana* (Passifloraceae)	Variety of wild cucumber	Eaten fresh
Nellekai	*Phyllanthus emblica* L. (Euphorbiaceae)	Emblic myrobalan	Eaten fresh, pickled, or cooked
Nirule	*Syzygium cumini* (L.) Skeels (Myrtaceae)	Black plum	—
Saliruannau	*Flacourtia montana* J. Grah. (Flacourtiaceae)	Mountain sweet thorn	Fruits eaten fresh
Valli mango	*Ampelocissus latifolia* (Roxb.) Planch. (Vitaceae)	Jungle angoor	—

		Leaves	
Chullisopo	*Diplazium esculentum* (Retz.) Sw. (Athyriaceae)	Edible fern	The tips of the leaves are highly relished
Kaduyella	—	—	Used as a substitute for betel leaves

Kira sopo	*Amaranthus viridis* L. (Amaranthaceae)	Slender amaranth	Both the stems and leaves are cooked and eaten
Mullukira	*A. spinosus* L.	Prickly amaranth	Leaves and tender stems are cooked and eaten
Pal chembu	*Colocasia esculenta* (L.) Schott (Araceae)	Cocoyam	Both leaves and corms are eaten

II. Plants used for medicinal purposes

Awemade	*Arisaema leschenaultii* Blume (Araceae)	Common cobra lily	Root is ground and placed on snake bites
Bataluganazu	*Cyclea peltata* Hook. f. & Thoms. (Menispermaceae)	Pata root	Root is ground, mixed with water, and used for stomachache
Kirimade	—	—	Fruits are used for stomachache
Kurumade	*Oldenlandia auricularia* (L.) K. Schum. (Rubiaceae)	—	Leaves and stem are ground, made into a paste, and put on heat blisters
Mulliulli	—	—	Fruits are used for toothache
Mullimare	*Bombax ceiba* L. (Malvaceae)	Indian bombax	Bark is ground and used for toothache
Nannari	*Hemidesmus indicus* (L.) R. Br. var. *indicus* (Apocynaceae)	Country sarasaparilla	Roots are used to improve digestion
Nelliketole	—	—	Bark is used for toothache
Sunti	*Zingiber roseum* (Roxb.) Roscoe (Zingberaceae)	Ginger	Made into juice and used for stomachache
Yemenipuri	*Rauwolfia serpentina* (L.) Benth. ex Kurz. (Apocynaceae)	Serpentina	Used for snake bites

SOURCE: Specimens were collected on July 10, 1979. Adapted from Bird 1983a:55–57.

A medium in front of a spirit house. Photographed by the author (1978–79).

5. Nonhuman Kin

Unispecies Societies and Plural Communities

The hill-spirit visitor is angry. She complains, "We are not looked after well," and she continues to moan, "You have committed many faults, but you come and say everything is inflicted by us." She goes on, "The appa-varu, annavaru, tammavaru *[father people, older-brother people, younger-brother people] are all here, and you leave this place and go to live wherever you like, and you do not look after them." Chathen charges, "You do not look well after us, the* makalo *[children]. We have little sense, and if we did any* tappu *[~ fault], you should not be angry with us. You should still continue to protect us from illnesses."*

I broaden the analytical focus in this chapter to include many more of the relatives populating the local world than those considered in previous chapters. In doing so, I once again encounter the problem of terminology, of how to generally refer to those other-than-humans whom Chathen and his relatives regard, inter alia, as *sonta* (our own, relatives), *dodappanuawanu* (great parents), *dodavaru* (great people), and *devaru* (a term widely used for deities in South India but, here, in a sense that overlaps with the other local terms). Labeling them by common anthropological terms, such as *spirits, deities, nonhumans, supernatural beings, animistic beings, invisible beings,* and the like, skews their salient local register. Such tags present them as types of beings, members of diverse classes, "the same" as other members of those classes, who can exist anywhere. For Chathen and his relatives, however, they are first and foremost a range of vivid beings who live in the surrounding area and periodically visit "us," *sonta*. I must refer to these entities in some way, however, to write about them intelligibly, so I interchangeably use *other-than-humans* (the term is Irving Hallowell's; see 2012 [1995]), *nonhumans,* and *spirits,* and depending on the specific context, I occasionally append *kin* to convey the local relational and situational senses. Other-than-human kin, then, are the focus of this chapter, and I approach them in relation to theories of animistic personhood and relations and theories associated with the ontological turn in anthropology, especially the neostructuralist Amazonian models known as perspectivism and animism, which have superseded Claude Lévi-Strauss's key focus on the modern "nature-culture" binary. These theories suggest that local cosmos comprise unispecies societies—in Philippe Descola's (2013 [2005]) vision, isomorphic with human societies and, in Eduardo Viveiros de Castro's (2012) model, each with a distinctive situated perspective on the others. Consistent with today's pervasive scale-blind perspective, these theories do not factor in the scalar context. I do so in this chapter as I explore, through ethnography spanning spirit visits, myth, interspecies kinship, and classificatory practice, another ontological option, a local community of *diverse* beings constituted and reconstituted as relatives. This local project accommodates heterogeneous forms, habits, and perspectives rather than regimenting their plural diversity into unispecies classes.

. . .

Anthropologists have been intrigued by indigenous registers of natural entities as sentient beings for more than 150 years, indeed, since the inception of the discipline. The phenomenon was glossed by Edward Tylor (1958 [1871]) as "animism," a concept that early on exerted broad scholarly and popular influence and recently has drawn renewed interest (see Harvey 2013). Perspectives on these indigenous registers have gone through remarkable changes over the years.[1] In 1871—when Chathen's grandfather was a young man—Tylor bracketed indigenous people as primitives and their animistic beliefs as misguided, illusionary, and childish. Subsequently, some scholars tried to rehabilitate this image. In the early twentieth century, Émile Durkheim, for example, argued that the primitive soul-body sense of the person is not delusional but is, instead, a universal experience; only the primitive's view of natural entities as kin, he conceded, is delusional. Lévi-Strauss proposed in the mid-twentieth century that a binary distinction between nature and culture is a human universal and that totemic/kinship relations with objects of nature are symbolic constructs "good to think." By the late twentieth century, when Chathen's grandson was a young man, scholars had recognized native cosmologies as nondualist, nonmaterialist, and nonessentialist alternatives to the Western binary, challenging and expanding modern Western understandings (kinship with nonhumans had by then faded from analytical prominence in these discussions).

Good ethnographies evoke local lives, cultures, and ontologies, but they are artful syntheses. Although true for any ethnography, the illusion that is created is especially seductive for a tiny-scaled community lacking a collective's authoritative account of itself. The ethnographer of such tiny communities, like an alchemist, transforms personal situated perspectives into a collectively authored overview. Philippe Descola states this clearly when he observes that, in writing about "societies, which like the [Amazonian] Achuar, have no coherent canonical theories of the world, the structures for representing practices must be pieced together from a motley collection of clues" (1994: 3). Likewise, Signe Howell explicitly notes in her ethnography of the Southeast Asian Chewong that what she presents "is the result of hundreds of unconnected bits of information collected throughout the period of the fieldwork which are then gathered together under the general heading of cosmology" (1984: 59). As ethnographers try to put together a huge and complicated jigsaw puzzle out of "hundreds of unconnected bits of information," what frame do they use for the job? I am troubled by the use, in studies of small-scale and large-scale societies alike, of the same (large-scale) frame for fitting the pieces together. In this chapter, I probe cosmological issues, attentive to the previously overlooked disparity between the scalar contexts that gave rise to the modern idea of nature and to foragers' alternatives—and attentive too to local kinship ideas.

Kinship, personhood, and animism have recently reconverged in the work of some anthropologists. For example, Marshall Sahlins (2013: 2) has called for disentangling kinship studies from "the person" and, instead, examining kinship in terms of "mutuality of being" and "the participation of kin in each other's lives," and Viveiros de Castro (2009) has proposed that the study of animism can open new ways of approaching kinship. Reversely, yet resonating with these approaches, I approach animism through kinship, and in particular, I scale-sensitively suggest that "relatives" (in the plural) is a productive concept, more than large-scale serial notions of persons, relations, and societies, for exploring foragers' animistic cosmos.

Though *person* is not often a direct translation from vernacular cultures, it has been the touchstone of debates on the animistic cosmos since Irving Hallowell's (2012 [1955]) pioneering work. Hallowell asserted that the North American Ojibwa approach their world in terms of "who" rather than "what," that their world is populated by persons of all sorts, human and others. Reversing the Western taxonomic hierarchy (in which humans are distinguished from others and only they can be persons), Hallowell argued that "person" for Ojibwa is an overarching category that contains various types (human persons, animal persons, thunder persons, stone persons, etc.). The dualistic split between humans and others so resolved, this adjusted category of the "person" still instills distortive modern convictions in the animistic world. Though much effort has been invested in disassociating the *person* from its modern dominant form, the *individual,* and pluralizing and relationalizing it (e.g., arguing that the *person* is a composite of relations, a dividual), the modern basic sense of *person* as a singular entity has for the most part been left undisturbed (cf. Sahlins 2013). Moreover, it remains a serial concept, like individual, citizen, and member; multiplied, these entities make up society and (Hallowell's legacy) the world, a world comprising a series of "one beings." Hallowell's ingenious expansion on this idea was to acknowledge nonhuman persons in the animistic cosmos.

With the growing popularity of relational analysis, *relation* also has gained a prominent place in debates on the animistic cosmos. Some of my previous work belongs to and illustrates this focus. I argued that, for the Nayaka and for some other tropical forest hunter-gatherers, the forest is a parental being, that those who dwell in it are its children (Bird-David 1990, 2008).[2] I proposed that various kinship relations are salient in foragers' cosmos: parental, procreative, affinal, and namesake relations are respectively central in the animistic worlds of tropical forest, Australian Aboriginal, North American Indian, and South African hunter-gatherers (Bird-David 1990, 1993). I turned, then, following Hallowell's lead, to "the person" and argued that the animistic person, transcending human/nonhuman distinctions, is relational and situational (Bird-David 1999a). These arguments were not scale-sensitive enough, though factoring immediacy into the analysis was a start in that direction.[3] To say that the animistic person and the world more generally are constituted of relations is to shift from one serial concept (*person*) to another (*relation*), again, scale-blindly.

Recently, Descola (2013 [2005]) and Viveiros de Castro (2012) introduced the notion of "species societies" into debates on the animistic cosmos. Descola (2013 [2005]: 248) argued that, in the animistic cosmos, humans and nonhumans (who both have souls but different bodies) occupy separate isomorphic groups with parallel structures and properties. Descola describes them as "tribe-societies" (2006: 9), "tribe/species" (2013 [2005]: 259), and sometimes, "collectives" (2013 [2005]: 248, adopting Bruno Latour's term). Nonhumans, in this vision, live in "fully complete societies . . . [that] would appear to be covered by all the habitual rubrics of an ethnological monograph" (ibid.). Viveiros de Castro (1998, 2012) further argues that each species-society has its own perspectives on other societies, its members viewing the others through the habitus of their own distinctive bodies, through their own distinctive eyes. The perspectivist cosmos that he describes comprises multiple natures alongside multiple species-societies. The indigenous cosmos for both these theoreticians (both ethnographers of Amerindian peoples) is constituted of multiple human and nonhuman societies, that is, of differentiable aggregates of serial persons; in their formulations, then, "society" too is a serializable concept. To figure societies in this way is not trivial for people living in tiny groups, especially those living in tropical forest environments, most of all those who inhabit the rich Amazonian ecosystem where, rather than sameness, diversity of beings is striking in any particular locale.

Amerindian communities include a number that are comparable in size to forager groups elsewhere; some are remarkably tiny. For example, when Viveiros de Castro (1992 [1986]: 19) studied them in the early 1980s, the Arawete totaled 136 men, women, and children, all living in one village; in preceding decades, they had numbered 300 people living in four villages. The Amazonian-inspired theories of hunter-gatherer-cultivator cosmos do not take such minuscule size into account; they are scale-blind, a fact that has gone unnoted in incipient criticism of them.[4] Terry Turner cautions that the perspectivist thesis takes "the class as identity with only one, fixed perspective per species-class" (2009: 32). In concert with this point, I caution that, in focusing on "species-societies," both animism and perspectivism take each species-society's members to be essentially similar (same bodies and viewpoints) and accept that similarity as the basis of their belonging together. This principle of grouping resonates with that underlying a biological taxon's membership and, equally, a nation's. This intriguing resemblance in itself raises the specter of unwarranted universalizing of a particular plural mode. It especially does so in the context of the Amazonian forest environment that Descola so evocatively described: "Out of roughly fifty thousand species of vascular plants present in Amazonia, fewer than twenty or so grow spontaneously in groups together, and where they do, that is in many cases the accidental result of human interference" (2013 [2005]: 11). Descola went on to reflect on whether "immersed as they are in a monstrous plurality of life-forms that are seldom to be found together in homogenous groups, possibly the forest Indians gave up the idea of embracing as a whole the disparate conglomerations of entities that constantly clamor for the attention of their senses. . . . [T]hey perhaps found no way of dissociating themselves from nature because they could not discern its profound unity, which was obscured by the multiplicity of its singular manifestations" (ibid.).

One could further question whether those Indians who "found no way of dissociating themselves from nature . . . [and] discern[ing] its profound unity" could have found a way of conceptualizing homogenous species-societies. Could they have achieved such a perspective, confronted as they were with a forest of "mono-individuals" (to borrow Lévi-Strauss's [1962: 142] term, cited by Descola)? Could such tiny communities of relatives imagine species-societies? The modern concepts of nature and society are grounded in and reflect large-scale concerns and imaginations, and the scalar context cannot be left out of exploring alternatives, any more than it can be ignored in exploring other issues.

I bring kinship sensibilities into the analysis of foragers' animistic cosmos (rather than large-scale-derived ontological language of persons and societies), as foragers themselves do. Their cosmos, I suggest, consists of communities of relatives whose members are not necessarily identical in terms of species/kind just as they are not the same in terms of gender and kinship positionality. Plural belonging here, I argue, is more an issue of being *with* than of being *like* other members. Chathen and his relatives, I suggest, constitute a communal core open to and including diverse vivid creatures, human and others, all of whom are regarded as "our *sonta*" (our relatives) by dint of constantly plurirelating, each with the others. They do so most demonstratively during the "big animistic visit" (hereafter, "big visit"), the ethnographic anchor of this chapter, whose discussion in this context benefits from comparative reference to the Malaysian Chewong, an Asian forager-cultivator group and a much-vaunted case for the purchase of perspectivism beyond the Amazon.

The "big visit" is larger than any assembly described in previous chapters (including those convened on the occasions of birth and death; see chapter 2); in fact, it is the largest communal event that locals experience. The visitors on this occasion are humans and nonhumans, the latter participating primarily through mediums. The locals do not categorize attendees or even have a special name for this event, which lasts more than twenty-four hours, just as they do not use proper ethnonyms or personal names for themselves or any place-names. They refer to this event inter alia as *adendra* (gathering, get-together) and *kunyatta* (merrymaking).[5] I prefer to call it a "visit" to foreground the framework locals take as given. This assembly occurs in the hamlets where people ordinarily live, rotating from settlement to settlement. The residents are the hosts, and the spirits are their visitors. The cycle of "big visits" draws the various hamlets and their residents together. Other terms I use in relation to this event are *spirit possession* (in line with other ethnographers of South Indian foragers); *medium* (preferred over *shaman*, a specialist role carrying power; locals address the medium by the appropriate kinship term and, when necessary, by the Hindu term *pujari,* "priest"); *mediumistic performer* (because the medium is not a passive vehicle but actively "calls" the spirits); and lastly, *trance performer* (because the medium operates under trance). Research into the vast field glossed as spirit possessions has explored the beliefs that underpin them, how the healing that they effect "works," and personal understandings of these events.[6] I approach spirit possession here in the context of nonhuman kin visits, which are continuous with the daily visiting that constitutes and reconstitutes the foragers' community. Spirit possession has been productively approached as a prism through which to refract or undo naturalized constructs such as "person," "self," and "body,"[7] and I examine it as a prism on plural life, seeking new refractions of the construct of "community."

THE "BIG ANIMISTIC VISIT": PREPARATIONS

Our own [nonhuman] relatives (Take 1)

The "big visits" took place (in the late 1970s) only in hamlets comprising more than a single hut, which in itself is an index of "being many." They were held sequentially, the first always in TR hamlet, the second in TM, and the third in GR, following the order of their settlement.[8] The scheduling of the "big visits" was not predetermined. When preparations for a particular event neared completion, the day it was to begin was announced. The preparations were so low-key that a casual observer would not have been aware of them. I recognized they were underway in GR, where I lived, several weeks after they began.

One day, I observed Chathen (the *modale,* the first inhabitant of GR) and his wife returning to the hamlet from the forest carrying a large wooden pole. They stuck it in the ground upright, amid the outside hearths, the piles of firewood, the scattered pots and pans on the ground, the axes, the sickle knives, and all the other paraphernalia of everyday life that lay between and around the huts. Nothing happened over the next week or so, and I assumed they were building a new hut for themselves, working at the same relaxed pace I had grown used to. However, a week or so later, I observed Chathen's sister and her husband arrive in the hamlet with another wooden pole and erect it less than three meters away from the first. I had earlier observed young, agile, single persons helping a couple thatch their roof, but I had not seen couples cooperating in such a project and not in this independent manner. When, some days later, I observed Chathen's second sister and her husband also carry a pole into the hamlet and position it perpendicularly near the other two, as if marking a hut's third corner, I started to ask questions.

The preparations for the "big visit," I was told, were underway, and a hut was being constructed for the visitor spirits (a structure variably referred to as *devaru mane*, "spirit house," or *pandalu* [Tamil] or *ambalam* [Malayalam], "temple"). The spirit house was built in a leisurely fashion, just as dwellings usually were. All the hamlet's residents participated in its construction, yet the process involved no concerted collective effort and no supervision. This or that resident added another element: a pole, split-bamboo sheet, bunch of grass, and so on, until the hut was finished, with no one advising or instructing them or even monitoring what they did. The spirit house came into being through sequential and cumulative effort, the process often initiated (as in the case I observed) by the *modale*, whom others then followed at their discretion and in their own time.

The spirit house was built in the course of everyday life, as part of it, next to the other huts. It looked just like any other hut, if anything, being smaller than the largest among them. Significantly, *one* hut was built for the many spirits expected to attend the "big visit," a practical yet also symbolic act.[9] Diverse as these visitors were expected to be, they could (indeed, had to) live together.

Next, food for the visitors had to be obtained. Doing so was a far cry from documented Amazonian and Melanesian feasting preparations, which involved amassing surpluses (of pigs, yams, beer, etc.) for weeks, months, or even years in advance, the main purpose being to exhibit wealth and power and score political points. Among Chathen and his relatives, the hosts had only to prepare enough food to feed their visitors once, at the end of the "big visit." They required enough food for a meal to be shared by their pluripresent heterogeneous visitors, each one given an equal share, young and old, human and nonhuman. When the spirit house was nearing completion, Chathen, his siblings, and their spouses began to gather money from their relatives and from close associates living in the Gorge (myself, the plantation's local administrator, migrant neighbors, etc.). Contribution was discretionary; each donor contributed as much money as he or she could afford to.[10] Providing an ordinary meal of rice sufficed for the "big visit," as it did any other day, and in fact was another signal figuring the visit as nothing out of the ordinary even though it involved a more heterogeneous and larger than usual gathering. That *everyone* shared a meal was the most important point.

On the morning of the day set for the "big visit," Chathen climbed up the steep jungle path to buy rice from the market stalls on the road crossing through the region. Meanwhile, some of his relatives lined the spirit-house floor with plantain leaves, and on them, they placed an array of objects taken out of storage. These objects included both deceased predecessors' utilitarian items (e.g., knife, cup, bracelet) that had been ritually appropriated to serve as their namesakes (see chapter 2) and cheap consumer goods (e.g., likenesses of the Hindu deity Ganesha) associated as much with the predecessors who had procured them (see chapter 1) as with the deities they represent. Chathen's uncle (Old Attimathen), who had arrived that morning in GR, busied himself with painting geometrical patterns of dots and lines, in white, red, and black, on these objects and on the hut's poles, to beautify them, he explained to me. This was the only "big visit" for which I observed this kind of decorative effort. Chathen returned late in the afternoon, bringing rice, coconuts, and incense sticks; these, along with small portions of uncooked rice, were placed (in Hindu *puja* style) in front of each of the object occupants of the spirit house. The bulk of the rice was kept aside for the main meal. The ordinary rhythm of life continued around the spirit house: children played, one woman bathed her baby, a youngster cut firewood, a couple left to collect firewood, and so on. Visitors arrived throughout the day. . . .

DIVERSE VISITORS COME

Our own [nonhuman] relatives (Take 2)

The arrival of human relatives for the "big visit" is not marked any more than visits on other days (with the exception of the arrival of one old man, now living in a "satellite" hamlet, who has come to help as a medium and is graciously greeted). The newcomers trickle in and, as usual, join in the ordinary everyday run of things, but then, in the late afternoon, I notice something unusual. People begin to invite the invisible spirits around them to participate with them in whatever domestic activities they pursue. Chathen's brother-in-law and his wife go down to the river to fetch water, but before they set out they bow in all four directions, inviting the invisible visitors to join them. Two of Chathen's nieces bring water from the river, and along the way they sprinkle some in the four directions, sharing it with the invisible beings. Chathen's sister and her husband eat leftover food and throw small pieces of it in the four directions. Chathen's nephew and cousin sit down to rest and smoke *bidi* (tobacco flake wrapped in native plant leaves) at the entry to the spirit house; after the cousin leaves, the nephew remains there and takes a nap.[11] Through these minor gestures, Chathen and his (human) relatives express, and simultaneously grow increasingly aware of and open to, the presence of an invisible multitude of other beings around them. They invite not this or that particular spirit, or a particular kind of spirit, but all the spirits present in the surroundings (propinquity being a condition for the resulting diversity and plurality).

Darkness begins to set in, and musicians start playing (on a flute and two drums) next to the spirit house and the other huts. The music rouses residents and visitors who have been idling around, and they now gather around the players. Some begin to dance. Men follow one another and women follow women, forming two gender-segregated circles, the separation an unusual sight in this tiny community. However, within these revolving circles, the dance form reflects the same idea expressed in the construction of the spirit house. The dancers do not move as one body, or even uniformly, yet each is attuned to what the others are doing. No one holds hands. Each dancer independently turns in place, following the others at will and maintaining the revolving circle (cf. Jerome Lewis's [2013: 61] observation of similar patterns in BaYaka singing). When someone tires, he or she simply leaves the circle to rest, often joining his or her spouse. The musicians form their own separate circle. The music and the dances also attract nonhuman visitors, who are summoned into being through mediumistic performance.

I had eagerly awaited this performance. All my prior attempts to get a sense of the "who's who" in the local cosmos, in formal sessions and in spontaneous conversations, had yielded piecemeal and conflicting information, a familiar experience for ethnographers of Asian hunter-gatherer-cultivators (and undoubtedly not only them). Some have reported numerous inconsistences in the information they collected and have written of the slipperiness of classifications (e.g., see Kirk Endicott 1979: 26–28; Howell 1984: 211–39). Even my effort to talk with Karriyen (Chathen's wife's father), one of the oldest and most experienced persons I knew and a respected medium, had not produced helpful information. Aged about seventy-five, bent with the years and walking with a stick, he looked after his seventy-year-old wife, who was blind. He gathered forest roots and fruits for their subsistence and sold forest leaves to vendors in little roadside stalls in Pandalur (the vendors used the leaves as packing material for their cheap wares). He was patient and willing to talk with me for hours, and he always appreciated the food I brought him and his wife. Yet, for all his knowledge, willingness, and patience, I did not learn from him what I hoped I would. He did not list and describe, one by one, the spirits dwelling in the Gorge and possessing the mediums. Finally, he suggested that I personally meet the spirits for myself when they came for the "big visit."

Several mediums may perform at any one time next to one another —distinctively dressed, though not alike, bodies wrapped from the waist down and torsos naked. Each holds a bunch of thin branches or a knife, which he waves in the air as he turns in place, bowing in all four directions, inviting the spirits to come and socialize with those present. Some spirits arrive at the same time, each through a different medium, and others come one after another through the same medium. To the neophyte, their profusion is striking. They speak in different languages—in addition to *nama basha* (our tongue), they use an archaic version of the local language as well as Tamil, Malayalam, Badaga, and Kurumba. They have their own idiosyncratic speech styles: one talks fast and the next slowly, one shouts loudly and another speaks softly, yet another whispers. Their body language and mannerisms are also idiosyncratic, as are their personalities, likes, and dislikes: one demands *bidis*, the next professes its desire for chicken, another complains of neglect, and so on. No spirit introduces itself on arrival, and in fact, those present differentiate (or not) between the incoming spirits by their idiosyncratic behavior, each person according to his or her experience and interest.

Weeks after the "big visit," I transcribed my audio-recordings twice, with a different man each time (neither was a medium). Their accounts of the spirits proved strikingly different, as did accounts I heard in less contrived ways from other people (see more in Bird-David 2004a: 415–16). The first man, Chathen's brother-in-law, a charismatic man in his fifties and opinionated and extroverted by local standards, listened to an hour-long excerpt and distinguished a dozen different characters, including his wife's grandmother, his second cousin's father, a Kurumba man who had lived in the Gorge, an ancestral spirit (unspecified), and a hill spirit. The second man, a skillful honey collector in his thirties, listened to the same excerpt and distinguished a few kinds of spirits in very broad terms: "our" *sattavaru* (dead persons, predecessors), hill spirits, and Kurumba *sattavaru*. What one might regard as inconsistency between the two men's (and others') identifications, rather, expresses locals' overriding interest in plurirelating with spirit visitors rather than in identifying who each *is*.

"Who are you?" is a pervasive question in spirit-possession rituals at the margins of mainstream society in Tamil Nadu (Nabokov 2000: 7)—but not among these foragers at the farthest forest margins of this region. In the Tamil spirit possessions studied by Isabelle Nabokov (2000), the medium is often a liminal figure, who was alone and outside home and community when he or she was initially possessed and who performs alone. The medium exorcises and mediates with spirits who inflict harm on clients, working in a wide range of settings. A principal venue is a small, ad hoc gathering that takes place twice a week at a small temple site and is open to everybody. Strangers from different social, economic, and territorial backgrounds, in great distress and deeply dispirited, come to the medium seeking help. They constitute what Nabokov describes as an "intimate face-to-face 'congregation of suffering'" (5). The spirits are evoked or expelled in these sessions, each time for a specific client. Asking each spirit, "Who are you?" Nabokov suggests, registers the Tamil concern with individual identity, which is especially critical during these rituals, as the afflicted must know the names and identities of their possessing spirits to be able to appease or counteract them. This question structures spirit possessions in other settings described by Nabokov, such as the "congregation of kinship," an affair limited to a kin group, whose members consult a medium in their agricultural fields, especially during rites of passage, to resolve issues with this or that aggrieved ancestor. The Gorge's foragers present an altogether different scenario (though I also term what they do spirit possession), within which the question "Who are you?" has no place.

The foragers are deeply familiar with one another, a congregation of pluripresent relatives. The mediums come from their midst, and the first time they fall into trance they do so amid their close relatives, with whom they continue to live thereafter. The local spirits are familiar (or assumed to be so), the key ones including predecessors, ancestors, and hill spirits, and are recurring guests at "big visits." In any case, the individual introduction and interrogation of the multiple spirits who come is, for the most part, not feasible, and its absence is not irregular. Recall that human visitors to a hamlet do not introduce themselves but rather swiftly move in with their hosts and participate in the hamlet's life. Just as family members are not asked, "Where is your home?" (see chapter 2), so they are not asked, "Who are you?" Likewise, local visitor spirits are not strangers but "our own, relatives," repeatedly constituted and reconstituted through their recurrent visits. The local practice subsists in *relating with* the spirit visitors more than in talking *about* them, and within this setting, their diversity and their distinctions unfold.

Within the regime of scale-blind (de facto large-scale-biased) anthropology, ethnographers of tiny forager communities are expected to provide colleagues and readers with a coherent description of the society's collective representations and its members' shared perspectives. The data they collect during fieldwork often appear inconsistent and conflicting, yet they feel compelled to connect them, like jigsaw puzzle pieces, into a large-scale picture. Signe Howell's (1984) monograph on the Chewong, at once self-reflexive and rich, is the best example of this genre one can ask for.[12] The Chewong society is startlingly tiny; when Howell studied them in the

1970s, they numbered 131 people, fewer than the residents of an average-size apartment building in many towns (18, 15). Howell's analysis is based on "hundreds of unconnected bits of information" (59). The scalar context plays no part in the analysis she offers of the Chewong cosmos, whose eight Earths she maps (61) and whose nonhuman beings she lists (category by category, each typified by kind, where they live, and what they do [66–124]). She describes the different species belonging to each category (e.g., twenty-seven species of *bas*, a category of "many different beings who live on Earth Seven and who cause disease" [104–12]) and notes their attributes by tabulating parameters such as sex, helpful-harmful propensity, objects of attack, methods of attack, and so on (115–23). The analysis is systematic and impressive.

Taking a scale-sensitive perspective, one can argue that such maps, catalogs, and lists offer (per W.H.R. Rivers; see Downscale 3) "more definite and exact knowledge than is possible to a man who has lived for many years among the people," but, for all that, that they do not reflect the locals' own situational perspectives. Readers of this book, inhabitants of large-scale settings, continuously engage in everyday domestic mapping, cataloging, and tabulating (e.g., you open a fridge to see what you need, prepare your shopping list, compare shops, map a route to a new shop, park in a particular slot, grasp the shop's layout, travel down the aisles and pick up x items of y type, and so on). Foragers like the Chewong do not operate in this way; they have a very different home setting and mind setting (see chapter 1). Communicative artifacts like maps and lists act as large-scale Trojan horses in forager ethnographies. Without denying their value, I seek to leave the local cosmology unmapped and uncataloged and, instead, to heighten the principle of manyness and diversity expressed through and driving spirit possession, again turning to the Tamil format as a "good to think" counterpoint. Nabokov describes spirit possession in "congregations of suffering" as a series of singular affairs (each involving one medium, one client, one spirit coming from a faraway and populous space or time, and often, one issue that is resolved through one-to-one dialogue amid plural spectators). By contrast, Chathen and his relatives view spirit possession as a "few-many" affair, during which not one, not two, and not even a sequence of "ones" or a generalizable "many" spirits/deities come but a "few-many," pluripresent, each vividly and idiosyncratically distinct. They do not come from faraway places and times; they are local or from a "living past" and exist in the form of "first people" here and now (Bird-David 2004a). They are all around, if invisible, and accessible, if ordinarily only contacted in chance forest encounters and ad hoc low-key private mediumistic sessions.

During the "big visit," they come with fanfare to demonstratively be-with and talk-with "us," the pattern recalling the now-and-then spatiotemporal mode of parents and children that I discuss in chapter 4. It is to spirit-human pluralogues that I turn next.

PLURALOGUES

Our own [nonhuman] relatives (Take 3)

I earlier described a common communicational mode in the hamlet as pluralogue, wherein one addresses no one in particular; rather, one talks with one's plural intimates, any one of whom can respond if so moved. This mode also characterizes the communication that goes on between human and other-than-human participants in the "big visit." Much of the conversation with the visitor spirits takes this form, and many of the pluralogues are general chatter of a daily nature. From time to time, though, someone seizes the opportunity to raise a specific matter (a recent death, an illness, etc.) with a particular spirit, pursuing a dialogue that others eventually join in. These dialogues may grab the outside observer's attention, but they constitute brief moments within the ongoing pluralogues.

The interlocutors, or perhaps better, the plurilocutors, engage in a broad range of discursive behaviors (talking, joking, teasing, complaining, nagging, etc.), as has been described for other South Indian foragers in the little written about their spirit possession. For example, Hill Pandaram discussions with the spirits are "personal and friendly," conducted "in a very human fashion," the spirits approached as "very immediate beings" (Morris 1981: 206, 207). The conversations South Indian Paliyan foragers have with spirits include "a good bit of joking and light talk" (Gardner 1991b: 371). The tone of the discussion during the "big visit" moves from joking to negotiation, argumentation, and persuasion—again, as described for other South Indian foragers (e.g., see Demmer 2007) and small-scale societies more generally (e.g., see Roseman 1991; Demmer 2007).

During my transcription sessions with Chathen's brother-in-law and the honey collector, I implored them to translate each word they heard on my audiotapes into their spoken language (*nama basha*) before they added their interpretations of what was said. I asked them to accurately replicate what was recorded. But they resisted my request, telling me that the same phrases were uttered again and again. At first, I thought they were simply trying to evade a tedious job, but then I myself began noting how highly repetitive the recorded spirit-human pluralogues were. To no small extent, these pluralogues constituted metacommunication, important because they took place ("we were talking") more than because of the topic discussed. Keeping the discussion going was especially hard in the small hours of the night, as those in attendance, tired after eight or so hours of such effort, would sneak away into the darkness to try stealing a short nap, leaving others to engage the visitor spirits. As a dutiful ethnographer, I remained attentive throughout the night to record the spirits, and my continuous presence was seized on by some as an excuse to retreat for rest. At one point, I was left alone with the only medium still performing, who promptly collapsed; I dropped my tape recorder and rushed to hold him until the others returned.

One recurring theme within the generally repetitive pluralogues is reflexive reference to the "big visit" itself, to its conduct, past, present, and future. Ulrich Demmer noted that during ritual occasions among the Jenu Kurumba, "many of the most-often used verbal expressions are related to the performance of discourse and argumentation itself: 'speak out,' 'ask,' 'listen,' 'tell which way we should go,' 'give the account,' 'break up and narrate,' and so forth are all phrases that initiate and keep the ritual debate going" (2014: 119). His observation applies to my case; additionally, the pluralogues contain many references to the logistics of conducting the "big visit." For example, the spirits say (in endless permutations), "Much more food was offered on earlier visits," "Many more people danced," and "Music was played for longer time," and their human hosts retort, "These days, the days of the children, we have less food than in the days of the elders," "There are few people, many have died." There are many allusions to "parents-children" relations between the visitor spirits and the human hosts, in terms of which mutual demands and promises are made. For example, the humans promise to provide the spirits with food, and the spirits promise to protect the humans' health. In these discussions, several noteworthy terms recur, *aaita* (~ offense, wrong), *tetru* (~ mistake), and *tapu* (~ fault),[13] which are broadly interchangeable. For example, a spirit says, "This time, you have not made the *pandalu* [spirit house] well. You are not making things as the elders did. You are skipping things, you make mistakes." And a human responds, "This year it happened. We will not make it next year. This was a mistake; from next year onwards, we will do everything correctly. We have little *budi*, and if we did any fault, you should not be angry with us. You should still continue to protect us from illnesses."

Just as the locals do not neatly identify who the incoming spirits are, they do not clearly identify what actions are prohibited as mistakes. *Tapu* (and the other notions) appears to encompass content-free actions, referring broadly to whatever disturbs particular spirits, to what has happened to anger this or that spirit, as evidenced by such signs as otherwise unexplainable illnesses. The spirits' emotionality more than their physicality drives *tapu* (and I think this is probably the case for similar notions among other foragers-cultivators). Illnesses and misfortune signal the spirits' discontent, at times not even directly intended by them as punishment or retribution but simply expressing their hurt. Specific illnesses and misfortunes (*batha*) of unrecognized cause are raised now and then during the pluralogues, providing an occasion to reflexively connect these misfortunes to the hurt felt by the spirits, and this hurt to human deed (see more in Bird-David 2004b). Even these moments do not involve exclusive one-to-one spirit-client diagnostic and therapeutic dialogue; the problem and the cause are plurirelational issues.

Similar content-fluid notions are reported by Demmer (2007), and more complex versions referencing highly eclectic, even seemingly inconsistent, content are reported for Southeast Asian Orang Asli peoples, among others, the Chewong and the Batek (Howell 1984; Kirk Endicott 1979). The Batek *lawac*, for example, refers to acts punished by thunderstorms and the upwelling of subterranean waters; among acts deemed offensive are laughing at animals, cooking certain combinations of food over the same fire, pouring certain kinds of blood into the river, and improper sexual behavior (Kirk Endicott 1979: 70). Kirk Endicott suggested that the term is best understood by reference to the English notion of "illegality," which covers numerous acts, from murder to parking violations. Again, I argue that a scale-blind perspective distorts comprehension of these notions; they cannot be properly understood with large-scale society in mind, whose dispersed members nevertheless share recognized similarities, including conformity to a standard generalizable moral code. Taking the foragers' scalar context into analytical account is crucial, and on the basis of my simpler case within the Asian forager range, I propose that *tapu* (and kindred notions) are deeds that offend particular vivid and idiosyncratic beings rather than constituting deviations from a standardized code. These notions are person tailored, by which I mean not the generalized singular person but this or that particular vivid being, the more elaborate Orang Asli notions perhaps representing their incipient generalization to other encounterable beings. So read, *tapu* belongs with *nachika* (~ restraint; see chapter 3), *budi* (~ social tact; see chapter 4), and *palaka* (~ custom; see chapter 7), their content malleable, arising situationally and perpetuated within particular plurirelational contexts. Meanwhile, through this idiosyncratically tailored content, the singularities of the spirits and the humans emerge within the plurirelational context.

CROSS-SPECIES KINSHIP

Our own [nonhuman] relatives (Take 4)

Huge corpuses of myths and chants provide seemingly inexhaustible bases for exploring the Amerindian cosmos; the same cannot be said for Chathen and his relatives. Their main cultural effort being invested in relating with, rather than in talking about, the diverse dwellers of their *sime,* no myths are told during the "big visit" or in any other special gathering.[14] During his work with a Nayaka group in the Gudalur area (in 2003–4), Daniel Naveh recorded two stories, to which I turn next (my own fieldwork material does not include any stories of this nature). The man who told Naveh the first story had heard it from his grandmother as she was doing her chores, and the man who told him the second story had heard it from his grandfather. Both stories were related to Naveh in several sessions stretching over a few days and nights, when the narrators were pursuing their household chores (2007: 69). A synopsis of each story follows (for the full versions, see Naveh 2007: 68–73). The first one concerns a bear (*cardi*) and his human wife (a similar Paliyan story is described in Gardner 2000: 189–90).

A woman who was eight months pregnant went to the river to fetch water. Having filled her pot, she left it on the riverbank while she went to urinate. A bear took the pot during her absence and poured out half the water, replacing it with earth. When the woman returned, she could not lift the pot, and the bear offered to carry it for her, on one condition: that if she gave birth to a daughter, she would give that daughter to him to be his wife. The woman subsequently did give birth to a daughter, and when the child grew up, the bear came and took her to live with him in his cave. Increasingly aware of her different needs and tastes, he fed her with honey and robbed passing wagons for rice and cloth. His wife gave birth to two bear cubs, and her relatives came to the cave to visit her. Her bear husband was away, and she did not offer them food. They came again, and this time the bear was at home, and he offered them food and ate with them. However, they tricked the bear and killed him. The bear cubs ran into the forest, their mother returned to her human relatives, and ever since then, bears get angry when they encounter humans in the forest.

In the second story, a forest buffalo cow (*cati*) found an abandoned human baby girl. She took her and raised her. As the bear in the first story had with respect to his wife, the cow began to observe her daughter's different capabilities and needs: her daughter spoke, she liked to eat rice, and she wanted clothes and vessels. The cow mother stole all of these things for her human daughter from the village. The village people succeeded in tracking the cow back to her cave, and there they found the human daughter. They came to the cave several times when the cow was away collecting food, and they tried to convince the human daughter to come with them to their village. But she refused, saying she wanted to live with her cow mother, and she called out to her cow mother to come to her. The villagers finally laid a trap for the cow mother, who fell in it and died. They took the human daughter to the village, but when they told her what had happened, she ran to the trap and jumped in, dying with her cow mother.

Both stories dwell on particular, vivid cow and bear beings and their kinship relations with humans—not on buffalo or bear societies whose members share the same "buffalo" or "bear" body and perspective. The drama in the stories is *not* triggered by the protagonists' different bodily habitus—cow mother and human daughter, bear husband and human wife. The differences between the protagonists unfold as they live together (the buffalo mother raising her human daughter and the bear-husband looking after his human wife), and they are not just observed but accommodated (the cow observes that her human daughter likes rice and dresses and obtains these things for her, and the bear obtains the honey his human wife likes). The animal protagonists have no relatives of their kind that we hear about. They live in the forest within reach of the human "village," a word that probably refers to the kind of tiny forest settlements in which the storytelling grandparents lived. The human protagonist appears to have *a few* close relatives (a father, an uncle, three relatives, etc.). The drama in these stories is triggered by improper severing of contact with those relatives (the cow's daughter does not want to visit her human relatives; the bear's wife does not offer food to her visiting human relatives). These disrupted relations among human kin eventually lead to tragedy (the second story, especially, elaborates on the primacy of affective kinship over species-related difference). Instead of isomorphic, separate human and cow (or bear) "tribes-societies," these stories depict the extension of kinship relations from the human village outward into the surrounding forest.

These same themes reverberate in Chewong myths, eighteen of which are included in Howell's ethnography (1984: 253–77). The protagonists are diverse and include animals and plants (spider, elephant, mango, pandanus, etc.), and the stories often are about their desire to marry and/or have children, regardless of species differences, leading to interspecies pairings, mating, and the birth of offspring. The Chewong myths express more concern about bodily differences than the Nayaka stories. For example, they dwell on different sexual organs that complicate intercourse, like the vagina of the pandanus woman, which is full of thorns that kill humans who sleep with her. In the Nayaka story, we are not told of any problem the bear's organ presents to copulation with his human wife. Even in the Chewong stories, however, the protagonists are not strictly segregated, each keeping to his or her own kind. Instead, they negotiate and accommodate their distinctions; indeed, they can even strip off their animal bodies. Chewong regard the body as *bajo* (~ a cloak) that can be put on and taken off, a notion that may not be as illustrative of perspectivism as it might appear, for *bajo* is a Malay word used by the Chewong for types of garments that were not indigenous to them and that they usually only wore when they descended from the hills to Malay villages to sell their rattan (Howell 1984: 54). The Chewong *bajo* may indeed align with Amazonian perspectivist bodily notions—but it may also be more in keeping with Nayaka pragmatic pluralism.

The Chewong myths reflect a *small* multispecies community more than they do the multiple unispecies societies stipulated by perspectivist and animistic theories that take the Chewong as one of their prime exemplars beyond the Amazon. For example, a spider living with his aunt sends presents with her to the house of two unmarried human girls he wants to marry (Howell's myth 6). Even when the animal's home is described as a "land" that is "far" away, it is not so far as to preclude visiting. A man spears an elephant and follows the injured beast to its land (myth 10), a journey that takes him three days of walking in the jungle. And "land" here should not be taken to imply a vast area, another country, another world. Our man arrives at a singular elephant house, whose dwellers take him to another house. There he cures the injured elephant and, in return, is given the latter's two elephant daughters as wives. The man walks with his new elephant wives back toward his home place, but they take fright and return to their own home. He continues on to his home but, after a while, misses his wives and goes back with his mother to their place/land. More than separate worlds, this story suggests to me clusters of small settlements that are not too distant to be reached by an extended journey on foot but that are too distant to maintain daily contact with (a familiar dilemma in the Gorge that confronts in-marrying spouses; see chapter 3).

Everyday practice also reinforces Chathen and his relatives' sense of their community as multispecies. From time to time, they brought home from the forest fledgling creatures that had been deserted by their mothers, a practice also reported for Amerindian and other hunter-gatherer groups.[15] I observed the adoption of a variety of orphaned animals, including monitor lizards, parrots, squirrels, and mongoose. Women carried fledgling parrots and baby lizards wrapped in cloth tied around their waists. Lactating women extracted milk on the palm of the hand and fed it to these creatures. When I took photos of families who requested it, the forest creatures they were caring for were included in the shots, held by family members when groups posed for the camera. People also brought stones to the hamlet, saying they were bringing them to "live with us" (see more in Bird-David 1999a: 74). Naveh reported that, as a matter of routine, the Nayaka he studied talked with potentially dangerous animals they came across in the forest (from elephants to poisonous snakes), reminding them that "we all live together in this forest."[16] The Nayaka stories and the Chewong myths suggest, I think, that kinship relations override bodily dissimilarities, that species is simply one of an individual's attributes alongside gender (see chapter 4), age, and personality.

TO BE-WITH OR BE LIKE: PRINCIPLES OF GROUPING

Our own [nonhuman] relatives (Take 5)

Ethnographers have noted the lack of systematic taxonomies among various Asian forager peoples (e.g., see Morris 1976: 546 on Hill Pandaram). A scale-sensitive perspective can offer insights into the reasons for this lacuna, and so I turn briefly to a consideration of classification. While not a main focus of my fieldwork, it *was* one of Howell's main concerns. She was "dismayed" (she wrote) to discover that she "could not discern any taxonomies at all, or indeed establish what were the Chewong classificatory principles" (1984: 212). She even submitted her voluminous data to computerized principal component analysis, which did not reveal any significant patterns. Remarkably, Howell concluded that in the Chewong system "no other factor may be common among members of an assigned class beyond their membership of it, the criteria of membership being *contingent* " (177). In other words, beyond a common name, nothing else is shared by the members of a class; contingency alone explains membership in a class. For example, because "someone had laughed at [a] particular animal in the recent past, or in a myth . . . [and] a bad thunderstorm had ensued" (Howell 1984: 241), that animal is included in the class of those at which laughing is prohibited. Howell argued that the Chewong have no categorization (a system whereby items are classed together according to certain shared explicated properties) and no taxonomy (a special case of categorization in which classes are arranged hierarchically) (214). They have only nomenclature, in which members of a class have nothing more in common than their name. These Southeast Asians, with their multiple rules for grouping by name, present a more complex case from which to approach issues of forager taxonomy than the South Asians I work with. In its relative simplicity, the Nayaka case offers analytical advantages that I exploit in pursuing a hypothesis derived from Howell's argument.

Using shared attributes as the basis for categorization and taxonomy involves envisioning each object as distinctively autonomous; the number of such objects is unlimited, and their grouping is purely a mental construct. By contrast, contingency as the basis of nomenclature involves envisioning the object *within* its plurirelational context; the number of such objects that may be feasibly comprehended is limited, and a close correspondence exists between grouping "on the ground" and "in the mind." The botanical episode I describe in Downscale 4 illustrates these two classificatory options well. Chathen and his relatives brought to the hamlet the plants they eat, literally grouping them in a pile of edibility for me. The botanists to whom I took these specimens regrouped them according to Linnaean taxonomic conventions. The botanists' scientific language can be initially deceptive in referencing the "families" to which specimens belong and species as organisms that interbreed and produce fertile offspring. But in this case, "family," of course, means a taxonomic rank, and "producing fertile offspring" refers to innate essentialist potential. "Family," in this context, is about exclusive membership and sameness of separate members, about (in my terms) same-and-separate members. By contrast, in referring to "our family," including nonhuman beings, the foragers meant a body of varied members who lived together in the same home area—diverse-and-pluripresent members in my terms.

During my fieldwork, I did not formally research local classificatory activities. However, exploiting quiet moments I spent sitting with people around their hearths, I would playfully present them with four items (e.g., deer, monitor lizard, snake, and drum) and ask them which of these belonged together and which was the odd one out. One evening, after I had made several unsuccessful attempts to elicit a response that made sense to me, Kungan impatiently explained, "Your pen, your copybook [diary], and your bag; they all belong together because every day you write with the pen in your diary and put both in your bag" (or words to that effect).

Twenty-five years later, intrigued by my story and inspired by Roy Ellen's (1993) work on Nuaulu animal categories, Naveh (2007: 107–19) pursued a pilot classification test among the Nayaka with whom he worked, and he reported on the process and the results in detail. He did the "test" at a late stage of his fieldwork. By then, he had accumulated thirty-five photographs (his own and a few he purchased) that showed a great diversity of images, including wetland rice fields, a forest landscape, a nest of ants on a forest tree, a termite mound, a Nayaka boy, three domesticated chickens, three langur monkeys, a bonnet macaque monkey, a house, forest yams, two domesticated dogs, a rock (about the size of a boy), a group of metal pots, two tigers, a group of elephants, a snake, and a butterfly. Ten persons agreed to take part in Naveh's test; only seven persevered to the end, largely to help Naveh as their friend. With the photos spread on the ground, each participant was asked, in turn, to group the ones he or she felt belonged together and to explain the basis for the groupings. Frequently, test participants first tried to identify the *specific* object(s) in the photograph, asking, for example, where the photograph was taken or whether the rock it showed was the one found on the way to so-and-so's house. Their questions did not reflect simple curiosity; rather, Naveh's answers informed their grouping choices, which favored propinquity and pluripresence over distinctions of kind. For example, a man who grouped together the images of a termite mound, a snake, and a mongoose, explained that "the snake likes to live in termite mounds and often when he comes out the mongoose comes, catches the snake and eats it." Grouping together the images of two tigers, wild dogs, and two deer, another man explained that "the tigers and wild dogs eat the deer." Likewise, an explanation provided for grouping together the images of the bear, the snake, and the rock was that "the bear digs under the rock and later the snake comes to stay there" (116).

Naveh's work suggests to me something beyond propinquity: the idea (in Jean-Luc Nancy's [2000] sense) of a "community of being," a local heterogeneous community whose members cooperate with or accommodate themselves to one another, rather than "being of a community," its members in "parts-and-whole" relations—in fact, "*same*-parts-and-whole" relations—with their class. "Your pen, your copybook, and your bag," "a termite mound, a snake, and a mongoose," and "a bear, a snake, and a rock" are associations of pluripresent-and-diverse entities. Their underscoring principle resonates with that of family members living together despite and because of their diversity, whose manifold distinctions become apparent in their living together—the opposite, in some sense, of a taxonomic family whose all-but-indistinguishable members live apart, and of the concept of "family resemblance," which mellows the strict definition of the taxonomic family, peculiarly, by picking from the interpersonal "family" the factor of members' genetically produced partial similarities. The forager basis of grouping foregrounds not those who are *like* each other but, rather, those who like each other (*like* indexing shared attributes in the first case and interpersonal affect, tolerance, or mutual accommodation in the second case). This basis for grouping is not as exotic or exclusive as one might think. If Lévi-Strauss famously used "engineer" and "*bricoleur*" as analogies, in today's consumer society, I suppose, one can look to Ikea's ground-floor warehouse and upper-floor "room" displays for inspiration: the first exemplifies grouping by essential kind, by sameness of commodities, and the second by assemblages of diverse commodities that "go well" together and with which prospective human dwellers can "live well." These two principles are combined, if less dramatically, in every consumer home, which has its respective storage and living components.

If the forager society does not exclude but, to the contrary, includes non-human kin, is it not, the reader might ask, a huge society?[17] Since a multitude of life-forms exist in the tropical forest (in Amazonia, Descola asserts, there are "fifty thousand species" of vascular plants alone), are foragers' human-and-nonhuman communities really so minuscule? This question is a fair one, and I can, at this stage, only respond to it with speculation. In Antoine de Saint-Exupéry's memorable *Little Prince* (1943), each in the cast of characters lives on his or her own tiny planet, and one of them, a businessman, obsessively counts all the stars in the universe. The setting poetically expresses the modern idea of pregiven separate individuals, each autonomous and a world unto him- or herself, an ideology that, further-more, conceals the fact of existing-with as the condition of existing at all. Surely, the businessman tends his planet and, thus, any other beings—whatever their form—he shares it with, to keep himself alive and able to continue surveying all the stars in the universe. This idea resonates with the contrast I present in Downscale 4 between Chathen and his relatives' view of the local flora and the government botanists' view. These two groups cannot be differentiated, respectively, as practitioners versus theoreticians, fieldworkers versus office personnel, or à la Lévi-Strauss, bricoleurs versus engineers. As I stress in that interlude, some of the botanists were experienced fieldworkers and were genuinely interested in the local flora, and *at the same time*, they saw each specimen as standing for an entire class that fit into large-scale regional and national classificatory schemes and into a global hierarchy of taxonomic ranks. Their vast horizons of concerns and imaginations enabled as much as they were enabled by the perception of these specimens as distinctively autonomous, classifiable by shared attributes, countable, and groupable with imagined faraway similar others. For Saint-Exupéry's businessman on his planet, the universe includes millions of stars. For the botanists, the forest includes tens of thousands of life-forms. Whether it does so for the foragers, whether their scales of concern and imaginations go beyond the plurally given forms they live with, is a subject for inquiry and one that, I think, may be key to understanding processes of cultural objectification and societalization. Forager-cultivator societies are tiny in terms of human numbers. Perhaps, processes of cultural objectification and societalization in these contexts are initially fueled by recognition and imagination of more and more nonhuman beings, which can help to explain why tiny Amazonian groups have extraordinarily complex cosmologies compared with tiny forager communities such as the Nayaka.[18]

Developing universal theories from regionally based observation is common practice in anthropology and a common mode of the discipline's dialectic development, as alternative models from other regions are subsequently presented. The broad purchase of the Amazon-born perspectivist and animistic theories is tested by consideration of such cases as the Asian Chewong. My analysis and ethnography in this chapter suggest a cosmology that departs from the Amazonian, one that appears more appropriate to the Nayaka (and the Chewong) than the Amazonian model is: a universe of tiny-scale multispecies communities of relatives whose plural mode is supported by a "diverse-and-together" rather than a "same-and-separate" logic.

Downscale 5

Family and Ethnonym

Back from the field and writing my thesis in the Social Anthropology Department at Cambridge, I had to choose an ethnonym by which to refer to Kungan and his relatives. I shared a room in the department with students back from fieldwork all over the world: Ghana, Fiji, Malta, Amazonia, and elsewhere. Photographs, maps, and genealogy charts hung on the walls facing our desks. Fieldwork material cluttered desks and filled burgeoning drawers and boxes on the floor. We asked each other the questions anthropologists invariably pose on first meeting: "Where did you work?" followed by "*Whom* did you work with?" The "whom" is presumed to be "a people," and the expected reply is "the X (an ethnonym) of Y (a geographical region)." The ethnonym identifies the "people" you studied—and, by extension, you as a scholar. You enter the ranks of the profession as an ethnographer of X. Each week in the Friday Seminar, the chief gathering of the Cambridge department's staff and research students, a different scholar would present the results of fieldwork with his or her X, and the audience would comment on it. Often, the comments were prefaced by, "Among the X group that I studied . . ." Scenes similar to these 1980s Cambridge seminars can still be observed today in departments of anthropology around the world. An ethnographer's performance in speech and text, formally and informally, commonly includes the ethnonym of the people with whom he or she did fieldwork.

I spent many days in the PhD student room sorting through name options for Kungan and his relatives. They were not isolated in their local world, as others were living there too, and although no government authorities had yet reached them, the existence of forest people in the vicinity of the Gorge was generally known. The foragers' neighbors and self-appointed authorities have variously named them over the years, and I turned to previous scholarship and administrative output to help me select a name.

Distinguishing between ethnic groups was critical to colonial governmentality whatever the context. In India, this work occurred on a colossal scale. Cultures, societies, religions, castes, tribes, and languages were distinguished and listed in the course of the mammoth process of developing the Indian census, starting with nonsynchronous data collection in 1820–70 and continuing through more systematic, comprehensive enumerations in 1871–1901. The British put the census to various political uses in the early twentieth century, a practice continued by the Government of India after independence. The Nilgiris region, in particular, has enjoyed—or, some would say, suffered from—an unusual amount of scholarly and administrative attention. By 1978, it was one of the most-studied areas for its size in all of Asia (see Hockings 1978, 1996). Its steep forested hills and its foothills rife with malaria had ensured the relative isolation of its tribal population until the British arrived in the early nineteenth century. Rapid colonization of the area then began (every year the seat of the government of the Presidency of Madras was moved to the cool hills for six months), accompanied by voluminous reports on and studies of the local tribal inhabitants. Some of these tribal populations were relatively large and/or clearly named (e.g., Badaga and Toda). But many others were tiny communities scattered through the forests, whom explorers, travelers, British administrators, and later, anthropologists expended considerable effort trying to distinguish and name.

In the literature on these tiny forest-foraging groups, one recurring ethnonym is "Kurumba" or close variations thereof, with prefixes multiplying from study to study. The renowned ethnographer of tribal India, Christoph von Fürer-Haimendorf, remarked of its use that Kurumba "is one of those tribal names which have done so much to obscure the ethnic picture of many Indian regions" (1952: 19). In one of the earliest works on the region, Francis Buchanan (1807) proposed two divisions of "Kurumba" (Cad- and Betta-Curubaru, cited in Thurston 1909, 4:163–64). Over half a century later, James Wilkinson Breeks (1873) mentioned four divisions (Botta-, Kambale-, Mullu-, and Anda-Kurumbas). And a mere seven years after Breeks, H. B. Grigg (1880), in the massive *A Manual of the Nilagiri District in the Madras Presidency*, enumerated six divisions (Eda-, Karmadiya-, Male-, and Pal-Kurumba, Kurumba proper, and Kurumba Okkiliya, none of these divisions overlapping with Breeks's four). About the time of my 1978–79 fieldwork, linguist Dieter Kapp (1978a, 1978b) suggested there were *seven* "Kurumba tribes" in the Nilgiris (Muduga and Alu-, Palu-, Bette-, Jenu-, Mullu-, and Urali-Kurumba). To further confuse matters, in reports relating to the Nilgiri-Wynaad—the part of the Nilgiris farthest from the British seat and the least studied (where Kungan and his relatives lived)—the ethnonym "Naiken," variously spelled and prefixed, was used interchangeably with Jenu- and Cadu-Kurumba (*jenu* means honey and *cadu*, forest). The permutations included Naikr, Naicken, Nayaka, Kattunayaka (*katu* being a variant of the forest prefix), Shola-Nayaka (*shola* means "woods"), and the poetic Jenu Koyy Shola Nayaka (translated as "honey-cutting lords of the woods").

Reading between the lines of the earliest accounts, one can sense that the names appearing in them did not come from the indigenous peoples themselves. Breeks, for example, mentions before offering his authoritative typology that "it is difficult to get a complete account of the tribal divisions recognized by them. One man will name you one (his own); another two divisions; another three, and so on" (1873: 48). Their villages, he adds, "are so dispersed over the slopes and base of the hills, that the inhabitants of one locality know nothing of those at a distance" (50). A planter in the Nilgiri-Wynaad, a Mr. Fletcher, wrote, "Although the two colonies are within five miles as the crow flies . . . the low country Nayaka . . . speech is a patois of Malayalam. The Nayaka on the hills above . . . speaks a dialect of his own . . . derived from Kanarese" (quoted in Thurston 1909: 77). Such observations were lost in the flood of successive attempts to map and name the Nilgiris' scattered forest inhabitants. Ethnographers subsequently worked their way through the "forest of names" that had grown up in colonial times, sometimes adding to the tangled nomenclature and sometimes reinforcing earlier terms. Elsewhere (Bird 1987), I have suggested this process was akin to Winnie the Pooh circling a tree and, spotting more and more footprints (his own), reading them as growing evidence that a mysterious animal, a Heffalump, has been there before him. Generations of observers took the labored and shaky divisions mapped by their predecessors as evidence of what "really" existed, of how things (or rather, groups, in this case) "really" were.

At the end of my literary expedition into the tangled thicket of naming options, I chose to use "Naiken," the term by which nonforagers living in the Gorge in the late 1970s were calling the foragers there. Kungan and his relatives were themselves aware of this name and occasionally used it themselves, if only in dealing with these neighbors. Luckily, "Naiken" has no derogatory meanings, unlike so many names by which hunter-gatherer peoples elsewhere are known. Indeed, it derives from a Sanskrit word meaning "leader" or "chief," rendering the name inoffensive and even respectful. In 1990, I changed the spelling to Nayaka, the spelling increasingly used officially (usually prefixed by *Kattu*), even though Nayaka, spelled as such, was the name of various ruling dynasties in South India in the seventeenth century. I have since then used Nayaka in my work and continue to do so in this book. As I discuss in chapter 7, in the 2000s the name Kattunayaka has come to obscure the ethnic picture of whole states, just as Kurumba confused the ethnic picture of many regions in the last century.

The ethnonym an ethnographer chooses for her study group becomes part of her professional "visiting card," appearing in the title of her thesis, publications, and presentations. All of the articles I have written about Kungan and his relatives have begun with their introduction as Naiken/ Nayaka/Kattunayaka of the Nilgiris/Nilgiri-Wynaad/South India. The first sentence I wrote as a PhD student read, "This thesis is concerned with the tribal Naiken who inhabit a forested area in the Nilgiri region" (Bird 1983a: 1). In this book, a late ethnography that enables subversive moves, the ethnonym itself is a subject of inquiry. In the next chapter, I ethnographically explore Kungan and his relatives' relations with nonforagers living in the Gorge, considering, among other issues, their respective onomastic praxes.

Couple fishing and plantation workers watching. Photographed by the author (1978–79).

6. A Continuum of Relatives

Othering and Us-ing

Kethan and his wife walk alongside the river and reach the bridge (the local gloss for two heavy logs that span the stream, balanced on rocks protruding from the water). A lorry is preparing to cross it, the climax of its slow descent down a slippery makeshift road (a man walks ahead of the vehicle laying bamboo poles over small brooks and muddy slopes to facilitate its passage). A small crowd of helpers and spectators from the plantation stand around to watch. Kethan and his wife join them, standing next to Musa, a Mappila migrant who had lived next to them for several months in a vacated hut in their hamlet while he and his family built a house nearby. They watch the lorry cross the river, then Kethan and his wife matter-of-factly wade through the water to the opposite shore and continue on their way through the forest to visit a cousin in UP.

In this chapter, I expand my analysis of the foragers' tiny-scaled world to include their relations with their migrant neighbors, a dozen or so people who lived on forestland in the Gorge not far from the foragers' hamlets. As Marshall Sahlins once remarked, modern hunter-gatherers no longer live in a world where they are surrounded by other hunter-gatherers, and consequently, their relations with neighboring peoples (farmers, pastoralists, and others) have constituted a major topic of study. These relations often are framed in terms of two societies, and their analysis focuses on particular interpersonal encounters as instantiations of intergroup relations. In this chapter, I pause to generally question this approach and its accompanying conceptual baggage, including putative universal groupness, ethnic boundaries, and "us-them" imaginations. In my ethnographic analysis, I show that Kethan and his relatives extend their concept of *sonta* to the corporeal limits of pluripresence and actively "us" (as opposed to "other") migrants with whom they closely associate. For their part, even as some migrants engage in close dyadic friendships with foragers, they "other" the foragers as members of a "Nayaka primitive tribe" and constitute their own plural identity through membership in their imagined communities of origin and, within the Gorge, as "non-Nayaka."[1]

• • •

Many foragers commonly engage with outsiders, especially (but not only) those described by James Woodburn (1997) as "encapsulated," those who have lived for a long time in the midst of other populations and whose relations with their neighbors are much debated. Debates focus on the antiquity of such relations; how they have affected foragers' ways of life; whether foragers have exploited or been exploited by neighboring farmers; whether foragers have depended on farmers for food; and specifically regarding the tropical forest, whether it is even possible to subsist solely on hunting and gathering in this environment or whether some interaction with food producers is necessary.[2] Triggered by archaeological and ethnohistorical findings suggesting long-term contact between Kalahari foragers and their neighbors, a major controversy even led some scholars of the late 1980s to question the validity of the "hunter-gatherer" category in ethnographic contexts.[3] In this chapter, I pay attention to the ontological "group" basis of these discussions and to their disregard for scale. To explicate my concerns as simply as I can, I turn for background to one of the earliest and probably still one of the best-known ethnographies of forager-farmer relations, Colin Turnbull's (1965) study of the relations between Mbuti (Pygmy) and their neighboring Bira villagers in the Ituri forest of Central Africa.

Turnbull cautiously introduced his fieldwork as a "one-band study," explaining that the "sacrifice of a whole year to the study of one small band was essential ... demanding of the fieldworker the utmost persistence in both physical and intellectual pursuit" (5). His aim had been, he wrote, a study of "the general nature of Mbuti society," an entity he assumes to exist and of which he takes his "one band" to be a subset. He assumes such an entity despite two major difficulties (26): firstly, Mbuti's "inseparability" from surrounding forest cultivators and, secondly, the lack of any basis for estimating the population of Mbuti society at large since no tiny local forager group has "any political identity.... [The] only effective political unit is the band" (in my terms, those Turnbull imagines as Mbuti do not have a sense of Mbuti as an imagined community). On the basis of conversations with colonial missionaries and administrators—self-appointed identity experts like those who, in South India, mapped and remapped forager communities (see Downscale 5)—Turnbull hazards a guess that there are about forty thousand Mbuti, but at the same time, intriguingly, his lengthy monograph on a single band provides no information on its size (Mbuti bands are elsewhere estimated to comprise twenty to one hundred individuals).[4] His work's title, *Wayward Servants*, prefigures the book's main thesis that, although the village farmers regard their Mbuti associates as servants, the foragers opportunistically engage with the farmers and retreat to the forest at will, while its subtitle, *The Two Worlds of the African Pygmies*, prefigures the "African Pygmies" as the broad group-subject, as is common in ethnography of small-scale societies.

Thirty years later, Roy Richard Grinker (1994) criticized Turnbull not for analyzing relations in terms of groups but, to the contrary, for *insufficiently* addressing the ethnic dimension. Grinker argued that Turnbull and other students of forager-farmer relations identify groups by their subsistence pursuits instead of taking an ethnic perspective on them. In his own ethnography of relations between Lese farmers and their forager Efe (Pygmy) neighbors (also Ituri forest dwellers), Grinker posits two ethnic groups that define their respective collective identities dialectically in relation to each other. He also describes the Lese sense of household as ideally including an Efe (male) partner, symbolically regarded as another household female, and asserts that the Lese feminize the Efe as a group. To be fair to both Turnbull and Grinker, it is possible, judging by changes over time in my own study area, that Grinker simply overlooks how local discourse had become more ethnically focused between the 1950s, Turnbull's era, and the late 1980s, his own era, reflecting global as well as local developments. Nevertheless, Grinker's critique—insofar as it is taken generally, as he intended it—entrenches the study of forager-other relations in terms of ethnic collectivities, failing to allow for foragers' alternative plural modes. Grinker's necessary use of ethnic labels prefigures the subjects of study as two ethnically imagined groups, Lese and Efe, complicating inquiry into their own plural categories and imaginations, if not precluding it.

These Central African studies provide ethnographic foils for my theoretical concerns—yet not before I cue in the scalar context. Paradoxically, one can live in a large city, imagined and known to be heterogeneous, its members belonging to many ethnicities and classes, and still spend every day surrounded by people who are the "same" as oneself. Any sizable "Chinatown" or African migrant neighborhood in a Euro-American capital illustrates this scalar duality. The occasional others who come into such neighborhoods stand out as odd strangers against the "sameness" of the locals. Meanwhile, in the forager nanoworld, dissimilarity is vividly present and conspicuous. Kethan and his relatives observe and value the diversity of dwellers in the Gorge, both human and nonhuman, and I expect other foragers do so as well. If they did not imagine themselves as an ethnically named group, why would they so imagine their neighbors? Why would they imagine the trickle of diverse migrants into the Gorge (even if it later turned into a flood) as "same-and-separate" members of this or that ethnic group?

General terms of analysis that spill into scale-blinded hunter-gatherer analysis might convey such wrong impressions. Foragers' relations with neighbors *are* largely discussed in terms of relations between groups identified by ethnonyms, and even the interactions between particular persons are couched in terms of intergroup relations—as if the most salient feature of those particular persons is their membership in different groups (e.g., an Efe man and a Lese man). The group basis of these discussions blurs the multiplicity of relatives/persons constituting each community as well as the matrix of unfolding social relations within and across them. In modern ontological terms, furthermore, each group figures as a whole, a singular entity, bounded and distinctive—and so, its relations with another group figure as those between two persons (e.g., Efe-Lese relations). The group basis of these discussions, then, also supports examining forager-farmer relations in "self-other" language (e.g., see Stewart, Barnard, and Tanaka 2002), a common way of speaking about intergroup relations in anthropology generally and consistent with references to a group's *self*-identity, *self*-interest, and so on. The professional concept capturing "self-other" group language is *alterity*. The word itself comes from the Latin *alter*, meaning "the other of two," and the concept it designates is one of what Nigel Rapport and Joanna Overing (2000) consider the sixty key concepts in contemporary social and cultural anthropology. "Self-other" language is often used to refer to even huge social aggregates, for example, in critiques of anthropology's early concern with "the primitive *other* relative to Europe's civilized *self*," and it infuses anthropologists' argument that "all systems of otherness are structures of identity and difference that have more to do with the establishment of *self*-identity than with the empirical reality of the other" (Rapport and Overing 2000: 12, my emphasis).

In addition to being imagined as a single being, a social group is often imagined as a body, social or political, an image that recurs in studies of forager-cultivators' relations with outsiders. This image is especially prominent in Amazonian research, informing comparisons between tiny Amazonian and Western societies (their scalar disparity disregarded). Claude Lévi-Strauss (1973 [1952]) famously distinguished between anthropophagic Amerindian societies that deal with strangers by swallowing them up, making them their own and gaining strength from them, and anthropoemic (from the Greek *emein*, to vomit) Western society, which excludes strangers. Eduardo Viveiros de Castro (1992 [1986]) elaborated on the Amazonian option, arguing for the Amerindian "cannibal cogito," an assimilation of the other (body and person) as a means of incorporating the other's external gaze on oneself (*other* can refer to each agent in the group and to the group as agent).[5]

From the modern Western perspective, boundedness is universalized and so also are bounded ethnic groups and "us-them" distinctions (see Lamont and Molnár 2002). Fredrik Barth (1969) is regarded as having helped pioneer the prolific discussion of ethnicity and boundaries in anthropology, and therefore his later (2000) retrospective critical reflections on the uses and abuses of the concepts involved are particularly refreshing and serve my ethnographic analysis well. Barth cautions that "boundary" has consistently been a concept of Western anthropologists, made to serve their analytical purposes. The English concept of "boundary," he notes, "is really a quite complex cultural model ... [that] carries massive cultural entailments" (2000: 20). It embraces, he suggests, three levels of abstraction: first and most literarily, boundaries are imagined lines that divide territories "on the ground." Second, more abstractly, boundaries set limits, marking social groups off from each other. Third, most abstractly, boundaries provide a template for separating distinct categories of the mind, offering "a schema for conceptualizing the very idea of distinction" (ibid.). In none of these senses, Barth asserts, should anthropologists assume that boundaries are universal. In many instances, he cautions, we only imagine that we are identifying preexisting boundaries. We should more productively ask what concepts and mental operations the people we study use in constructing their worlds and, in particular, whether they deploy the concept of boundaries for thinking about territories, social groups, and categorical distinctions.

Boundaries, intergroup, self–other, body—the conceptual terminology so common in anthropological discussions of groups and intergroup relations—do not translate well into the Gorge's nanoworld, and I doubt they fit the nanoworlds of hunter-gatherers more generally. I question the distortive effect of using these terms in a world where, as described in previous chapters and usefully recalled here, a single body sleeping alone is pathological and the salient experience is, rather, one of multiple bodies close to one another (cuddling together at night for sleep, sitting close together beside open hearths, following one another along forest trails, etc.). Huts are not marked off from their surroundings by fences or other physical or symbolic means, they often are not walled and lack interior divisions, and domestic life takes place around outside hearths that structure space in terms of closeness–distance (not inside–outside) and focality (not barriers). *Sime* (~ home area) is understood as the area surrounding a focal point, in contrast to the sense of a bounded territory conveyed by the same word in other parts of the Nilgiris, and streams constitute not geographical boundaries but rather meeting points where relatives bathe, wash cloths, and draw water. To the forest trekker on the way to visit relatives, a stream is something to be matter-of-factly waded through.

In previous chapters, I explored Kethan and his relatives' malleable territorial notions and touched on their alternatives to categorical distinctions. In this chapter, I turn to how they figure what their ethnographers examine as their relations with putative "outsiders," the very term presupposing boundaries marking them off from insiders. I explore how they engaged in the late 1970s with their neighbors in the Gorge and how they imagined them. I begin, however, with a contemporary vignette.

BOUNDARY: A NEW LOCAL WORD

Our own [diverse] relatives (Take 1)

Noa Lavi did fieldwork in TM in 2010 and 2012; Kethan was still living there at the time. She regularly heard TM people using the term *boundary*, always in the singular; one incident she recorded especially struck me. She related that she had asked Kethan about the local word for *boundary* and he had insisted that boundary *was* a local word (Lavi 2012: 7–8). When she asked him if that word was used in the early days, he laughed, saying that there had been no "boundary" in the forest when "your mother" (referring to me) was here, so the word was not here either.[6] Daniel Naveh (personal communication) also heard the English word *boundary* during his fieldwork (2003–4) with another Nayaka group, and when he asked for the local equivalent, he was told that it *was* a local word. When he pressed the point that *boundary* is an English word, he was told emphatically that it was a local word right from the days of the forefathers.

In the 2000s, Kathen and his relatives in TM used the word *boundary* when they referred to the electric fence surrounding their houses and coffee plants (erected by an NGO to protect the coffee from wild elephants) and to fences enclosing nearby plantations that were expanding into the forest. They also used it when mentioning the imagined Tamil-Kerala border, which they traversed when traveling through the forest to visit relatives in UP. The area deep in the forest through which the boundary ran, as marked on official maps, was not under government control in the 1970s. In the 2000s, that area began to draw police attention, as a result of interstate smuggling of goods and the entry of bandits from Kerala into Tamil Nadu.

In chapter 7, I address some of these changes (see also Lavi 2012). Here, I continue to focus mainly on the mid- to late 1970s, *before* there were boundaries, and a word for them, in Kethan and his relatives' world. My ethnographic analysis of those years continues to move outward from the core of pluripresent relatives, and I focus, firstly, on in-marrying relatives from outside the Gorge, then in-marrying non-kin (who identify them-selves as other ethnic subjects), and finally, nonforager neighbors living alongside Kethan and his relatives. I thus step back in time to the 1970s, when Kethan was young(er)—and I was too. . . .

RELATIVES OF RELATIVES

Our own [diverse] relatives (Take 2)

In a tiny, highly inbred community, one would expect an in-marrying spouse, by default, to quickly become connected through kinship ties to everybody in the community. An appropriate kinship term for a relative's spouse is easily inferred from the appropriate terms for the relative him- or herself in most kinship terminologies, especially in Dravidian ones, which revolve around alliances. However, in the Gorge, the "kinshipization" of an in-marrying spouse involved a process that could take many weeks because not only *knowledge of* the relation but also *familiarity with* the specific person was at stake. One expression of this process was the gradual use of kinship terms as appellations for a newly arrived distant relative. I was able to observe the tail end of the process after Kalan came to GR and married Kalliyani (see chapter 3).

Recall that Kalan had come by way of a "satellite" hamlet (DV) from a more distant hamlet (SF) that was well beyond the orbit of regular visits by the Gorge's residents. No one had known Kalan before he came. They only knew that he was a nephew of a man in DV who occasionally came to GR. Kalan was recognized *as a relative* of a relative, and furthermore, he was generally adept in some of the local ways and traditions. He was a skillful honey collector and was conversant with the locals' mode of spirit posses-sion, and he quickly adjusted to the local dialect, which was only slightly different from his own, reflecting the greater influence of Kannada speak-ers in the Gorge and of Malayalam speakers in SF. But for all this, his absorption into *nama sonta* (our own, relatives) was gradual. At first, his wife's relatives mainly spoke to and about him using the name Kalan, by which he was registered as a new worker on the plantation. When I asked why they used this name and not the appropriate kinship term, as they commonly did among themselves, and which they could easily figure out from their respective relations with his wife, they explained that they "did not know him well as yet" (or words to that effect).

The insistence on familiarity can partly be understood by considering what it meant to live in a tiny community of relatives, in which everyone was multiply related to all the others. Familiarity was imperative for learning which kinship term to use for whom, firstly, because multiple kinship routes connected people, and therefore, there were optional terms from which to choose. To make things more complex, kinship terms were chosen tactically, in response to changing circumstances, needs, and strategies. Moreover, a relative's switching between optional kinship terms could have a cascading effect, reshuffling and reconstituting the field of kinship routes and choices. In any case, marriage, as the incomer's pivotal link, was itself a fluctuating state until the birth of a child. Lastly, no one would, or could, have presented Kalan with the kind of orderly diagram of kinship relations that I provide in Downscale 3. He had to gradually grow familiar with his wife's intricate, diverse, manifold, and fluid plural relations—by *being-with* them as they addressed and referred to one another, dynamically, tactically, and instrumentally.

It took some time, therefore, before he grew familiar with each of them and each of them with him, separately and vividly, as pluripresent relatives rather than known relations. The issue was not one of admission into the group, of crossing boundaries and being accepted *in*. Rather, it was one of engaging *with* each person, consonant with how each of them engaged with one another. The process involved not belonging to a group, through this or that dyadic tie with specific members, but belonging with each and all of these relatives in unmediated ways by plurirelating with them.

Kalan also had to gradually grow familiar with the spirits living in the Gorge, and I observed a particularly dramatic expression of his progress during a "big animistic visit" in which I participated. The incident in question was highly unusual, happening only once during the three such events I attended. Generally familiar with spirit possessions, as they were also held in his place of origin (SF), Kalan began his preparations to fall into trance: he wrapped the cloth around his slim body and chose a particularly large knife. His face grew solemn, and his half-naked body started to shake fiercely. He continued shaking and waving the knife in the air for some time, but nothing happened. No local spirit entered his body. After ten minutes or so, he finally gave up, took off the cloth, and lay the knife down.[7] Kalan was familiar with this spirit-possession tradition, had the know-how to participate, and was entitled to perform. No one prevented his performance or, as it turned out, his attempt to do so. His failure may have been attributable to specific reasons of which I was unaware (I did not pursue the issue with him or others at the time). But it may also signal that the local spirits did not know him yet and that he did not yet know them well, in terms of their peculiarities, their idiosyncratic manners, gestures, and languages. This incident was doubly significant as, during the same "big visit," Kalan *did* perform, and very well indeed, in the ritual of reversal, which involves the visit of two *pichachio* (~ spirit Others) who invert the normal respectful ways of being and being-with others. He took on the role of the male figure in the visiting pair (see chapter 4). By the end of my fieldwork, Kalan was generally addressed and referred to by everyone in the Gorge as a relative, through kinship terms that were dynamically and tactically deployed.[8] In large-scale Euro-American societies, using kinship terms instead of personal names can highlight kinship roles and authority, and using personal names instead of kinship terms can, reversely, individualize and personalize a relative (e.g., see Strathern 1992a: 17–21). By comparison, the foragers' gradual shift to using kinship terms for Kalan marked his becoming one of "our own," our *sonta*, a relative among relatives. When his marriage later produced a trail of further marriages between his relatives in DV and his wife's relatives, he gradually came to occupy a key node in the local matrix of relatives.

NEW RELATIVES

Our own [diverse] relatives (Take 3)

Occasionally, people married into the local community who were not, like Kalan, relatives of relatives. Usually men, they were non-Nayaka in terms of the ethnic divisions recognized in the area and they did not know the local traditions and forest ways.[9] Nevertheless, they were gradually regarded as *nama sonta*, just as Kalan was, if they joined their spouse and lived with her relatives. A crucial difference between Kalan and such a man—for which reason I call the first "relative of relatives" and the second "new relative"—was that marriage in the second case could not produce a trail of visits and subsequent marriages and so reshape the contours of "our *sonta*." The family of a new relative, especially one with a higher position in the regionally recognized hierarchy of castes and/or tribes—say, a Malayali man—would not regularly visit him at his wife's forest hamlet, nor would his wife's relatives visit his family in their village. Marriage with a new relative was a one-off episode that could not affect the network of relatives the way marriage with a relative of relatives did, through ensuing frequent visits and further marriages. For the foragers, this was the salient difference between the two cases of in-marrying spouses, not the degree of "sameness" to "us" (in terms of physical look, traditions, language, etc.).

Readers living in the modern nationalist era might be reluctant to accept my proposal that sameness was immaterial to acceptance among the Gorge's foragers. In the midst of writing this chapter, struggling to make a persuasive case for this proposition, I happened to see a news story about a convention of redheaded people taking place in a European city,[10] a useful event for putting my point across. Redheads had come from all over the world to be together at the convention. One man spoke of how wonderful it was to be with people "like him" and not to "stand out"; redheads are usually a minority in their respective communities, he added, and at the convention there were "so many." His comments take to an extreme the idea of sameness as a basis of identity and belonging, an idea readers might instinctively find more congenial than the idea of an indigenous community welcoming a different-looking person from another local community, or, indeed, a very different-looking white person, as one of "our own." In Kethan and his relatives' terms, feeling a sense of shared identity with red-haired people one had never lived with or visited would have been strange. Red hair would have been, for Kethan, just one of a person's idiosyncrasies that, in registering and normalizing diversity, he might have commented on. But then, in his small world, he would never have seen thousands of redheads together, their sameness striking by dint of numbers, downplaying multiple other differences. Had there been a redhead, as there was a white-skinned person and a frizzle-haired Paniya, among "our own"—only a few dozen people at most—this difference might have stood out no more prominently than any other.

Another way of putting the point across is through the counterpoint concept of *naturalization*, the official term for a state's conferral on an "alien" of the rights and privileges of citizenship.[11] Naturalization is about forging an individual's allegiance to society, and becoming *nama sonta* involves forging personal relations with plural relatives. Marriage with a native can be a sufficient criterion for naturalization, but plurirelating with the spouse's relatives by living next door to them is not a prerequisite. Rather, insofar as naturalization enables living in a country with the spouse's relatives, it comes *before* and enables engagement with them. In Kethan's world, "becoming our own" involves no policing of boundaries, no membership application, and no administrative and legal determination. Living with the spouse's relatives and growing personally familiar with each of them are inseparably the means, the process, and the proof of becoming our *sonta*.

One day, well into my fieldwork, a Mappila migrant neighbor gossiped to me that Kethan was one of three children born to a Nayaka woman from affairs she had had with three migrant men, a single child with each man. My Mappila interlocutor identified one of the men as Malayali and the other two as Tamil. None of them stayed on and lived with the Nayaka woman, he told me.

On another occasion, I was told on a visit to the plantation's office that Chathen's father was a Paniya (the name by which another Nilgiri-Wynaad tribal people are known). The plantation's bookkeeper had known the GR people for more than two decades, and in his office, he related that Chathen's grandfather had been the first man to settle on the GR side of the Gorge and the first man to occasionally work on the plantation. That man's first-born daughter, the bookkeeper continued, married a Paniya man, who stayed on in GR and lived there with her and her relatives. Chathen was their firstborn, and subsequently the two had three daughters; one daughter died and the other three children continued to live in GR.

I returned to the hamlet and asked Kungan if the information was accurate. He matter-of-factly confirmed it and wondered why I was surprised. The father's Paniya origin was for Kungan a biographical fact, part of his history, one of Chathen's personal traits and idiosyncrasies. That Chathen's father had been born Paniya (in regional terms) did not weigh on Chathen's position among his relatives any more than his height or disposition did. It was not regarded as a prime marker of his identity, constituting him as a member of this or that ethnic group, bounded and named, nor was it a marker of a class he belonged to, identifying him as someone likely to be and do this or that. In fact, as the firstborn of his mother, herself the firstborn of the man who had originally settled in the GR area, Chathen was the *modale* (discussed in chapter 3), expected to head the preparations for the "big visit" in GR, the one whom others could follow and join, the first around whom their interactions, each with all the others, including him, unfolded.

Kungan's wonder at my surprise led me to ask him what made a person "Nayaka" (still thinking then about my study group in terms of the ethnonym by which they were known in the area). His masterly reply ingeniously bridged his terms and mine. He said essentially that Nayaka are those who live with us, like us, in our *sime*. He referred not to sameness of look or origin but, recursively, to living with us, as we do, all with all. His allusion to those living "in our *sime*" was not a simple territorial stipulation. *Sime* did not have territorial boundaries; it generally referred, rather, to the site of living together, to the local area in which "our own" live together. *Sime* and *sonta*, in this sense, are inseparable concepts (like the Pintupi *walytja* and *ngurra;* see Myers 1986: 48). Kungan's answer triply emphasizes plural enmeshment, referring to (1) *this* place, where (2) we all *live with* one another, and which (3) is our place *because* we live here together.

WAYWARD RELATIVES

Our own [diverse] relatives (Take 4)

By the late 1970s, the number of migrants who lived permanently in the Gorge (some of them since the 1950s) was nearly double that of the local inhabitants. Still, given that Kethan and his relatives numbered around seventy, the migrant community was small. The majority of its members lived within the coffee plantation's bounds, but a slowly growing number of families (eight in 1979) had encroached on forestland and built small houses there, interspersed among the Nayaka hamlets. I continue to train my attention outward from the tiny group of foragers with whom I lived and now bring those migrants into the bounds of analysis.

One simply cannot overemphasize the everyday constant presence in one another's lives of the Gorge's pluridwellers, who could be (and are by some) distinguished as Nayaka and non-Nayaka. Of the four core couples living longest in GR, three had close relations with particular migrants (the fourth, Kungan and his wife, had a close relation with me). These relations varied remarkably from couple to couple, but all involved intimate interpersonal engagement. Below I profile three of the migrants involved in those relationships and consider how the foragers regarded them and how they in turn regarded the foragers.

Musa and his wife had come to the Gorge in 1955 from Kerala, in the first wave of Mappila workers. An enterprising man, Musa opened the first tea shack at the border of the plantation, where, in addition to tea, he offered snacks and meals that his wife cooked for workers and occasional visitors. In 1969, they were the first to leave the laborers' accommodations on the plantation, settling temporarily in a vacant hut in one of the foragers' hamlets, near which they planted bananas and some coffee. At that time, the foragers still followed a nomadic lifestyle, and when that hamlet's occupants moved to another place, Musa and his family stayed on, eventually building a brick-and-mortar house. During the first several months of their residence in the hamlet, before the foragers left, Musa and his family befriended one couple in particular, Kochikalan and his wife, with whom they maintained close relations well into 1979. I observed Musa's children fishing with Kochikalan's children; Musa hunting with Kochikalan (several times); Kochikalan and his wife attending Musa's daughter's marriage; and Musa's wife attending Kochikalan's daughter's birth (which she did, she explained to me, in accordance with "Nayaka custom"). Musa's advice was always well received by Kochikalan and his wife; for example, when Kochikalan's wife's sister died, Musa advised and helped her son to buy a cow with the gratuity money the family got from the plantation where the deceased had been working on and off.

Mathew, the second migrant I profile, was a Syrian Christian from Kerala who had come to the Gorge in 1955, leaving his family in his natal village and returning to visit them once or twice a year. By a bureaucratic quirk, the barely viable, isolated plantation in the Gorge was classified by the state as an "industry" (it started as a rubber plantation) and was obligated to keep employment and pay records for all workers. Mathew's job was to keep records of the workers' marriages, births, and deaths as well as of their attendance at work and their pay. Life on the plantation, "far from anywhere," as he described it, was monotonous for Mathew, and he looked forward to the daily mail, brought down through the forest from Pandalur, for diversion. The life of the native inhabitants, a few of whom worked as casual laborers on the plantation, was a source of constant interest for him. In another life, he could perhaps have been an anthropologist. He delved into the foragers' personal lives and their kinship and residential connections far beyond the call of duty, with a bookkeeper's eye for detail. Their lives provided him much-appreciated diversion from his tedious and repetitive days in the out-of-the-way Gorge. When they did not come to work, he went to their hamlets to find out why and to urge them to come. He contributed to and participated in their "big visits." He was closest to Chathen, who worked as the watchman on the plantation. The two had afternoon chats each day before Chathen returned to his home. One episode illustrating their close tie involves the cow that Musa had helped Kochikalan's nephew buy. This story, which unfolded over several months during my fieldwork, is an ethnographic gold mine on many issues, but I tell it here to provide a sense of how locals engaged with the migrants (for more on the cow episode, see Naveh and Bird-David 2014).

This cow was, to the best of my knowledge, the first ever to be kept in any of the hamlets in the Gorge, if *kept* can even be used in this case, for the animal roamed freely in GR, with no one trying to milk it and everybody helping to feed it. It "lived with" GR people for several months, until the son of the deceased plantation worker, with whose gratuity money the cow had been bought, married a girl in DV and moved there to live with her and her relatives. He wanted to take the cow with him, but his relatives objected, especially Chathen, the deceased's elder brother. The cow had been living with them in GR, Chathen said, and it belonged to all of them, as one of them. Musa (who had advised acquiring the cow and who had helped buy it) was asked for his opinion, and he suggested the cow belonged to the deceased's husband. His suggestion made no local sense; the widower, in any case, was no longer living in GR (he had moved to MR in search of a new partner). Musa then got an offer from a trader in Pandalur to buy the cow, and he suggested that the residents of GR could divide the money from its sale among themselves. This proposal was rejected too; it was said that the cow was "living with us," was one of our own and, thus, could not be sold. (The cow was also regarded as a sort of keepsake of the deceased relative.) Finally, Mathew bought the cow, which was acceptable because of his close relationship with Chathen and other GR residents. He was "one of us" to a sufficient degree for everybody in GR to feel comfortable with the cow's move to his household, which was nearby.

The third migrant I focus on is Kumar, a Tamil man, one of the seasonal timber workers who camped near the so-called Depo (where the timber was stored until its pickup); their numbers fluctuated between one and several dozen, depending on the scale of timber work in the forest. He befriended Chathen's brother-in-law, who lived in GR and whom he frequently visited, sitting with him, his wife, and their daughter on their veranda. From my hut, a few meters down the hillside, I could hear their bursts of laughter, as they talked, joked, and shared betel nuts. A mean rumor spread among some migrants that Kumar had had an affair with the wife, but he simply enjoyed passing his free time with the couple and their daughter, and they all enjoyed his company as well.

These three migrants could hardly be more different in their own terms: a low-caste Keralite Muslim small landowner and shopkeeper; an educated Keralite Syrian Christian (effectively, the plantation boss); and a Hindu Tamil seasonal worker. Yet the foragers in the Gorge extended to all three their sense of *sonta*, doing so by means of what I call "*sonta* discourse." *Sonta* discourse included talking about interactions in terms of helping the migrants and being helped by them and in terms of being able "to visit them" and "sleep and eat with them" and, furthermore, to do the same with their relatives. For example, to express his closeness to Musa, Kungan told me he was helping Musa fence his household plot (downplaying the daily wage Musa paid him for this work). And, he said, he could eat and sleep at Musa's place, transitively extending these terms to Musa's relatives. If he asked Musa for something that Musa did not have, Kungan said, Musa would ask his relatives for it and give it to him. The last-mentioned idiom reflected Kungan's paradigmatic sense of relatives as pluripresent and plur-irelational, obligated each to all, so that sharing and helping had cascading effects. To a certain extent, *sonta* discourse can be understood as involving semiotic labor to include among "our own" co-others like the three migrants I have profiled.

Sonta discourse was also extended to more remote persons, and it was more striking at the edges of the local nanoworld. I observed this on the rare occasions that I walked with Kethan to Pandalur, when people would approach him to ask about me, as the sight of a white woman was rare in this far corner of the Nilgiris in those days (and still is today). Kethan was delighted with the attention and boasted to me about how well he knew these people. He could sleep and eat with them, he said, to make his point. Some of Kethan's relatives referred to the "government" in terms of *sonta* discourse. Complaining to me about the hardship "now, in these days," as I was tape-recording him, one man added, with great pathos, "With whom shall we go now to live? Shall we go and sleep with the government?" (Fred Myers [1986: 282–84], similarly, describes how Pintupi expect various government bodies and white people to "help" and "care for" them.) Such figures of speech also apply to the past. The short period during which Kethan's uncle and a few other relatives worked in the Nelliyalam Rani's elephant stables (see chapter 3) is recalled as the time they stayed with the Rani and she gave them food. Insofar as I could ascertain from contemporary records and interviews with the Rani's descendants, a few Nayaka men from the Gorge probably worked for a few years in the Rani's elephant stables. However, it is inconceivable that a member of a local feudal family of high caste, living in a place of immense grandeur in local terms, would have looked after the lowly tribal stable workers. Nayaka described this period in *sonta* discourse terms (see more in Bird-David 2004a).

Again, I turn to the "big visit" as a kind of potent litmus test detecting cultural patterns, an event that shows more than just semiotic means of including others among "our own." Everyone that GR people engaged with was asked to contribute money to help underwrite the "big visit" in GR (residents of other hamlets did the same in their turn). Everyone who was solicited was also invited to attend. In fact, anyone could attend—no one was excluded—but few wanted to come and could reach the dispersed tiny hamlets in the midst of the forest. In particular, Musa, Mathew, Kumar, and

I were all asked to contribute money toward the "big visit" to be held in GR. Mathew and I could and did give money, and during the spirit-possession sessions we were introduced to the visiting spirits as the new people who had brought offerings on that occasion. We were introduced—in terms of *sonta* discourse—as the new people who had come and joined the firstcomers, that is, not just coming to and dwelling *in* this place but dwelling *with* those already living together there. The logic underscoring *sonta* as a mode of "many" potentiated its extension to a substantial degree, freeing it to include instead of exclude others who are not "the same" as "we" are, to include others as diverse as "us" and so add to our diversity. *Sonta* consisted of relatives who, different though they may have been from one another, were proximate and plurirelated. Through plurirelational work, they became "us."

The migrants occupied the fuzzy end of *sonta* because they did not plurirelate with all local relatives but only with this or that Nayaka family, and they did not figure themselves as the foragers' relatives but only as their friends (they had other notions of kinship). For this reason, the migrants can be described (paraphrasing Turnbull and shifting to the forager viewpoint) as "wayward relatives."

SONTA AND NAYAKA IN THE GORGE

Our own [diverse] relatives (Take 5)

While Kethan and his relatives extended their concept of *sonta* and, then, their *sonta* discourse, to include migrants, migrants approached the foragers in a duplex way: individually, as kinds of friends, and collectively, as "Nayaka people" and, moreover, as a "forest people" and a "primitive tribe" (deploying labels commonly used in the region and in India generally). The migrants were not concerned about contradictions between the two views, if they were even aware of any. The foragers' and the migrants' two modes of pluralizing were, to use Eyal Ben-Ari's words, "continually produced and reproduced despite different interpretations of these same relations by the participants" (1987: 168).

The migrant population was heterogeneous; though two-thirds were Mappila (a poor Muslim caste), they had come from nine different villages in Kerala. Living in the out-of-the-way forested Gorge, the migrant families mingled with one another. The adults worked together on the plantation and socialized after work in the small tea shack run by a few enterprising laborers. Their children grew up together. Hypothetically, the migrants and their families might have been expected to develop the same sense of belonging with one another that Kungan and his relatives did. However, they primarily saw themselves as members of large-scale imagined communities; the Gorge figured as a small place, a detail in the large canvasses of their imaginations. The migrants conceived of themselves in terms of their places of origin (Kerala, Tamil Nadu, their specific villages), their ethnicities and religions (Mappila Muslim, Hindu, and Christian), their "mother tongues" (Malayali, Tamil), and in occupational class terms (plantation laborers). They collectivized indigenous inhabitants of the Gorge as "Nayaka" and, correspondingly, themselves as "non-Nayaka." A neater textbook case for a symbolic construction of community (e.g., Cohen 2000) can hardly be imagined. The migrants unified their diverse and unrelated selves by means of the Nayaka as Other. They generated a sense of "sameness" beyond their common locale in contrast to the Nayaka, alongside and sometimes overriding the close interpersonal relations some of them had with individual Nayaka.

Consider what Musa told me in the late 1970s about how the Nayaka had lived in the late 1950s, when he first arrived in the Gorge (the following is a summary, in which I attempt to retain the original rambling flavor):

> They did not bother about each other. They just collected food in the forest, each one to themselves. Even the children collected their own food and made themselves a small fire. And parents would come back from the forest, and their child was already asleep. If father and son sat near each other and one ate and the other did not, it did not matter. They did not quarrel. They did not bother about it. There were twenty families at that time. If death occurred, the entire hamlet moved. They did not bother about rain and sun, and just wandered everywhere. They only bothered about oil for their hair, which they got from selling honey. During those days, they found work for three to four months a year, clearing the shrubs between the rubber trees, and for the rest stayed in the forest.

In this account, as in others I heard from migrants, facts and fantasy mix together. No doubt, when Musa first met them, Kethan and his relatives had been more nomadic than in later years and had largely subsisted by foraging. His description becomes more questionable when it touches on local social life and, especially, family relationships. He depicts an anomic society, lacking bonding social ties: families who do not eat together and do not care for each other; homeless people who move aimlessly about; people with no concern for their economic security or that of their families. I heard other accounts that further accentuated what was constructed as primitiveness, describing how Nayaka slept in trees, were not scared by wild animals, and so on. All this Musa related, when, at the same time, he had lived with these people in their hamlet for several months, he had invited Kochikalan and his wife to his daughter's wedding, his wife had attended their grandson's birth, and his children had fished with their children. In his more learned style, Mathew, who enjoyed his afternoon chats with Chathen at the end of his workday, also regaled me with stories about "Nayaka customs," for example, that Nayaka nomadically moved to another site every year or so, that eloping with a woman into the forest was a customary Nayaka form of marriage, and that Nayaka believed in hill spirits. Mathew, Musa, and the other migrants had not met any Nayaka beyond the pluripresent locals in the Gorge. Nevertheless, they figured the individuals they had met as members of an imagined Nayaka tribe, an entity existing in India, expecting all its members, wherever they might be found, to typically have the same general characteristics and behaviors.

For their part, Kethan and his relatives keenly observed idiosyncratic distinctions unfolding in the Gorge among those plurally living there. At the same time, they were not inattentive to patterns—they observed what they called *palaka,* a word that I initially struggled to understand. After repeated attempts to get an explanation, I was delighted when, one day, Kethan volunteered the following: "For us," he said, "going with a *dhoti,* like this [pointing at his dress], is *palaka;* building huts with bamboo, like this [pointing at his hut], is *palaka.*" Then he added, pointing at my notebook, "For you, writing every day in this notebook is *palaka.*" Reflecting a little, he smilingly added, "Now, using this tape recorder [pointing to it] is *palaka* to me."

A content-free notion, *palaka* can be translated as "custom," although only in one of that word's two meanings, which easily blur in large-scale settings. Resonating with "path" (see chapter 2), "custom" means, firstly, a "habitual practice," which one is "accustomed to, habituated to, [has] become familiar with," and secondly, "a practice so long established that it has the force of law."[12] A collective of some sort is assumed in the second case, whereas in the first case no such body need exist. *Palaka* glosses patterns of behavior with some anticipated purchase in the future but that are not fixed and are open to change. The concept applies equally to one person and to few-many whom one can personally observe. When applied to few-many, *palaka* describes neither what they do as a collective nor a standardized behavior that all must follow but what each, individually, chooses to do, again and again. *Palaka* is of a kind with the notions of *nachika* (avoidance, reticence; see chapter 3), *budi* (~ social skill, tact; see chapter 4), and *aaita* and *tapu* (~ offenses and mistakes; see chapter 5), all of them situational, relational, and personal.

Mathew had a printed map in his office showing the boundaries of his plantation and the other plantations in the region, and he also had a map in his mind showing ethnic boundaries. In the 1970s, Kethan and his relatives had no map showing distinct bounded territories and no mental map of ethnic groups and divisions. They moved along paths of relations, their pluripersonal itineraries constituting their *sonta*. *Sonta*, firstly, is not constituted by boundaries marking insiders off from outsiders, in the complex Euro-American cultural sense. Barth (2000) has suggested that groups can be conceptualized by other means, citing as one option the nomadic Basseri of Persia, who move as a herd, "as a body through open space." *Sonta* presents yet another option, the image "good to think" here being a hearth around which people gather and plurirelate, connoting immediate-to-horizon, close-to-distant, and (almost literally) warm-to-cold vectors of belonging. *Sonta*, secondly, is not constituted by constructing an Other in contrast to whom a group's members are recognized by their perceived sameness. Kethan and his relatives' cultural effort is not invested in sorting people into different "kinds," in imagining series of ethnic beings that they perceive as somehow identical to each other. Their attention is attuned to those vivid beings (of all sorts) with whom they share the same place, attentive to *convivial* life-together (borrowing Overing and Passes's [2000] term), those with whom they (metaphorically) plurirelate around the same hearth. In Lévi-Strauss's picturesque terms—which, so extended, reveal the peculiarity of universalizing groups as collectives with selves and bodies—the *sonta* community is neither anthropophagic nor anthropoemic but, one could say, instead, commensal. *Sonta* encompasses vivid dissimilar beings, whose singularities and distinctions continuously unfold. In the next chapter, I explore locals' changing plural modes and imaginations as they accommodate themselves to each other.

7. The State's Foragers

The Scale of Multiculturalism

One day in 1998 I received an e-mail from an engineer working in Tiruchipalli who, to my astonishment, introduced himself as a Nayaka. He was interested in the anthropology of his people, he wrote, and requested copies of my publications. Straightaway, I sent him a dozen articles, and at the first opportunity, after a spell of fieldwork with Kungan's relatives in 2001, I made the eight-hour train journey from the Nilgiris to Tiruchipalli to meet him. From that city's Central Railway Station we traveled by bus for two hours or so to his natal village, which turned out to be a collection of shabby houses surrounded by agricultural fields amid the vast Tamil Plains. Dozens of men, women, and children awaited us. As we made our way to the village center, they surrounded us, the youngsters pushing each other to get as close as they could, daring each other to inspect my gear and urging me to videotape them. The crowd eventually parted to make way for several older men carrying hunting and snaring equipment. Making sure my video camera was on, they exhibited this equipment, the crowd cheering and hailing them. Then, amid growing hilarity, the men demonstrated their traditional hunting method, a young man enacting an animal chased by hunters into a net. I was still catching my breath from this episode, when, followed by the throng, I was led to a small hut and shown idols and other ritual paraphernalia arranged on shelves and on the floor. My engineer host—whom I call Rajiv—stayed by my side at all times and constantly commented on what we saw. He frequently directed my attention to the resemblance between what we were looking at and what I had described in my articles (in this or that publication, he specified, at times citing page numbers). Back at the railway station at the end of the day, he asked me if I could write a report testifying that his community was Kattunayaka.

When Rajiv wrote to me, nobody in the Gorge was familiar with the indigenous political context that was evolving in large-scale legislative and judicial arenas far from the Nilgiri-Wynaad forests. Pluriscaling my perspective, in this final chapter I explore these arenas and focus on changing imaginations of belonging. I broaden my analytical lens to include the state of India (about 2.4 percent of the world's land mass and home in 2014 to 17.5 percent of the world's population)—its administrators, policy makers, lawyers, and anthropologists—and the tens of thousands of people claiming to be Kattunayaka within India's scale-blind multicultural distributive justice system. The rapidly growing number of these claimants has become a major concern for the state, and here I consider the practical as much as the theoretical need to recognize diverse ontological modes of communal belonging and to acknowledge the scalability of inclusiveness. I especially explore the conflicting plural imaginations instantiated in the state's "Scheduled Tribe" mode and the foragers' "us, relatives" mode, the first replicating the "national" style of imagining communities and the second reflecting an alternative style. Within this chapter's multiscalar analysis, the concept of pluripresence and the issues created by scholarship's scalar blindness not only are further sharpened but also gain relevance in broader discussions of indigeneity and multiculturalism.

· · ·

Accompanying Rajiv to his natal village was a dizzying experience, to say the least: a sort of reverse spirit possession, in which the anthropologist was made to perform herself, and her anthropological writings were invoked as the spirits to be engaged with (cf. Rabinow 2007; Bilu 2000). This encounter was a reminder that, at the end of the day, ethnographers of even the tiniest communities write about them within—and write them into—large-scale anthropology, large-scale nations, and large-scale politics. Ethnonyms can travel far and claim new life beyond local horizons, playing a role within the large-scale imagined orders that encompass and affect local nanoworlds. An ethnonym can forge identity freed from pluripresence, the social linchpin of Kungan's world. When it does so, it can have unimagined, escalating consequences.

To explore these consequences and, more generally, multiscalar intersections of communal horizons and identities, I adopt a key analytical metaphor from Bruno Latour (2005): travel by roadway. Latour exploits the fact that different kinds of roads, from highways to country lanes, afford the traveler different speeds and panoramas, indeed, different experiences and senses of the surroundings. The driver's choice of roadway illustrates

Latour's assertion that scale/scaling is an actor's own achievement, performed through spacing and contextualizing (see the introduction).
Footpaths remain outside the template provided by Latour, an ethnographer of the (very large-scaled) "Moderns." My case requires me to add foot
travel (and attendant speed, panorama, and experience) to this analytical
allegory and to nudge readers to recall that highways, country roads, *and*
footpaths may intersect in urban and rural settings and, sometimes, in forests too. Major highways go through forests, and alongside and underneath
them footpath travel continues. I compare the pathway travel of *sonta* in
the Gorge and the highway travel of *Kattunayaka* in India at the turn of
the twenty-first century, focusing on actors' scalar work.

This expanded travel-based allegory offers a nuanced framework for
intervening in discussions of indigeneity, the state, and multiculturalism.
Ethnographers of hunter-gatherer-cultivators sometimes are accused of
ignoring the powerful influence of the state and overromanticizing the
autonomy of the local group, a close relative of the argument that they
overlook foragers' long-term contact with nonforaging peoples (see chapter
6). In her ethnography of the Meratus of Indonesia, people who could be
typed as forager-cultivators, Anna Lowenhaupt Tsing (1993) explored the
extent of state influence on them from their position as marginal "out-of-
the-way" people. She argued that their marginality was a factor that cru-
cially shaped their culture and lifeways (as well as affording the anthropologist unique analytical perspectives on the state). Her "out-of-the-way"
viewpoint evoked the highway running between the state's center and its
margins but did not explicitly articulate what her ethnography also richly
showed: that the Meratus's world of mountain pathways exists alongside
and also intersects with the (metaphorical) state highway.[1] Tsing (2005)
went on to develop a multiscalar analytical framework in a subsequent ethnography that focused on Meratus rainforests, their exploitation, and the
intervention of environmentalist movements, in which she insightfully
examined how local, national, and global scale-making projects intersect.
Such a multiscalar viewpoint can provide a nuanced perspective on indigenous peoples who are *at once* forager-cultivators and marginal subjects of
the state.

For me, Tsing's account of choosing an ethnonym for her group strongly
suggests the fruitfulness of extending a multiscalar approach to the study of
small forager-cultivator groups incorporated within contemporary nation-
states. Tsing's study people were called Bukti by their Banjar neighbors, a
name connoting "hillbilly" and insulting to them. Searching for another
name, she consulted with her research assistant, Bingan Sabda (the first of

his people, to her knowledge, to have gained a postgraduate education). They agreed on the name Meratus for strikingly different, if not contrary, reasons. Tsing favored Meratus "because it refers to Dayak inhabitants of the Meratus Mountains" (1993: 52), deriving the ethnonym from a nationally known place-name (a reasonable choice in a nationalist era, when names of population and territory often coincide) yet, from my standpoint, serializing and standardizing the population by reference to a replicable Meratus person. For his part, Bingan Sabda approved of it because, for him, "*Meratus*, with its root *ratus* ('hundreds') evokes the diversity of the people"; he liked Meratus, he said, as "a kind of *anti-ethnic* label, a label for a group of people who are all *very different* from each other" (ibid., my emphasis). His reason would have appealed to Kungan's plural sensibilities.

In postcolonial states, indigenous subjects who claim recognition as such paradoxically face an impossible standard when it comes to demonstrating that they are bearers of authentic traditional culture (Povinelli 2002). This said (and I could have used my experience with Rajiv to support and pursue this line of argument), my further concern in this chapter is the obliviousness to scalar disparity at the base of multiculturalism and the attendant universalization of the ethnonymic grammar of plural life. Multicultural discourse and policy are based on the tenet of equal treatment of all cultures, which translates into a "whole-and-parts" social language—and, I would add, into a language of "One and ones," in which the "whole" is personified and its "parts" are always serialized, whatever the scale of the group. Members of the group are regarded as persons of the same cultural/ethnic kind; their kind matters regardless of where they are or with whom. In this multiculturalist register, for example, there exist separate Kattunayaka persons who can live anywhere, one conceivably in the Nilgiris and another 300 kilometers away in Tiruchipalli (or, stretching the point, 2,250 kilometers away in Delhi, or 8,000 kilometers away in Cambridge). In the name of cultural equity, indigenous communities' alternative and subversive styles of imagining themselves and their scalabilities are denied. As I show below, even when an indigenous population undergoes an apparently rapid exponential increase, as has happened in the Kattunayaka case, false claims of identity are suspected, not the faultiness of an identity's presumed ontological basis.

India provides a particularly interesting case for intervening in discussions of indigeneity, the state, and multiculturalism. Postcolonial India imagines itself a pluralistic society. Cultural diversity is its cornerstone (Khilnani 1997; Kholi 2001), and in some views its constitution is a multiculturalist text (Bhargava, Bagghi, and Sudarshan 1999; Rudolph and

Rudolph 2002). Its diversity is governmentalized by a massive distributive justice system embedded in the constitution. This system includes extending affirmative-action advantages to Scheduled Tribes (STs), Scheduled Castes (SCs), and Other Backward Classes (OBCs); prominent among these advantages are employment quotas in government posts, reserved places in institutions of higher education, and special "tribal" development packages. The so-called race to the bottom by many marginalized communities who claim ST status is propelled not only by the lure of the benefits accruing to it but also by a desire to establish a firm anchor in Indian society through ethnopolitical recognition of indigeneity (see Shani 2011: 307–9). This "race" has resulted so far in recognition of over seven hundred STs, and an estimated one thousand communities are currently vying for recognition (Middleton 2013: 13).

The official list of STs goes back to the 1930s and is based on descriptions of tribes living in India compiled during the course of the comprehensive survey started by the British in the nineteenth century and continued by the Indian government after independence. The ambiguities local administrators and their employees encountered on the ground (see Downscale 5) were smoothed over the higher up the bureaucratic ladder indigenous ethnonyms traveled. From the shifting and situated local uses described in the previous chapter, ethnonyms climbed up well beyond the region, the district, and even the state level, to New Delhi itself. These ethnonyms—including those used by or for a few hundred or a few thousand people living in small, highly localized, dispersed communities—entered the all-India list of tribes that later were entitled to reservations. The list is managed and controlled in New Delhi. Authority to amend it is given to the central government in consultation with local states. The list is just that, a list of names recognized by state. Reading the entries, one can easily forget the origin of some at the improbable juncture (metaphorically speaking but, to some extent, also literally) of the tiniest possible jungle footpaths and the largest grid imagined by the functionaries of the British Raj, the points where local people, anthropologists, administrators, and policy makers intersected. Adding a new ethnonym to the official ST list, or even a differently prefixed name, is an immensely difficult administrative, legal, and political feat that can take decades (in some cases, over forty years; see Kapila 2008 on the Kangra Gaddis). The process involves all ranks of the state's hierarchy: from state-level research institutes, welfare departments, and chief minister's offices, through the federal-level Ministry of Tribal Affairs, Ministry of Law and Justice, and Ministry of Finance, right up to the upper and lower houses of Parliament and the president of India him- or herself.[2] Anthropologists play an active role in ST claims as government officers and expert witnesses (see Middleton 2011a, 2011b, 2013).

Minority mobilization for ST status has drawn scholarly attention in recent years,[3] and what I find especially striking about related studies is their unquestioned ethnonymic basis. These studies are consistent both with India's scale-blind governmentality of cultural diversity and with anthropology's scale-blind regime. The Indian constitution lists STs by ethnonym, state by state, without regard for a group's population size, even though some STs are tiny communities of hunting and food-gathering people, and the strings of names by which they are known, variously prefixed and spelled, clearly hint at the confusion surrounding their designation by others. The constitution's list of names is the touchstone of the vibrant and volatile political discourse swirling around STs in India, and it is also the undisputed basis of ethnographic study of the ST phenomenon. Related research includes case studies of the Gorkha of Darjeeling (Middleton 2011a), the Gaddis of the Western Himalayas (Kapila 2008), and the Dhanka of Rajasthan (Moodie 2015). Consistent with ethnographic precedent, scale does not figure prominently in these works—one has to search for the one or two lines that refer to population size (e.g., see Moodie 2015: 9; Kapila 2008: 123; and general discussion in the introduction).

Scale-blind studies of ST claims in India have dwelled on "governmental epistemologies of identity" (Middleton 2011b). For example, Townsend Middleton (2013) has studied government anthropologists tasked with verifying the identity of groups claiming ST status in Darjeeling. He analyzes the "classificatory moment," including how those anthropologists "deploy, demand, and ultimately instantiate" particular ethnographic forms and develop their own unofficial guide for recognizing authentic tribalness (see also Kapila 2008). In line with the general study of indigeneity claims in a multiculturalist era (e.g., Povinelli 2002), I think that anthropologists examining ST claims in India need to critically examine (paraphrasing Middleton) the "governmental ontologies of identity" that are unthinkingly extended to the indigenous subject. That is, beyond studying how peoples are governmentally recognized to have "authentic" culture, it is important to also study alternative modes of "being people." The latter has been one of my main concerns throughout this book, and here it emerges as pertinent to yet another context of study.

My case provides a good basis for me to explore governmental ontologies of identity. Unlike previous studies of ST claims, which have focused largely on "new" groups, (i.e., groups petitioning for indigenous recognition and for their names to be added to the official ST list), my study concerns the case of applicants claiming membership in an already recognized ST—"Kattunayaka," a name that appears in the original constitution list. In fact, the Gorge's foragers are recognized not only as an ST but also as one of the most disadvantaged of such groups, a PTG (Particularly Vulnerable Tribal Group; originally, Primitive Tribal Group). In this chapter, then, I scale-sensitively examine Rajiv's effort to claim Kattunayaka ST status. His case brings into sharp relief the contrast between the forager ontological mode of communal belonging and the universalized idea of "community" that underscores India's multiculturalist policy of distributive justice and the issue of scalability.

THE STATE'S JUNGLE OF ETHNONYMS

Multiscaled plural life (Take 1)

Rajiv's initial ambition was to achieve ST status to access higher education. He lived and operated in a world in which his official recognition as a member of an ST could assist him in fulfilling this ambition and affect his social and economic prospects. He had fought for such recognition for over two decades, pursuing it and related entailments up the administrative and juridical ladder to the Supreme Court in New Delhi. He did so with great determination and growing knowledge of this institutional world. He approached me at the end of the 1990s, when he was well into the process. By then he had deeply immersed himself in the relevant anthropological literature and had even thought about establishing a Kattunayaka tribal museum in his home village. He was concerned about the flood of what he regarded as "bogus" applications for recognition of Kattunayaka status.

There are many ways to view cases like Rajiv's. My interest here lies in the cultural logic that his case (and others I know of) displays and how it leads to an ethnic vertigo, to viral multiplication of the ethnic identity carried by an individual (wherever he or she goes, among or beyond others of his or her imagined community). My interest also extends to the absurd entailments generated by confusing plural scales and overlooking the work and effects of scaling. I begin with Rajiv's experience of the immensely complex bureaucratic jungle that has grown up in India around affirmative-action advantages, popularly known as reservations, that accrue to ST status.

Hundreds of densely populated kilometers from the Gorge, Rajiv's natal community is known as Dellanayaka (*Della-* is a fictive prefix). The seemingly small difference between the prefixes *Kattu-* and *Della-* has serious implications in Tamil Nadu. The first entitles Rajiv to a reserved place in higher-education institutions and in certain workplaces, and the second does not. Among Kungan and his relatives, one was "our own" in all respects by joining and living *with* "us"—with "all of us," the plurality of relatives—not just one or another person. This performative, relational, and plural basis of belonging superseded and accommodated individual differences of origin and kind, extending to other humans and nonhumans alike (see chapters 5 and 6). In Tamil Nadu, a state of close to 74 million (in 2013),[4] reservations cannot, of course, be administered on such a basis. To qualify for entitlements, Rajiv had to *prove* that he belonged to an appropriate ST community, evidenced by what is called in India a "community certificate."

Paradoxically, the Nilgiri foragers who are called Kattunayaka were not even close to understanding what the reservations entitled them to, as options or even fantasies, when Rajiv applied for a Kattunayaka community certificate in the 1980s. It was still the case in 2012 that no one living in GR and TM had more than a few years of primary education. The same is probably true today for other originally listed STs, and especially those few, like the Kattunayaka, who are designated PTGs. For the most part, they are communities of traditionally hunting and food-gathering people.

Rajiv too is faced with the cross-scale irony of the system. As I mention above, adding a new ethnonym to the official ST list, or even a differently prefixed name, is an immensely difficult administrative, legal, and political feat that involves all ranks of the state's hierarchy and can take decades. If people like Rajiv want to benefit from the reservations, an easier choice, on the face of things, is to prove that they belong to an already listed ST, and this involves applying for an ST community certificate. "Kattunayaka," an official entry on the ST list, is, in Christoph von Fürer-Haimendorf's words (see Downscale 5), "one of those tribal names which have done so much to obscure the ethnic picture of many Indian regions" and, in fact, even states. The Constitution (Schedule Tribe) Order of 1950 includes multiple entries for Nayaka/Kattunayaka (in one spelling or another, prefixed this way or that) in Tamil Nadu (item 9: "Kattunayakan") and in no fewer than five other states: Kerala (item 9: "Kattunayakan"); Karnataka (item 20: "Kattunaykan" and item 38: "Naikda, Nayaka, Chollivala Nayaka, Kapadia Nayaka, Mota Nayaka, Nana Nayaka"); Andhra Pradesh (item 13: "Kattunaykan"); Maharashtra (item 35: "Naikda, Nayaka, Cholivala Nayaka, Kapadia Nayaka, Mota Nayaka, Nana Nayaka"); and, Rajasthan (item 10: "Naikda, Nayaka, Cholivala Nayaka, Kapadia Nayaka, Mota Nayaka, Nana Nayaka"). As if this plethora were not enough to complicate the appellatory jungle through which applicants like Rajiv must work their way, Naik and Naiken are terms by which various castes are known in South India. Recall also that these terms derive from a Sanskrit word meaning "leader" or "chief" and that Nayaka was the name of various ruling dynasties in South India in the seventeenth century (see Downscale 5).

Rajiv applied for a certificate recognizing him as Kattunayaka. He had never visited the Nilgiris; he had never met any of the local people known there as Kattunayaka. Moreover, he did not know more than a few of the more than 20,000 people already registered in Tamil Nadu as Kattunayaka when he applied for the certificate. According to census figures, the number of registered Kattunayaka rose from 5,042 in 1971 to 26,383 in 1981. More than half of those enrolled were urban dwellers, and only 1,245 were living in the Nilgiris (Singh 1994: 483). In 2001, their numbers had nearly doubled, reaching 45,221.[5]

In the course of his two-decades-long mission, Rajiv met a host of officials, professionals, functionaries, and anthropologists. The persons he engaged with, sometimes face-to-face, "spoke for" and "represented" large-scale entities: the courts, the government, the tribal association, the anthropological community, and so on. He engaged with them interpersonally, but his claim was for membership not in their communities but in a community he and his interlocutors coimagined. Those with whom he dealt were, for him, "faces" of the system, individuals he approached as occupants of institutional positions but who, now and then, for brief moments, were also persons he closely engaged with, including me (we have kept in touch since we first met in 1998). He fought for inclusion in very different terms from those forming the basis for joining Kungan's pluripresent forest community.

Around the impossible juncture between the tiniest jungle footpaths and the all-India highway grid, there evolved a weird institutional praxis and culture according to whose terms Rajiv had to work, the terms by which belonging to an ethnic group was authorized (or not). I cannot do justice in a few sentences to the highly complicated and still-evolving bureaucratic and legal system intended to keep in check the growing flood of applications for ST community certificates. People who, like Rajiv, end up pursuing their cases in court hire lawyers to help them through the corridors and past the hurdles of the judicial system, during which their cases are subjected to the legal code of evidence. My take on this complex process focuses on the special terminology developed and used in these procedures.

People like Rajiv are "applicants" in this system. They apply for "community certificates" stating their tribal affiliation. Their applications have to be approved by "competent authorities," the prerogative over the years of ever-higher-ranking officials on the administrative ladder. In Tamil Nadu, for example, following a change in the law in 2007, this authority was taken away from the district collector, as it previously had been from tahsildars and revenue divisional officers/subcollectors. A State Level Scrutiny Committee (SLTC) now deals with claims for ST community certificates, and includes no less than the secretary to the department of Adi Dravidar and Tribal Welfare (chairman) and the director/commissioner of Tribal Welfare (member secretary); an anthropologist also serves as a member. Appeals concerning its decisions can only be made to the High Court of Tamil Nadu and, then, the Supreme Court in New Delhi.[6] The charter of the committee speaks for itself: the SLTC is to "scrutinize" and "ascertain" if a claim for ST status is "genuine," "doubtful," or "spurious," if a claim is "falsely" or "wrongly" made, or if a certificate is "falsely" or "wrongly" issued. If the certificate obtained or social status claimed is found to be fraudulent, a "prosecution" follows for making a "false claim." As the offense is regarded as involving moral turpitude, conviction is grounds for disqualification from elective posts or offices in any local body or state legislature or in the national parliament.

"Belonging to a community" at this scalar level has become a matter of certification and also an issue of binaries: yes/no, in/out, true/false. It is an individually based claim, filtered through the image of a community, an imagined community that rebounds on the individual. Ironically, there are echoes here of the "follow-and-join" logic at work in the forager community but operating at another scale of abstraction and in a complicated, hybrid way. If Rajiv succeeds in his claim and secures a community certificate recognizing him as Kattunayaka, then it will be easier for his relatives and other community members to do so, drawing on his case in claiming their own individual entitlements.

THE STATE DEFINES THE "REAL" KATTUNAYAKA

Multiscaled plural life (Take 2)

One might think that securing an official grant of membership in a community, a yes/no binary decision, would take far less time than becoming "one of us," one of the forest forager community, a process achieved through living-with, togetherness, and pluripresence. One would be wrong. Rajiv's experience shows how complicated the process can be. Rajiv initially was granted a Kattunayaka community certificate. But the authority of the district officer (tashildar) who issued it was later questioned. Rajiv had already enrolled in an institution of higher education under an ST quota when this occurred. He argued that he had appealed for a legitimate certificate and would provide it when available, and on that basis, he continued his studies. The certificate was still pending when Rajiv graduated and was given a quota job in a large company. He was employed, again on the understanding that he would shortly provide his community certificate. Two decades passed. Rajiv was promoted several times. Now his promotions, salary, and future pension were entangled with his receiving the long-awaited community certificate. He was reaching retirement when his complicated legal suit reached the Supreme Court in New Delhi and was finally resolved.

I pause at only one point in this long and complex battle, the point at which a district collector decreed that Rajiv belonged to a certain Hindu community and was not Kattunayaka. Rajiv did not speak the dialect associated with the recognized ST, a point against him. But Rajiv appealed to the high court in Chennai, which overruled the district collector's objection on the grounds that there could be many reasons, such as educational advancement and migration, for a person being unable to speak the language of his "native" community. A similar case reported in the *Hindu* (November 27, 2009) amplifies the priority given in court to previous certificates over command of language. A lower-ranking official had issued a Kattunayaka certificate that was later canceled on the grounds of "a negative opinion" given by an anthropologist who pointed out that the applicant did not speak his community's language. The Chennai High Court did not accept the cancellation on those grounds and, instead, gave priority to the voluminous community certificates of the applicant's brothers, sisters, and other relatives and, especially, an early primary school certificate of an older brother that gave his ethnic affiliation as Kattunayaka.

Rajiv did not just provide school certificates of relatives. He also compiled, he wrote to me, "a big report containing the Anthropological analysis," which, he explained, was based on "your literature" (i.e., my publications) and on books in Tamil citing my work and that of others. The main points he extracted from these studies are illuminating; they look outlandish to outsiders but are consistent with the legal/administrative code of evidence. The first is the similarity of the shorthand ethnonym used in his locality and that appearing in the anthropological studies: Dellanayaka are locally known as Nayaka, just as, anthropologists have shown, the Nilgiris Kattunayaka, the indisputable ST, are. The second point is similarity of "profession": the Dellanayaka traditionally hunted animals and birds (in addition to other pursuits), and anthropologists describe the Kattunayaka "profession" to be hunting and gathering. Lastly, anthropologists describe the Nilgiris Kattunayaka as nomadic: arguably, their peripatetic descendants could by now have made their way more than 300 kilometers from the tribe's "homeland" to the area where the Dellanayaka live.

Authenticating ST community membership involves more than ethnonyms and state-issued certificates. "Culture" can play a serious role too, especially the first time a claim is made, when there are no preexisting certificates to draw on. Within the complex praxis of issuing community certificates, accepted procedures have evolved for proving cultural "authenticity," including the use of anthropologists as expert witnesses (recall that the Tamil Nadu government also employs them as mandatory members of the committees authorizing or denying claims). The official constitutional criteria that provide the basis for these procedures reflect how early to mid-twentieth-century legislators envisioned unprivileged groups in need of "upliftment": "primitive traits," "distinctive culture," "geographical isolation," "shyness of contact with public at large," and "backwardness—social and economic."[7] Unofficial criteria now guiding anthropologists in the Registrar General of India Office include demarcated territory, use of primitive technology, animist or totemic religion, and practice of endogamy (see Kapila 2008: 131). I turn to another case for a sense of the format (Rajiv's claim was resolved without recourse to it).

The applicant in the case lives near Maduari, 350 kilometers from the Gorge. The anthropologist submitting expert testimony in his case is Dr. P., head of a government tribal research center situated high in the Nilgiri Hills yet far removed from the sloping Nilgiri-Wynaad valleys where Kattunayaka people live. Like Rajiv, Dr. P. works within a system he did not help create but whose reproduction he contributes to. His four-page report on the applicant's case, submitted to court in 2003,[8] has all the trimmings of an official document, with government and case reference numbers at the top. The title is "A Report on Community Tribal Status (Case Study)," and the findings are summed up as "Ethnography of the Community and Other Particulars of the Case." The report states that the ethnography is based on a one-day visit to the applicant's community, 215 houses in so-and-so town. The anthropologist visited the applicant at his house, toured the area with him, and then went with him to another house to meet fourteen informants (all individually named in the report). The informants, all men, were interviewed as a group about "their culture and society." On the basis of what they said, the anthropologist reports that the community's members were once nomads who gradually became seminomads after settling in villages and towns. They speak the Telugu language but read and write in Tamil. The men append the title "Naicken" to their names. They use traditional hunting implements to catch birds and jackals. The anthropologist testifies that he inspected each house and found everyone to have hunting implements. He goes on to describe their social structure (e.g., division into endogamous groups; exogamous marriage; child marriage; marriage by capture, by elopement, by service, and sometimes by negotiation), their political system, their life rituals, their Hindu beliefs, and so on, going through the standard old-fashioned ethnological rubrics (again, all within a four-page report). The conclusion is unequivocal: "The above narrated ethnographic details of the studied community in cultural anthropological frame work reveal that this community is having the characteristics of a Schedule Tribe called as Kattunayakans or KattuNaickens. So the appellant belong to the Kattunayakan's community."

THE ANTHROPOLOGIST'S (DIS)SERVICE TO THE STATE

Multiscaled plural life (Take 3)

An anthropologist should be circumspect when working in a country other than his or her own and should respect its traditions—to a degree. I am spared the dilemma of how to remark on these kinds of reports by minutes (easily found online) of discussions on the matter by the highest authorities in India.[9] The secretary of the National Commission for Scheduled Tribes (NCST) in New Delhi came to Chennai on an official visit (January 7–9, 2014) to discuss verification of tribal identity and related issues with the Tamil Nadu director of Tribal Welfare. The meeting was also attended by a Madras University anthropologist, a former director of the tribal research center in Ooty, a law officer, and representatives of *two* Kattunayaka tribal welfare associations. One of these Kattunayaka tribal welfare associations operated in Vellore (a more than eight-hour drive from the Nilgiris) and the other in Mylapore (a further two-and-a-half-hour drive, the town being located a few kilometers from Chennai). All the attendants expressed deep concern over "the extraordinary increase" in the number of persons officially granted ST status, especially but not only as Kattunayakas. The contribution of anthropologists to this increase is bluntly pointed out: "Various communities with convenient prefixes to their names were making claims of belonging to ST communities and in this matter, different anthropologists were offering divergent interpretations. This had created considerable problems particularly in respect of Kattunayakans who were only available in the Nilgiris" (2). "Some of the anthropologists have not understood the scope of the Acts or were acting at the instance of partisan interests and they had consequently erred in their recommendation" (5). The NCST secretary himself suggested that the state government "should be more circumspect in the kind of anthropologists they appoint to the State Level Scrutiny Committee and avoid those who had committed such errors on previous occasions and who had now become the focus of complaints" (5).

The viral spread of "Kattunayakaness" can be judgmentally or cynically viewed and the motives of actors such as Dr. P. and Rajiv questioned. The phenomenon may be compared with "convenience" applications for citizenship in many contemporary nation-states, for example, through fictive marriages or descent from immigrant citizens. The case can even be compared, as an academic issue, with recourse in the United States to "blood quantum laws" for determining membership in Native American nations (based on the Indian Reorganization Act of 1934, which variously stipulates one-half, one-quarter, one-eighth, or one-sixteenth blood quantum for membership in listed tribes; see Spruhan 2006). The anthropologist can observe that applicants in the United States and India submit, respectively, genealogical evidence and reports on their community's culture, reflecting the difference between Western egocentric and Asian sociocentric senses of self (e.g., see Nisbett 2004) and an American individualistic ethos (and genetic sense of kinship) at odds with an Indian sense of primary belonging to a caste/group within a hierarchical structure. However, the explosion in validation of ST claims also should alert professional anthropologists to the need to critically examine—beyond the malpractice and poor judgment of this or that particular practitioner—their own theoretical paradigm.

I contend that, through its scale-blind confusion of the pluripresent and imagined modes of plurality, anthropology is an accomplice in creating this ethnic vertigo in India. The "population explosion" in India's hunter-gatherer-cultivator communities originates in the naming of these communities and in indifference to the existence and effects of distinctive scalar conditions at the tiny end of the social spectrum. It is fed by the sanctioning of ethnonyms as markers of communal identity, whatever the community, including the one whose members we-designate as *sonta*, as "our own, our relatives." Using an ethnonym for such a community reifies "our [diverse-and-related] own" as an entity-in-the-world and creates the basis for popular and legal discussions of individually based criteria of belonging, for distinguishing between real and spurious claims, and for debating the authenticity of a "group's" culture. Tiny communities end up subjected to the ontological terms of the "imagined community" mode of plurality, their own terms overlooked. Anthropologists could, instead, explore clashing ontologies of "being many" in multiculturalist India. I do so here by focusing on the ontology underscoring the idea of Kattunayaka, which mirrors modern national ideas of society and is the inverse of the foragers' we-imagination as *sonta*.

As I argue throughout this book, *sonta* describes relatives dwelling together, whose all-with-all relations are the essence of social life. They constantly work at these relations, at relations connecting each with (almost) all of the others. They engender these relations through a whole range of everyday practices and cultural traditions, from their mode of domicile and perpetual visiting to modes of child care, conjugality, and siblingship; subsistence; and spirit possession and animism. I have used the term *pluripresence* to characterize the essence and condition of their communal practice and of their cultural project and ideal. Its scalar implications are crucial and should be kept in mind. A mode of we-ness and shared identity that subsists in all-with-all relations, that is perpetuated through such plurirelations, and that depends on each being-*with* the others, it is at once elastic and limited. A community that perceives and defines itself in this way can include beings *of all sorts* but cannot grow beyond certain limits (whether because of neurological restrictions, as Dunbar [1993] proposes, or simply because of pragmatic considerations: one cannot live full-time with and perpetually visit more than a certain number of relatives).[10] Against this plural mode, the three most common "proofs" raised in court by applicants for Kattunayaka status are jarring. The Nilgiri Kattunayaka sense of community did not primarily reside in the ethnonym—an outsider term, in any case. It did not primarily inhere in hunting as a shared and characteristic "occupation" or "profession"—Kungan and his relatives sanctioned diversity, and in fact, they engaged in hunting far less than they did honey collecting and foraging. Their "nomadism" was not about moving *away* from their home area but about visiting and being-with relatives, human and nonhuman, and by this means, constituting and co-constituting their community. By this praxis, and by imaginaries that are not far extended beyond immediate bodily horizons, they scaled their community down to those who were pluripresent (or who visited).

The secretary of the NCST made an insightful suggestion, noted in the minutes of the January 2014 meeting in Chennai, that begins to speak to the local plural mode and we-imagination. He suggested that "the burden of proof *[of belonging to the community]* was not fulfilled merely upon production of an ST certificate issued to some relatives but there should be a clear connection between the person and the community which had been made entitled originally in the Presidential Orders of 1950/1956" (2, my emphasis). "Clear connection" can be understood by reference to Kungan's response, when I once asked him who is a Nayaka ("Naiken"), and he responded, "Those who live with us, like us, in our *sime*," referring not to sameness of look, origin, or any other attribute but, recursively, to all those living and engaging together (see chapter 6). His suggestion begins to scale down the government's concept of "authorized Kattunayaka" to the real dimensions of life among tiny indigenous groups and to respect their mode of pluripresent community over the mode of imagined community. Under the latter mode, the registered number of Kattunayaka has increased to more than forty thousand, each of whom has relatives who can also claim this ethnic status, as can their children, present and future. Under the pluripresent mode, the community is constantly scaled down to those who live with (or continually visit) clusters of close relatives. The imagined and pluripresent modes are, respectively, large-scaling and small-scaling projects. If anthropology takes serious notice of the tiny scale of indigenous traditional worlds and their plural modes, rather than contribute to the viral spread of Kattunayakaization, it could contribute to checking it. Doing so would go a long way toward redressing its role as an accomplice in rewriting ethnic reality in Tamil Nadu. Multiscalar anthropology, then, could help clarify murky and complex issues surrounding reservations in India and, perhaps, similar issues elsewhere, as well as a host of other state-indigenous matters.

THE LARGE-SCALE ENTERS THE GORGE

Multiscaled plural life (Take 4)

Paul Nadasdy (2012) argues that having to make their territorial claims in a language intelligible to agents of the Canadian state—a language, in that case, of territorial sovereignty—has seriously devalued Yukon First Nation peoples' forms of sociopolitical organization and propelled unintended radical change of their societies. I fear that claiming rights in the state's language of "groupism" (see Brubaker 2004 and discussion in the introduction) could have much the same effect in India on tiny communities of relatives like Kungan's.[11]

It cannot be overstated that Kungan's people had *not* lived in isolation before the state and NGOs entered the Nilgiri-Wynaad areas in the late 1980s. Their representatives are just the latest arrivals in a long history of incomers into the Gorge's surroundings (see Bird-David 1994b, 2004b). One need only recall the two Scots who established the rubber plantation at the bottom of the Gorge in the mid-nineteenth century; the hundreds of prospectors who crowded into Pandalur in 1881–82, when rumors spread of rich gold deposits in the area; the work done by Kungan's father and other men in the elephant stable of the Nelliyalam Rani in the 1930s; or the migrant laborers who settled in the Gorge in the 1950s. However, up to the late twentieth century, outsiders who entered the Gorge—including those who might have appeared especially alien to the locals (like the Scottish planters in the mid-1800s and, a century later, myself)—did not approach Kungan's relatives as spokespersons for large organizations or authorities. Nor did they try to mobilize them as members of an indigenous population pressing claims for state recognition and rights.

In some parts of the world, "first contacts" were dramatic and exceptional: for example, Captain Cook, on arrival in Hawaii, was deified as Lono, the circumstances of his arrival, by a series of coincidences, neatly fitting with this god's local script (Sahlins 1985). Far less dramatic and picturesque encounters happened in the Gorge—and far fewer people were involved on each side. The banality of these encounters as reflected in local recollections was, in fact, their most striking characteristic. These recollections suggest that even the strangest newcomer was perceived as a being-with: someone who had relatives, with whom people could interpersonally relate, and who could potentially become "our relative." I was told, for example, that the two white men who "were here before you" (the Scottish rubber planters) had lived in a nearby bungalow. According to my oldest "relative" in the hamlet, the wife and children of one of the white men once had come to visit him, and they all lived together in the bungalow (see more in Bird-David 2004b). Replace "white men" with a kinship term (e.g., "my uncle") or a local personal name (e.g., Mathen) and this same sentence could easily refer to locals' own flesh-and-blood relatives. Consider, at the same time, how Kungan's people *might* have registered the arrival of the two white men who dressed and behaved so differently and whose activities, in establishing their rubber plantation, involved never-before-seen sights and sounds associated with clearing five hundred acres of forest and building a bungalow. The advice sometimes given to public speakers stricken by fear of their audience can perhaps help in conceptualizing my point: imagine each member of the audience naked, one is advised, as a reminder that the audience is made up of human beings no different than oneself. Kungan's relatives "saw" their interlocutors as people with relatives like themselves, whom they could approach in much the same way they approached one another in their own community. They did not even need to imagine them stripped of their clothing, belongings, and conduct. These accoutrements were not imagined as signs of belonging to a faraway class or group. I cannot overemphasize that each person in the forager nanoworld was odd (i.e., distinctive) and that no one was an "odd man out." Each person was unique, a mono-being, and no one was deviant compared with a standardized "many." Bingan Sabda, Tsing's Meratus research assistant, could have seen them as Meratus according to his understanding of that name.

Development organizations arriving in the Nilgiri-Wynaad in the late 1980s and reaching the Gorge's foragers in the late 1990s brought with them large-scale multicultural language and group ontology. From the start, the target and scalar framework for some were the region's *adivasis* (original inhabitants, a term brought to the region by several of those activists) and for others the region's *tribal people* (the common official term in India). The first organization to arrive, Action for Community Organization,

Rehabilitation and Development (ACCORD), was started in 1986 by activists from Bangalore and Calcutta who set up their office in Gudalur. The second organization, Center for Rural Development Trust (CTRD), followed in 1988; it was started by an activist from a rural area in a faraway part of Tamil Nadu and was based near Pandalur. Initially ACCORD and CTRD informally carved up Gudalur and Pandalur (by then, two separate administrative units) into their respective "development" spheres, and both mainly worked through the mid-late 1990s with the more accessible communities in these areas: Paniya, Betta Kurumba, Mullu Kurumba, and Irula. ACCORD recruited young people from these various tribal groups as "animators" to "awaken" and galvanize their respective peoples, each as a distinct cultural group and all as Nilgiri-Wynaad *adivasi*. Remarkably, ACCORD succeeded in 1989 in mobilizing a reported ten thousand people (mainly from the above-listed communities) to march through the small township of Gudalur and demonstrate for their land rights. Their march was a spectacular materialization of an emergent pan-regional entity.

Historically, outsiders had approached Kungan's people as exotic inhabitants, as a potential labor force, and as neighbors. The development organizations and, after them, various government offices began to approach them as *communities* of tribal people/*adivasi* and subjects of the state, as well as, interrelatedly, *individuals* constitutive of those communities and carrying their identity. Population surveys were the next logical step, the process itself an ethnographic moment showing the materialization of new ontologies of being and identity. I observed some aspects of that "moment" in my 2001 visit in the area.

As well as visiting my old friends in the Gorge, I visited ACCORD's regional office in Gudalur, relocated that year to a large building with a tribal hospital and a tribal school annexed to it. The site hummed with the coming and going of animators discussing their interests as *adivasis* and, at the same time, distinguishing themselves by ethnic affiliation, speaking for their respective tribal/ethnic groups. No Nayaka animator had yet been recruited; very few Nayaka kids attended the school; Nayaka patients only sporadically came for treatment at the hospital. But a survey was under way of Gudalur's *adivasis*, including the forest Nayaka. I sat with Menon, one of the volunteers, in front of an old computer screen in a small office, and he showed me data collected by twenty students from Chennai (from the Institute for Development Alternatives [IDA]) sent to survey Gudalur's tribal population. The tribal animators had helped the students reach an estimated 75 percent of the hamlets in the Gudalur area, hamlet by hamlet, many of them by foot. The surveyors wrote the date and the household number on each house's exterior wall, a local material expression of its serialization, though the overt practical purpose was to mark the house as having been surveyed.

The unpublished raw information Menon showed me, on a pre-Excel computer spreadsheet, was organized in tabular form, with one line per family and multiple columns for data. One column was for the tribal name, three others for the names of nested administrative units: village, pancha-yat, and hamlet. Several dozen columns were allotted to information for each family member (husband, wife, and up to ten children): name, age, sex, occupation, and income. Out of the survey at large, sixty-four men, women, and children were listed as K. Naikr (an appellation corresponding to Nayaka and Kattunayaka). This population was distributed among four hamlets: in the first, eight families, thirty-five individuals; the second, one family, eight individuals; in the third, two families, eight individuals; and in the fourth, five families, twenty individuals. One can safely assume they were relatives, a salient point this representation obliterated; these data also obscured how few they were and what this meant experientially. Through this process, which served as the basis of distribution of various kinds of development aid (from health and education plans to parcels of kerosene and rice), communities of relatives were reconstituted as Kattunayaka families and individuals, subjects of the multiculturalist Tamil Nadu state. The survey set the grounds for the replication of many more Kattunayaka members, spinning Kungan's people into another scalar imaginary. The *large-scale perspective* of the latest arrivals to the Gorge's surroundings may induce more dramatic change than their physical pres-ence does.

During the nearly four decades I have known Kungan's people, I have seen their *sonta* ontology outlast their casual wage work on plantations (see Bird 1983b; Bird-David 1992b), their contract labor for a timber com-pany (Bird-David 1992b), and even their settlement in "modern" concrete-and-mortar houses built by the government and NGOs (see Bird-David 2008; Lavi and Bird-David 2014). I am not sure whether or how their *sonta* logic will survive their changing scale of imagination, the addition of a highway to their footpath perspective. Kungan and his relatives have begun to imagine themselves as members of the Kattaunayaka Scheduled Tribe as well as *sonta*, the articulation of these perspectives yet to unfold.

Epilogue

Pluripresent and Imagined Communities

Each time I left Kungan and his relatives at the end of a spell of fieldwork, I would not, like one included within *sonta*, hike to another tiny hamlet in the forest to visit and stay with relatives there. Neither would I climb the steep path to sell forest produce to vendors running market stalls along the country road that passed through the area. Rather, I would set out on that road and travel for 20 kilometers or so to the township of Gudalur (which the Gorge's foragers rarely visit even today), then continue on from there to Bangalore airport. In the air, I would watch the vast South Indian plains disappear from sight below me, and not long after, I would find myself once again in my university office, thousands of kilometers from the foragers' few dozen huts in the forest. At my desk, I would resume writing about their intimate plural world to imagined readers, my words aimed at those concerned with anthropology's large-scale comparative project and with understanding human social evolution.

Writing ethnography involves determining, translating, and articulating scales. As we determine the scales of our fieldwork and analysis, we often ignore what Bruno Latour (2005: 184) described as "the actor's own achievement"—that is, that those we study have their own scales of practice and imagination, their own "scale-making projects." If my concern at the beginning of this book was the distortive effect of scale blindness in the ethnography of foraging societies, at its end I am convinced more than ever of the need to clearly confront how anthropologists' and foragers' scale-making projects collide. My conviction grew as I consistently paid attention in my writing to scale and scaling, as I critically reflected on scalar blindness in previous hunter-gatherer studies, and as I focused special attention on those

(Facing page) A honey collector. Photographed by the author (1978–79).

aspects of Kungan and his relatives' tiny-scale plural structures and imagi-nations that have been most heavily obscured by the analytical language of the large-scale. It solidified when I engaged with the complex political situ-ation the Gorge's foragers currently face and when I realized the implica-tions of the clash between the state's large-scale projects and the foragers' own horizons. Anthropologists have long looked to indigenous forager-cultivator cultures for insights into the spectrum of human lifeways, and I am convinced now that our failure to appreciate indigenous horizons of concern and, in cross-cultural comparisons, to factor in enormous dispari-ties in population size distorts the insights these societies offer us.

The tiny-scale world I began studying in the late 1970s (and whose spa-tial reach and horizons of imagination I deliberately chose to maintain in this analysis) is Kungan and his relatives' own achievement. They engen-der it by constantly engaging with one another and with other local beings, both human and nonhuman. Its scale is predicated not only on a minuscule population but also on a mode of living as a sustained community of rela-tives: *sustained* because its members are plurally pregiven but must also work to remain connected; *community* because the group is presingular and starts with "being many"; and *relatives* because its members culturally configure and refigure themselves as plurally constituted beings. The idea of *pluripresence* encompasses these senses as much as it does the immedi-acy of belonging discussed throughout this book.

As I thought about their mode of plural life, 10,000 kilometers from their forest footpath view, I began to consider what kinds of "good to think" con-cepts I could abstract from my ethnographic encounter with them. Kungan and his relatives' prenational sense of themselves as *sonta*, I came to realize, provides a good starting point for examining the basis of all those we-desig-nations that recur cross-culturally among tiny indigenous communities: "we, relatives," "family," "real people," and so on. The putative appellatory syno-nym for the Gorge's foragers, the ethnonymic "Nayaka"—and at the state level, "Kattunayaka" (forest Nayaka)—is, at the same time, a good counter-point against which to try to conceptualize the subversive alternative.

"Kattunayaka people" configures this community as a collective of so many singular beings who share an identity, a Kattunayakaness. Each singu-lar being within it is a Kattunayaka, "the same as" all the others. The hypo-thetical eventuality that one last Kattunayaka person could remain in the world is ontologically conceivable from this perspective and so is the even-tuality (which, in fact, has become a reality under India's distributive justice system) that the number of Kattunayaka persons could exponentially grow and include far more "same" persons than one could possibly meet or even know of during one's lifetime. Imagining "Kattunayaka people" involves, in Benedict Anderson's words, "serialization: the assumption that the world [is] made up of replicable plurals" (1991 [1983]: 184). Computer engineers use the term *scalability* to describe how well a solution to a problem works when the size of the problem or the number of clients it affects increases. One could say that the "nation" is a solution of extremely high scalability with respect to the problem of plural belonging; indeed, it was an ingenious solution in the early modern world and into predigital modern times.

The *sonta* solution is one of extremely low scalability. Its context is the tiny community of relatives whose social project is maintaining the presence of each in the lives of all the others. Recall that, from the large-scale "modern" perspective, *relatives* can function in ways that are directly opposed to the functioning of *sonta*, although the English word itself is a fair translation of the latter term. Modern kinship seems to have adopted effective forms from the "national" mode that underwrites large-scale society, just as nationalism has appropriated affective symbols from kinship. From a singular "relative" a series of "relatives" can be derived, a series of individuals who may be widely dispersed but who share genes. Similarly, *family* is a source metaphor for entities that are separate yet share resemblance. *Sonta* foregrounds almost the opposite aspects, though surely familiar ones in any kinship experience: diversity, plurirelationships, and withness.

Sonta constitutes an inherently heterogeneous community, turning on its head the stereotype of the small-scale community in which people have the same identity and background and share common norms and values. *Sonta* encompasses diverse beings, human and nonhuman, irrespective of origin, previous life history, and embodied form, so long as they live and plurirelate with "us," the core of relatives, in person or through spirit possession and so become "our relatives" too.

As well as being sociocentric and heterogeneous, *sonta* is an inclusive concept, a far cry from the putative unified group that reproduces itself by maintaining boundaries and members' commonalities in opposition to imagined Others. *Sonta* engenders itself by extending outward from its pregiven core of plural relatives; its edges are fuzzy, and its horizons are those of pluripresence. Its members perform and re-perform their community through plurirelational work (coresidence, visits, sharing, gatherings, etc.), and through this work they downscale their community and each one asserts his or her respective singularity, a singularity within the pregiven plurality. So performed and re-performed, the *sonta*/kinship community could be described (freely using Jean-Luc Nancy's phrase) as a "community of being" rather than a "being of community."

Sonta's inherent diversity goes hand in hand with the scalar limits of pluripresence. The trade-off between *sonta* and the "national" mode is that between diversity and freedom from such limits. Large-scale postplural society prides itself on its diversity, but its diversity is that of imagined groups; even those who are pluripresent in certain settings can be regarded as members of other imagined groups, and in some scholarly perspectives, each singular being within that society embodies many imagined groups/ categories. The scale-blind multiculturalist ethos sanctions the equity of all cultures, but it allows for only one mode of "being many," an approach that, in some theories of radical indigenous cosmos, is also extended to nonhuman societies: the large-scale-borne mode. In the subversive *sonta*/kinship mode of plural community, members can be conspicuously different as long as they (or at least, the core members) constantly plurirelate. The forager *sonta* boasts a multiplicity of mono-beings, who are not serialized replicable plurals but, instead, diverse and plurirelated beings within the scalar bounds of pluripresence. It is tempting to cast such a community (to paraphrase Marshall Sahlins) as the Original Plural Society. Or again, freely using Nancy's terms, maybe here we can see, ontologically, a state of "being singular plural" as opposed to "being plural singular," a state not unique to but, feasibly, privileged at the forager scalar range.

An appreciation for the *sonta*/kinship mode of "being many," for me, brings this study to closure. It provides an answer of sorts to the three-decades-old question with which I started this book: why did a community of forest foragers nonchalantly accept as one of their own a stranger whose like they had never before seen, when neighboring Tamil plantation workers gazed on that same stranger with fascination and bemusement? In the *sonta*/kinship mode, either no one is the "odd one out" or everyone is. Even the appearance of a white ethnographer—a novelty—was taken in stride within that mode, her whiteness registering simply as one of her many observable features. Certainly, for Kungan and his relatives, it was not a marker of the large imagined community from which she hailed. In their plural mode, the ethnographer was configured as a white-skinned relative, not a member of an imagined group of faraway Whites.

As I engaged their perspective more broadly with my professional craft, I continued to consider what it could offer the large-scale project of anthropology. My conceptualization of the *sonta*/kinship mode might suggest to some readers a radical forager world, one perhaps even incommensurate with our own, a view of indigenous worlds that has enjoyed popularity during the discipline's "ontological turn." My experience convinces me, to the contrary, that scale-blind ethnography has turned the evident commensal basis of fieldwork settings into texts on exotic indigenous worlds that scale-blind comparisons have further radicalized. Anthropology's multiculturalist scale-blind ethos has blown indigenous structures up to monstrous proportions, beyond locals' scales of practice and imaginations and beyond those structures' scalability. *Incommensurate* is used by anthropologists, along with linguists and philosophers, to emphasize the untranslatability of other peoples' worlds (see Povinelli 2001). Somewhat prophetically, certainly ironically, *incommensurate* means *disproportionate* in ordinary usage. We need to ask ourselves, I contend, whether, in fact, the practice of multiculturalist scale-blind anthropology has been incommensurate with its indigenous subjects; whether, by failing to take into account the scale in which it embeds their analysis, much of the cultural anthropology of the past century has potentiated the perception of tiny-scale indigenous communities as radically alter.

A scale-sensitive ethnography moves us toward confronting this problem; the broader vision must be, I think, the realization of a multiscalar anthropology, including scale-sensitive cross-cultural comparison—one aligned with the scalar turn in the social sciences more broadly. Proponents of this approach, nascent in anthropology, have begun to study the large-scale modern world and global phenomena from a multiscalar perspective, but we need to recognize that indigenous communities too merit this approach, both ethnographically and in cross-cultural comparison. Unless we do so, members of indigenous societies will find themselves caught within the large-scale webs not only of national bureaucracies and global connections but also of anthropology and the modern imagination of plural life. It is important to continue to examine the ways modern scalar discourse, alongside temporal discourse (Fabian 1983), has shaped how anthropology makes such peoples its object. A study of this kind is critical for understanding indigenous peoples' pasts and, equally, their futures.

My forager ethnography suggests to me that a productive starting point for such a project is to distinguish among modes of "being many," removing the blinders that constrain multiculturalist anthropology's approach to social belonging. The modern imagination of huge communities as "nations," with its individualistic and groupist certainties, is only one such mode, and this ethnography suggests *pluripresence* and related vocabulary (*plurirelations*, *pluralogues*, *pluriresidents*, etc.) as productive language for exploring other modes, especially but not only those of tiny indigenous societies. My analysis suggests to me that the concept and language of pluripresence redress more than a lacuna in the large-scale sociological language centered on the singular being, the related two, and the group, and more than the myopia of the national imagination of community keyed to serialization and replicable plurals. The idea of pluripresence, I suggest, brings into focus a range of plural life that is perhaps universal in human experience, a matter of everyday praxis oppressed by as much as it resists other plural modes, not least in nation-societies that generate their own intimate modalities (see Herzfeld 1997). Though pluripresence may be an ordinary and commonplace experience, it is probably nowhere so intense or pervasive, and surely not so determinative of culture and ontology, as it is among forager and other tiny-scale indigenous communities. To the extent that their autonomy (not to be read as isolation) allows, these tiny indigenous communities have maintained traditions engendered within pluripresent arenas and present a repertoire of plurally inflected cultural structures elaborated over time, some intricately so. No equivalent-size groups of relatives in larger-scaled settings, who constitute microarenas in which they enact and reproduce macrostructures, can match them in this achievement.

The mode of communal belonging shown by these foragers may have broad analytical purchase for the study of human plural life today, and also past and future. *Past* because studies of human prehistory can benefit from theoretical grounding in a plural mode like *sonta* instead of "nation," that is, from conceiving of early societies as pluripresent communities of diverse-and-related kin instead of as groups of serial men, women, and children, and from taking into account scale, scaling, and scalability. Lending such communities their "hunters and gatherers" category name, their mode of subsistence has proven a poor predictor of common sociocultural forms. A mode of "being many," like *sonta*, I believe, affords more immediate entrée into their social worlds. And *future* because "pluripresent community" and "imagined community" are, I am convinced, "good to think" plural modes of "being many" that can articulate in complex ways we have yet to explore. The importance of studying their articulations is increasing in an age when digital technologies radically expand a kind of pluripresence among millions of e-mail, Facebook, and Twitter users, an age that generates plural and cultural structures that are nested within, articulate and negotiate with, challenge and resist, and sometimes succumb to the large-scale national mode—structures that may outlive the "national" mode.

Conceptualizing foragers' modes of plural life is challenging in an age when nations are taken to be so natural that, as Ernest Gellner observed, "having a nation" is like "having a nose and two ears" (2008: 6). It is perhaps even more challenging a task than exploring indigenous alternatives to the Western concept of nature, the impetus of much recent study of foraging groups. However, the challenge must be taken up. We owe it to those tiny groups we have ushered onto the world stage through ethnonyms we have chosen and whose plural modes we have effaced in the process.

Acknowledgments

This book is dedicated to all those who over the many years of its gestation have constituted my communities of belonging. I am indebted more than I can say to the several dozen South Indian foragers who taught me to appreciate their own powerful mode of belonging: an "us-ness" that trains attention on singularity within pregiven plurality, on diversity rather than sameness, on a community of being. And I am deeply indebted to my teachers and peers in the Department of Social Anthropology at Cambridge University, who welcomed a foreign graduate in economics and mathematics and helped me acquire the professional skills and intellectual freedom to make sense of my experience with those foragers: to Alan Macfarlane (my supervisor), Caroline Humphrey, Steven Hugh-Jones, Marilyn Strathern, and James Woodburn, among others. Sincere thanks also to Michael Herzfeld, who, decades later, hosted me on sabbatical at Harvard (in the other Cambridge), where I figured how to freshly theorize my fieldwork experience. I am indebted to colleagues and friends in India, especially Phillip Mulley, Pramode Misra, Stan and Mari Thekaekara, Anita Varghese, and members of ACCORD, Keystone, and CTRD for engaging with my research in productive conversation, and I thank M. Lakshmanan, P.O. Phillip, and V. Karunakaran for their help with specific aspects of my study. Many colleagues, friends, and students (who have since become colleagues and friends) have provided me with an affable and stimulating intellectual environment over the years, among them, Debbi Bernstein, Françoise Dussart, Mina Evron-Weinstein, Yuval Feinstein, Judith Fichman, Peter Gardner, Tsipi Ivri, Tamar Katriel, Carol Kidron, Noa Lavi, Brian Morris, Daniel Naveh, Haya Shpayer-Makov, Amalia Sa'ar, Wendy Sadler, and Vicky Umansky.

For their insightful intervention at critical stages in finalizing this book, and for their helpful readings of draft versions, I am deeply thankful to Eyal

Ben-Ari, Françoise Dussart, Signe Howell, Noa Lavi, Tanya Luhrmann, and Matan Shapiro. My language editor, Linda Forman, has been a wonderful companion on this project; her skills, patience, and kindness have contributed much to it, as have Osnat Boo's timely assistance with artwork and counsel on visual communication, and the professional final touches of the Press's editorial team, Reed Malcolm, Dore Brown, and Elizabeth Berg.

I happily acknowledge my debt to members of my far-flung family in Israel, England, the United States, and Switzerland: to Gabriel and Hedva Ben-David, Daniel Bird, Osnat Sharf, and Avishai Ben-David, Michael Bird, Rachel Bird, Yaron Sharf, and last but not least, Shlomo Bar-Ilan, for their unwavering support and patience over the course of this project, and to Naama and Ethan Dekel-Bird; Betsy Burin; Jan and Adam Boo; David, Rotem, Haleli, Tamara, Asael, and Devora Bar-Ilan; and Yael, Chen, Achinoam, Alma, and Uria Fisher for their presence in my life.

Readers of this book will determine what it says to them and its value, and that too is a contribution for which I am grateful. The book ultimately belongs to that imagined community alongside those whose vivid presence in my life so enriched me as I worked on it.

Notes

PROLOGUE

1. *Sonta*, the word Kungan uses here, is also commonly used by neighboring speakers of South Dravidian languages to refer to one's intimate circle of family and close relatives. In this book I explore its meaning specifically for Kungan and his kin.

INTRODUCTION

1. Another, more popular, cultural survey, National Geographic's *Book of Peoples of the World* (2008), is unabashedly advertised as covering "more than 200 ethnic groups—some as obscure as the Kallawaya of the Peruvian Andes, numbering fewer than 1,000; others as widespread as the Bengalis of India, 172 million strong." See http://www.amazon.com/Book-Peoples-World-Guide-Cultures/dp/1426202385 (accessed January 3, 2014).

2. Smith and Wishnie (2000: 493) cite Bodley 1996: 12. See also Spielmann 2002: 195.

3. On comparison in anthropology generally, see Gingrich and Fox 2002; Holý 1987; Nader 1994; and Ivri 2010. See also Bird-David 1995b for a review of types of comparison in hunter-gatherer studies (regional, grand, heuristic, evolutionary-ecological, and ethno- comparisons).

4. For a review of these studies, see Kelly 1995: ch. 6.

5. I take the term *identity expert* from Viveiros de Castro 2012: 98.

6. With local group size tied to their mode of subsistence, their tininess appears to be a core element of their lifeway, not the outcome of catastrophic contact with outsiders.

7. For recent works, see Ingold 1999; Bird-David 1999a; Willerslev 2007; Viveiros de Castro 2012; and Descola 2013 (2005).

8. For example, Steward 1936, 1969; Johnson 2003 (which recently revived Steward's "family-level of social integration"); Damas 1969; Gardner 1966,

1991a; Burch 1975; Myers 1986; Bird-David 1994a; Overing and Passes 2000; and Walker 2013.

9. Viveiros de Castro 2012; see my discussion in chapter 5.

10. Over the past two decades, social geographers have intensively engaged with issues of scale (see, among many others, Jones 1998, Howitt 2002, Masuda and Crooks 2007, Moore 2008, and Giesbrecht et al. 2010). Anthropologists have considered scale more sporadically (see, among others, Berreman 1987; Strathern 1991, 1995; Ferguson and Gupta 2002; Latour 2005, esp. 183–5; Philips 2013).

11. In previous publications, I translated *sonta* as "our own, family," partly because in the major Dravidian languages spoken in the area this word is translated as "family." Here, I opt for the translation "relatives" as more adequate for and conceptually open to exploring the foragers' senses of their pluripresent community and world.

12. See, for another exception, Praet 2013, who also cross-culturally surveys similar notions. He approaches these categories as indexes of animistic systems.

13. "Ethnonym," Dictionary.com, www.dictionary.com/browse/ethnonym? s=t, accessed April 2015.

14. The notion of imagination is variably used in anthropology. Some scholars regard imagination as overarching cognitive script (see Taylor 2002, 2004 on "social imaginary"), others as activity through which "individuals create and recreate the essence of their being, making themselves what they are, were, and will become" (Rapport and Overing 2000: 4). Two special journal issues have been dedicated to the subject of imagination, and their editors provide good overviews of this subject: see Gaonkar 2002; and Sneath, Holbraad, and Pederson 2009. See Axel 2003 for a critique of Anderson's lack of an explicit theory of imagination, and see Sneath, Holbraad, and Pederson for commendation of his approach as an "antidote" recognizing that "imagination can be investigated empirically as a process that, though always present in social life, may have variable characteristics" (2009: 9). I concur with Anderson and Sneath et al. while dwelling on what could be described as body-technique involving visits, gatherings, and spirit-visits/possession.

15. Irad Malkin (2011: 15) suggests that the ancient Greek civilization as we know it became more "Greek" the more widely its people dispersed; thus, ethnic sentiments may have been predicated on spatial dispersal as early as classical times.

16. The "first nations" discourse comes from and serves natives' desire to be recognized as peoples who exercised sovereignty over territories, especially in North America, that Europeans declared *terra nullius* on first encountering them. Some native communities are/were larger than the tiny hunter-gatherer groups on which I focus in this book. Even in those cases, however, careful attention should be paid to who counts and who is counted as native, to the fluidity of ethnic names informing demographic surveys, and to confederations that include multiple groups under one name.

17. Compare Schneider 1969. On gendered aspects of the nationalistic use of kinship terms, see, among others, Delaney 1995; Yuval-Davis 1997; and Bryant 2002.

18. Steven Pinker (2007: 138) discusses "one-two-many systems." See more in chapter 2.

19. Marshall Sahlins's "The Original Affluent Society," the opening chapter of his canonical *Stone Age Economics* (1972), is the best-known work. See Bird-David 1992a for its review; see also Altman 1984; and Kaplan 2000, among others.

20. A case readily argued in Maurice Merleau-Ponty's terms.

21. Nisbett 2004; and Markus and Kitayama 1991. See Lindholm 1997 for an anthropologist's criticism of the latter.

22. Strathern elaborates on these notions in various works, e.g., 1988, 1991, 1992b, 2004. See Marriott 1976, 1990 for early uses of *dividual* in the Indian context.

23. For an illuminating perspective on Simmel's thesis, see Pyyhtinen 2009.

24. See Strathern 1992a, 1992b; Kuper 1992; and Ingold 1999, among others. See Ingold 1999 on how modern understandings of society shaped the study of hunter-gatherer-band social relations.

25. See Overing and Passes 2000 for a direct statement on the anthropological struggle with notions of "society" and for resolving it by exploring, at the microlevel of emotions and intersubjectivity, local Amazonian theories of the "good life." One could consider as exceptions to anthropology's relative neglect of alternative forms of social belonging Evans-Pritchard's (1940) study of the Nuer segmentary lineage system and Fei's work in the 1940s comparing Western and Chinese grouping structures (for an English translation, see Fei 1992); cf. also Descola 1994.

26. See Brubaker 2004 on disentangling "nation" as a category of practice from "nation" as a category of analysis, the latter too often a default in scholarly social scientific research.

27. "Collective," suggested by Bruno Latour (2005), and used by Descola (2013 [2005]), to my understanding indicates the existence of agents who "collect" and produce "the collective," and it seems to be a more productive term to apply to large-scale settings than to hunter-gatherers' tiny-scale realities. I introduce *pluripresence* to capture precisely the opposite idea: the sense of a pregiven, irreducible, uncollectible pluralness.

28. For example, see Fine and Harrington 2004; Fine 2012; and Stolte, Fine, and Cook 2001. Fine also uses the phrase "tiny publics."

29. See note 8. Ingold 1999 provides a review of this literature, and an overview can be also found in Bird-David 1994a.

30. Available at http://censusindia.gov.in/.

31. See Paul Hockings's *A Comprehensive Bibliography for the Nilgiri Hills of Southern India, 1603–1996* (1996).

32. See Bird 1987; Bird-David 1989, 1994b, 1996, 1999b.

33. Their recognition has gradually grown since the mid-twentieth century. Two tribal communities of India that have been studied as hunter-gatherers

234 / Notes to Pages 25-29

made appearances in the *Man the Hunter* symposium: the Paliyan and the Birhor (Lee and DeVore 1968). However, only in 1999 did South Asian foragers enter the canon as a regional class, introduced by Bird-David (1999b) in *The Cambridge Encyclopedia of Hunter-Gatherers* (Lee and Daly 1999). That entry incorporated further groups—the Nayaka, the Hill Pandaram (Morris 1982), and the Chenchu, Vedda, and Kadar, the last three studied early in the twentieth century by some of tribal India's most renowned ethnographers (Fürer-Haimendorf 1943; Seligman and Seligman 1911; and Ehrenfels 1952). Other groups later joining the class include Andaman Islanders (e.g., Pandya 1993), the Raute of Nepal (e.g., Fortier 2009b), the Jenu Kurumba of Tamil Nadu (e.g., Demmer 2001, 2014; Misra 1977), and the Chola Nayaka of Kerala (Mathur 1977; Bhanu 1982; and Kakkoth 2005). Not until 2009 were "South Asian foragers" established as a major category in mainstream anthropology, the subject of an essay in the *Annual Review of Anthropology* (Fortier 2009a). Recently, Peter Gardner (2013) reported their startling proportion among the world hunter-gatherer population. A special issue of *Eastern Anthropologist* (2014, vol. 67, nos. 3-4) is dedicated to South Indian foragers.

34. The estimates are problematic on conceptual and logistical grounds yet are thought provoking. The estimates are based partly on official and partly on unofficial publications, and Gardner attributes the relatively large number of hunter-gatherer groups in South Asia to the accommodating nature of the Hindu culture, which may have served to protect these foragers from assimilation pressure until the twentieth century.

35. Daniel Naveh (2007) did PhD fieldwork during 2003-2004 among a nearby group, and Noa Lavi (2012) did MA fieldwork in one of my study group's hamlets in 2010 and again in 2012 and 2014. She is currently writing her PhD thesis. See Naveh 2007; Bird-David and Naveh 2008; Naveh and Bird-David 2013, 2014; Lavi 2012; Lavi and Bird-David 2014.

36. The temporal focus of this ethnography largely overlaps with the period in which, for example, Howell (1984), Descola (1994), and Viveiros de Castro (1992 [1986]) did their baseline fieldwork.

37. For studies of changes in the local world, see Bird-David 1992b; Naveh 2007; Lavi 2012; Naveh and Bird-David 2014; Lavi and Bird-David 2014.

38. The debated positions are known as "formalist" and "substantivist," the latter endorsed by scholars like Paul Bohannan (1955) and Sahlins (1972) and inspired by the work of the economic historian Karl Polanyi (1957).

39. On the tactical use of kinship terms among foragers, see also, among others, Bird 1982; Dussart 1988; Bodenhorn 2000; Nuttall 1992; cf. Barnard 1978.

40. I managed the local dialect well enough for living with Kungan and his relatives, benefiting from occasional visits by an experienced translator, the late Mr. Lakshmanan, who assisted me in delving into metaphysical issues.

CHAPTER 1. AT HOME

1. See, for example, Wilson 1988; Whitelaw 1994; Ingold 2000; Bird-David 2009; Lavi and Bird-David 2014.

2. These studies have multiplied in recent years, although the anthropology of the house has yet to take its place alongside established subfields such as the anthropology of kinship, cosmology, consumption, and so on. For ethnographic studies of houses in the Western context, see, among others, Birdwell-Pheasant and Lawrence-Zuniga 1999; Csikszentmihalyi and Rochberg-Halton 1981; for studies of houses in South and Central America, see, among others, Robben 1989; Pader 1993; Colloredo-Mansfeld 1994; Leinaweaver 2009; Holston 1991; and for East and Southeast Asia, see Daniel 1984; Waterson 1990; Fox 2006; Keane 1995; Fleischer 2007. See also Humphrey 1974.

3. The group Daniel Naveh studied in 2003–4 lived in a larger settlement than Kungan and his relatives did, one comprising scattered huts. I am unsure whether to consider these structures one hamlet or several. We cannot know how their occupants lived in the late 1970s, the period I focus on in this ethnography.

4. In traditional contexts, Kungan and his relatives used *apare* both for countable entities beyond four (e.g., huts) and for uncountable entities (e.g., water). They borrowed large-number words from neighboring Dravidian languages (as they did many other words in their dialect) in speaking about wages, purchases, and earnings from forest produce sale. But this does not mean that, say, a hundred-rupee payment was understood as one hundred times one rupee (see Bird 1983b: 76 for locals' views and uses of money).

5. See Gordon 2004 and Everett 2005 on the Amazonian Pirahã.

6. I thank Noa Lavi for this insight.

7. *Home* means, inter alia, a place of dwelling and nurturing; a place to which one properly belongs; the center of one's affections; a place where one finds rest, refuge, or satisfaction; a place where one's ancestors dwelt; a place associated with family; a place of origin; a place of ultimate return; a place one feels at home in, familiar with, and comfortable in (abstracted from *Oxford English Dictionary*, 3rd edition, s.v. "home"; see also Hollander 1991). See Mallett 2004 for a review of interdisciplinary scholarship on "home."

8. As Strathern (1992a: 90) observes, *house* and *home* are often used synonymously, for example, in "home for sale."

9. Phillip Mulley, personal communication.

10. Precisely this sense was expressed—and perpetuated—in the series of "big visits" that took place in the Gorge's hamlets. The core dwellers of a hamlet where the event was to be held took special responsibility for its happening, but relatives gathered from all the neighboring hamlets to take part in it, as did all the invisible beings in the valley (see chapter 5).

11. The underlying structural logic resembles (unnervingly so) the classic anthropological model of "segmentary opposition" associated with African unilineal societies (e.g., see Evans-Pritchard 1940).

12. See note 7.

CHAPTER 2. LIVING PLURALLY

1. Johnson's 2003 ethnography is based on his fieldwork with Matsigenka of the Peruvian Amazon in the 1970s.

2. *Collins School Dictionary,* 1990, s.v. "visit."

3. *Oxford Dictionary of English,* 3rd edition, 1973, s.v. "visit."

4. In his own Hadza case, he drew on informants' statements (Woodburn 1982: 188); on the Baka death, on information provided by Robert Dodd, who, in turn, relied on informants' statements (ibid., 194–96); on the Mbuti Pygmy, on Colin Turnbull's work (esp. 1965: 143–45, which does not specify the source of the information); and on the !Kung, on Lorna Marshall's work (1962: 243), largely making an argument on the basis of her silence on the subject in the context of her otherwise exceptionally rich ethnography.

5. The group Naveh (2007: 35) studied fluctuated at the time between thirty-four and forty-nine people.

6. Naveh observed an "oil" ritual in which a bamboo vessel rather than a pit was used. Similar rituals are reported elsewhere in the region (e.g., see Breeks 1873; see also Francis's *Madras District Gazeteers* [1908: 153]).

7. I remained unsure about the temporal order of the "oil" ritual and the "ring" ritual. Perhaps, as often was the case with other activities, there was no clear protocol, and practical considerations influenced what was done first.

8. Benu's relatives did not explicate the meanings of this rite beyond stating that it is how things are done.

9. Naveh also noted the relatively quick resumption of routine in the hamlet where he was living after the sudden deaths of the husband and wife, which left their nine-year-old child an orphan.

10. In previous work (e.g., Bird-David 1996, 1999a, 2004a, 2004b), I mainly refer to these events as "trance-gatherings."

11. Bonnie Hewlett (2005: 339) notes that although the forager Aka bury the body quickly and simply and that their cultivator Ngandu neighbors lay it out for viewing for several days and hold commemorative rituals for several years afterward, both groups experience sadness and a sense of loss.

12. I did not pursue with people their intense emotional response to the photographs.

CHAPTER 3. THE SIB MATRIX

1. *Sonta* functions here as a first person plural possessive, and *kudumba* is a common South Dravidian word usually translated as "family."

2. For literature on siblings, see, among other works, edited volumes focusing on groups in Oceania (M. Marshall 1979) and in Southeast Asia (Nuckolls 1993). For ethnographies that pay attention to siblings, see, among others, Basso 1973; J. Kaplan 1975; C. Hugh-Jones 1979; S. Hugh-Jones 1979; Århem 1981; Jackson 1983; and Myers 1986.

3. The "holy family" is a trinity of father, virgin mother, and child—no siblings here to cause unholy ruffles.

4. Biblical siblings originated separate people units, distinctive ethnic units in today's terms.

5. *Bereaved* has general purchase.

6. See Carsten 2000. Adoptees sometimes search for siblings as a means of finding their birth parents. In publicized debates on the rights of children born from sperm donation, the right to know the father's identity is the focus.

7. On my return visit in 2012, I toured hamlets in the Gudalur area that were linked to hamlets in which Daniel Naveh worked (2007). Of all the people I met in those hamlets, only one man recollected having once traveled to the Gorge area.

CHAPTER 4. COUPLES AND CHILDREN

1. For reviews of the literature, see Kelley 1995: ch. 7; Brightman 1996; and Karen Endicott 1999.

2. See also Slocum 1975; Hiatt 1970; Zihlman 1989; and Estioko-Griffin and Griffin 1981.

3. *Oxford English Dictionary,* 3rd edition, s.v. "together."

4. For examples, see studies of the Efe people of the Ituri forest in Zaire (Ivey 2000; Tronick, Morelli, and Winn 1987; Tronick, Morelli, and Ivey 1992; Barry Hewlett 1991). In some cases, babies are breastfed by women other than their birth mothers. See Hewlett and Winn 2014.

5. In conversations with me, people used *gandu* and *endru* (~ man and woman) and *okkalgaren* and *okkalgarati* (~ the man-in-the-house and the woman-in-the-house), common terms in the region.

6. My attempts to elicit local interpretations of this performance produced no result beyond statements that this is what has always been done, or that this is what our elders did, or words to that effect.

7. *Kura* (common deer) and *udu* (monitor lizard) were caught by dogs and beaten with sticks and billhooks, or they were snatched from the claws of forest predators, mostly *chennas* (wild dogs, *Cuon alpinus*). Birds and eggs were sought, adults and children thrusting their hands into tree hollows they passed. *Ame*, a small common land tortoise, was collected when noticed. Exceptionally, a few men constructed traps from bamboo in attempts to take jungle fowl; their efforts met with little success. I observed men and youths trying to bring birds down with stones, and I heard about applying a sticky paste to branches on which fruit was placed as bait for birds; they supposedly got stuck on the branches and could be collected by hand. Occasionally, fire was used to smoke out and burn *mulandi* (wild pig), which were then beaten by sticks. Observers in the late nineteenth century remarked that local foragers in the Nilgiris area did not hunt and had no arrows (Dubois 1897: 76).

8. Compare with hunting game as part of male initiation rites (e.g., Lee 1979: 205) and as associated with taboos (e.g., Woodburn 1968a: 52).

9. For example, Hill and Hurtado (1996: 219) and Kaplan and Dove (1987) on Ache of Paraguay, Endicott and Endicott (2008: 61) on Batek of Malaysia. See Melvin Konner's (2005) review of empirical findings of child-focused studies conducted in the 1970s on !Kung, Hadza, Efe, Aka, Ache, and Agta; and Hewlett and Lamb (2005a) for a review of more recent studies.

10. See Bird and Bird 2000, 2005 on Australian Aboriginal cases. On Hadza contrasted with !Kung, see Konner 2005: 21–30; Blurton Jones, Hawkes, and Draper 1994.

11. I observed children playing with dolls made out of short wooden sticks and wrapped in cloth (some had breasts fashioned from beeswax); sliding down the muddy slopes of the terraces on which the huts stood, two to five children sitting on a large plantain leaf, one nested against another and legs wide apart; and using a rope to pull a piece of bamboo, referred to as a "lorry" in imitation of the trucks that arrived occasionally to haul timber from the area.

12. See Christer Norström's 2003 follow-up study of the Paliyan, in which he generally argues for "counterbalancing" Gardner's strong emphasis on Paliyan "individualism" by also paying attention to their "collectivism."

13. Compare Demmer 2015 on indigenous South Indian "person" concepts. For example, among the Jenu Kurumba, according to Demmer, "the head, or buddi, is the site of the intellect and instrumental rationality. The *mansu*, located roughly where we situate the physical heart, is said to be the site of the faculties of will, ethical deliberation, moral orientation, ethical decisions to act, social attentiveness and social memory. The third organ is termed *otte*, or what we would call the stomach and is the site of emotions and feelings" (108). The Jenu Kurumba are former foragers in the Nilgiris, whom Demmer studied between 1987 and 2011.

14. Joanna Overing and Alan Passes (2000) suggest using "conviviality" as a key analytical term in analysis of Amazonian theories of social life. This concept, however, does not sufficiently enfold the nanoscalar context.

15. Walker estimates the total Urarina population to be around four thousand to six thousand, a rough figure since, as he describes it, "exact numbers are difficult to determine because relatively few have identity documents or are covered in the national surveys" (2013: 19–20).

16. Some scholars, widely reported in hunter-gatherer studies, argue that game sharing functions as collective insurance against natural fluctuations (e.g., see Lee 1968; Wiessner 1982; Cashdan 1985; Smith 1988). Compare my "culturalist" analysis (Bird-David 1990).

CHAPTER 5. NONHUMAN KIN

1. See Descola 2013 [2005] for a comprehensive review; and Bird-David 1999a for discussion of the notion of personhood involved.

2. See Ingold (2000: 42–44) and Descola (2013 [2005]: 250–52) on the issue of figurative and cognitive metaphors. Descola accepted that metaphors such as

"parent-child" constitute handy cognitive schemas for understanding relations between humans and nonhumans, and Ingold, approaching metaphor in a figurative rather than a cognitive sense, regarded it as an "as if" statement, a view that entrenches the modern split between nature and culture. That the "parent-child" metaphor conveys living-together before it does any hierarchical or reciprocal caregiving relation has not been pursued by scholars.

3. See also Bird-David and Naveh 2008; Naveh and Bird-David 2013, 2014.

4. See Turner 2009; Ramos 2012; Bessire and Bond 2014; and Vigh and Sausdal 2014 for critical reviews of perspectivism and animism. See Blaser 2009, 2013; and Holbraad, Pedersen, and Viveiros de Castro 2014 for political perspectives on the ontological turn.

5. Compare circumlocutions like the Cree "shaking tent ritual" and the Batek "fruit-season's singing session" (see, among others, Hallowell 2000 [1960]; Feit 1994; Brightman 1993; Kirk Endicott 1979).

6. See, among others, Csordas 1983; Dow 1986; Schieffelin 1985, 1996; Nabokov 2000. See Boddy 1994 for a comprehensive review.

7. See, among others, Kapferer 1979a, 1979b; Boddy 1989; Comaroff 1985; Janzen 1992; Lambek 1993; Ong 1987; Stoller 1989.

8. Dwellers in the one-hut BR and UP hamlets cooperated with those of GR and TR to host visitors.

9. Two huts were built in TR, one by its residents and the other by the residents of UP, then a one-hut hamlet whose people celebrated their "big visit" alongside the people of TR.

10. In the 1960s, some of these foragers took up casual wage work and "gathered wage" (see Bird 1983b; Bird-David 1992b). They spent their wages largely on food, and rice entered the regular diet interchangeably with the traditional staple food, forest yam.

11. Compare Demmer's (2001, 2007) description of similar elements among the Jenu Kurumba as religious: for example, walking to the river to rinse the idols as part of death rituals.

12. In this chapter I largely draw on Howell's monograph. For her recent publications on Chewong, see Howell 2011, 2013.

13. I did not pursue the semantic distinctions between these three notions.

14. See Bird-David (2004a, 2006) on locals' ideas, respectively, of time and knowledge precluding narratives and depictions.

15. For example, see Chen 1990: 41; Cormier 2003: 114; Rival 2002: 98; Seitz 2007: 185; Smole 1976: 185.

16. See specific examples in Naveh 2007; Naveh and Bird-David 2013, 2014.

17. I am indebted to Philippe Descola for suggesting this question to me.

18. The Amazonian ethnographies of Viveiros de Castro (1992 [1986]) and Descola (1996) and Myers's (1986) Australianist ethnography, in my reading, contain arguments that resonate with this hypothesis.

CHAPTER 6. A CONTINUUM OF RELATIVES

1. The migrants' pronunciation of the name in 1979 is better inscribed as *Naiken* but for consistency I continue to use *Nayaka* in this volume.

2. See Spielmann and Eder 1994 for a review essay on forager-farmer relations; see also Ikeya, Ogawa, and Mitchell, 2009. See Gardner (1985, 2013) and Fortier (2009a) for overviews of South Asian foragers' long-term contacts with mainstream Indian society. See Bird-David (1988, 1992b) for early commentary on these issues.

3. See, among many others, Barnard 1992, 2006; Schrire 1980; Solway and Lee 1990; Wilmsen 1989; Wilmsen and Denbow 1991.

4. Human Relations Area Files.

5. See Ramos 2012 for a critique of this argument and its political consequences.

6. Lavi explores the emergent social, territorial, and symbolic boundaries in the Gorge in her MA thesis (2012).

7. In 2003–4, Naveh observed failures to enter into trance in other circumstances.

8. On the tactical use of kinship terms among foragers, see also, among others, Bird 1982; Dussart 1988; Bodenhorn 2000; Nuttall 2000; cf. Barnard 1978.

9. I only know of cases involving in-marrying men, but I can imagine the local response had I asked my respondents to generalize: "Maybe in other places, other women also marry in."

10. "Just Don't Call Them Ginger," YouTube, www.youtube.com/watch?v=H0Yhe69ve2c, accessed September 30, 2013.

11. Compare the biological meaning of the term: "introducing organisms into a region and causing them to flourish as if native." "Naturalization," Dictionary.com, http://dictionary.reference.com/, accessed September 30, 2013.

12. "Custom," Dictionary.com, http://dictionary.reference.com/, accessed September 30, 2013.

CHAPTER 7. THE STATE'S FORAGERS

1. Lye Tuck-Po (2004) explores the lifeways of Batek foragers in Malaysia, across whose territory a major state highway now runs.

2. For an illustrative figure of the bureaucratic road involved, see Middleton 2013: 18.

3. See, among others, Bisht 1994; Kapila 2008; Middleton 2011a, 2011b; Middleton and Shneiderman 2008; Shneiderman 2009; Moodie 2015.

4. "Population of Tamil Nadu," India Online Pages, www.indiaonlinepages.com/population/tamil-nadu-population.html, accessed October 13, 2013.

5. National Commission for Scheduled Tribes New Delhi 110003, 28th January 2014, p. 3. http://ncst.nic.in/writereaddata/linkimages/Tour_Report_07–09Jan2014_Secretary3077152684.pdf, accessed December 22, 2014.

6. Compare this with the District Level Vigilance Committee for Scheduled Castes, which includes the district collector as chairman, a district Adi Dravidar and Tribal Welfare officer as member secretary, and an anthropologist.

7. Ministry of Tribal Affairs, Government of India, http://tribal.nic.in /index3.asp?subsublinkid=303&langid=1, accessed February 24, 2014.

8. I thank ACCORD (Action for Community Organization, Rehabilitation and Development) for providing me with this document.

9. Available at http://ncst.nic.in/writereaddata/linkimages/Tour_ Report_07–09Jan2014_Secretary3077152684.pdf, accessed February 24, 2014.

10. In the absence of a singularized social entity, there is no basis in the community for the accumulation of political power by any one individual or faction claiming to "speak for" the group and mobilizing it as a Network-Actor (in Latour's [2005] terms).

11. Compare Valkonen, Valkonen, and Koivurova 2016 on politics of indigeneity in Finland.

References

Alber, Erdmute, Cati Coe, and Tatjana Thelen, eds. 2013. *The Anthropology of Sibling Relations: Shared Parentage, Experience, and Exchange*. New York: Palgrave Macmillan.

Alford, Richard D. 1988. *Naming and Identity: A Cross-Cultural Study of Personal Naming Practices*. New Haven, CT: HRAF Press.

Alia, Valerie. 1994. *Names, Numbers and Northern Policy: Inuit, Project Surname, and the Politics of Identity*. Halifax, Nova Scotia: Fernwood.

————. 2007. *Names and Nunavit Culture and Identity in Arctic Canada*. New York: Berghahn.

Altman, Jon C. 1984. Hunter Gatherer Subsistence Production in Arnhem Land: The Original Affluence Hypothesis Re-Examined. *Mankind* 14 (3): 179–90.

Anderson, Benedict. 1991 [1983]. *Imagined Communities: Reflections on the Origin and Spread of Nationalism*. New York: Verso.

————. 2006 [1983]. *Imagined Communities: Reflections on the Origin and Spread of Nationalism*. New York: Verso.

Århem, Kaj. 1981. *Makuna Social Organization: A Study in Descent, Alliance and the Formation of Corporate Groups in the North-Western Amazon*. Uppsala: Academiae Ubsaliensis.

Asch, Michael, and Shirleen Smith. 1999. Slavey Dene. In *The Cambridge Encyclopedia of Hunters and Gatherers*, ed. R.B. Lee and R. Daly, 46–51. Cambridge: Cambridge University Press.

Axel, Brian Keith. 2003 Poverty of the Imagination. *Anthropological Quarterly* 76 (1): 111–33.

Barfield, Thomas, ed. 1997. *The Dictionary of Anthropology*. Oxford: Blackwell.

Barnard, Alan J. 1978. Universal Systems of Kin Categorization. *African Studies* 37 (1): 69–81.

————. 1992. *The Kalahari Debate: A Bibliographical Essay*. Occasional Papers, 35. Edinburgh: Centre of African Studies, Edinburgh University.

————. 2006. Kalahari Revisionism, Vienna and the "Indigenous Peoples" Debate. *Social Anthropology* 14 (1): 1–16.

Barnard, Alan, and Jonathan Spencer, eds. 1996. *Encyclopedia of Social and Cultural Anthropology.* London: Routledge.

Barth, Fredrik. 1969. *Ethnic Groups and Boundaries.* Boston: Little, Brown.

———. 2000. Boundaries and Connections. In *Signifying Identities: Anthropological Perspectives on Boundaries and Contested Values,* ed. A.P. Cohen, 17–36. London: Routledge.

Basso, Ellen. 1973. *The Kalapalo Indians in Central Brazil.* New York: Holt, Rinehart and Winston.

Bateson, Gregory. 1987 [1972]. *Steps to an Ecology of Mind: Collected Essays in Anthropology, Psychiatry, Evolution, and Epistemology.* Northvale, NJ: Jason Aronson.

Ben-Ari, Eyal. 1987. Pygmies and Villagers, Ritual or Play? On the Place of Contrasting Modes of Metacommunication in Social Systems. *Symbolic Interaction* 10 (2): 167–85.

Berreman, Gerald D. 1987. Scale and Social Relations: Thoughts and Three Examples. In *Scale and Social Organization,* ed. F. Barth, 41–77. Oslo: Universitetsforlaget.

Bessire, Lucas, and David Bond. 2014. Ontological Anthropology and the Deferral of Critique. *American Ethnologist* 41 (3): 440–56.

Bhanu, B.A. 1982. The Nomadic Cholanaickan of Kerala: An Analysis of Their Movement. In *Nomads in India,* ed. P.K. Misra and K.C. Malhotra, 215–26. Calcutta: Anthropological Survey of India.

———. 1989. *The Cholanaicken of Kerala.* Calcutta: Anthropological Survey of India.

Bhargava, R., R. Bagghi, and R. Sudarshan, eds. 1999. *Multiculturalism, Liberalism and Democracy in India.* Delhi: Oxford University Press.

Billig, Michael. 1995. *Banal Nationalism.* London: Sage.

Bilu, Yoram. 2000. *Without Bounds: The Life and Death of Rabbi Ya'aqov Wazana.* Detroit, MI: Wayne State University Press.

Bird, Douglas W., and Rebecca Bliege Bird. 2000. The Ethnoarchaeology of Juvenile Foragers: Shellfishing Strategies among Meriam Children. *Journal of Anthropological Archaeology* 19 (4): 461–76.

———. 2005. Mardu Children's Hunting Strategies in the Western Desert, Australia. In *Hunter-Gatherer Childhoods: Evolutionary, Developmental and Cultural Perspectives,* ed. B.S. Hewlett and M.E. Lamb, 129–46. New Brunswick, NJ: Aldine Transaction.

Bird, Nurit. 1982. Inside and Outside in Kinship Usage: The Hunter-Gatherer Naiken of South India. *Cambridge Anthropology* 7 (1–2): 47–57.

———. 1983a. Conjugal Families and Single Persons: An Analysis of the Naiken Social System. PhD diss., Department of Social Anthropology, University of Cambridge.

———. 1983b. Wage-Gathering: Socio-Economic Change and the Case of the Naiken of South India. In *Rural South Asia: Linkages, Changes and Development,* ed. P. Robb, 57–89. London: Curzon Press.

————. 1987. The Kurumbas of the Nilgiris: An Ethnographic Myth? *Modern Asian Studies* 21: 173–89.

Bird-David, Nurit. 1987. Single Persons and Social Cohesion in a Hunter-Gatherer Society. In *Dimensions of Social Life: Essays in Honour of David G. Mandelbaum*, ed. P. Hockings, 151–65. Berlin: Mouton.

————. 1988. Hunter-Gatherers and Other People: A Reexamination. In *Hunters and Gatherers: History, Evolution and Social Change*, ed. T. Ingold, D. Riches, and J. Woodburn, 17–31. Oxford: Berg.

————. 1989. The People and the Ethnographic Myth: An Introduction to the Study of the Naiken. In *Blue Mountains: The Ethnography and Biography of a South Indian Region*, ed. P. Hockings, 249–81. New Delhi: Oxford University Press.

————. 1990. The Giving Environment: Another Perspective on the Economic System of Gatherer-Hunters. *Current Anthropology* 31 (2): 183–96.

————. 1992a. Beyond the Original Affluent Society: A Culturalist Reformulation. *Current Anthropology* 33 (1): 25–47.

————. 1992b. Beyond the Hunting and Gathering Mode of Subsistence: Observations on the Nayaka and Other Modern Hunter-Gatherers. *Man*, n.s., 27 (1): 19–44.

————. 1993. Tribal Metaphorization of Human-Nature Relatedness: A Comparative Analysis. In *Environmentalism: The View from Anthropology*, ed. K. Milton, 112–25. London: Routledge.

————. 1994a. Sociality and Immediacy: Or Past and Present Conversations on Bands. *Man*, n.s., 29 (3): 583–603.

————. 1994b. The Nilgiri Tribal Systems: A View from Below. *Modern Asian Studies* 28 (2): 339–55.

————. 1995a. Hunter-Gatherers' Kinship Organization: Implicit Roles and Rules. In *Social Intelligence and Interaction: Expressions and Implications of the Social Bias in Human Intelligence*, ed. E. Goody, 68–84. Cambridge: Cambridge University Press.

————. 1995b. Hunter-Gatherer Research and Cultural Diversity. In *Cultural Diversity among Twentieth-Century Foragers: An African Perspective*, ed. S. Kent, 297–304. Cambridge: Cambridge University Press.

————. 1996. Puja or Sharing with the Gods? On Ritualized Possession among Nayaka of South India. *Eastern Anthropologist* 49 (3–4): 259–75.

————. 1999a. "Animism" Revisited: Personhood, Environment, and Relational Epistemology. *Current Anthropology* 40: S67–S91.

————. 1999b. Introduction. South Asia. In *Cambridge Encyclopedia of Hunters and Gatherers*, ed. R.B. Lee and R. Daly, 231–37. Cambridge: Cambridge University Press.

————. 2004a. No Past, No Present: A Critical-Nayaka Perspective on Cultural Remembering. *American Ethnologist* 31 (3): 406–21.

————. 2004b. Illness-Images and Joined Beings: A Critical/Nayaka Perspective on Intercorporeality. *Social Anthropology* 12 (3): 325–39.

————. 2005a. The Property of Relations: Modern Notions, Nayaka Contexts. In *Property and Equality*. Vol. 1, *Ritualization, Sharing, Egalitarianisn*, ed. T. Widlock and W.G. Tadesse, 201–16. Oxford: Berghahn.

————. 2005b. Studying Children in "Hunter-Gatherer" Societies: Reflections from a Nayaka Perspective. In *Hunter-Gatherer Childhoods: Evolutionary, Developmental and Cultural Perspectives*, ed. B.S. Hewlett and M.E. Lamb, 92–105. New Brunswick, NJ: Aldine Transaction.

————. 2006. Animistic Epistemology: Why Do Some Hunter-Gatherers Not Depict Animals? *Ethnos* 71 (1): 33–50.

————. 2008. Feeding Nayaka Children and English Readers: A Bifocal Ethnography of Parental Feeding in "the Giving Environment." *Anthropological Quarterly* 81 (3): 523–50.

————. 2009. Indigenous Architecture and Relational Senses of Personhood: A Cultural Reading of Changing Dwelling Styles among Forest-Dwelling Foragers. *Design Principles and Practices: An International Journal* 3 (5): 203–10.

————. 2015. Hunting and Gathering Societies in Anthropology. In *The International Encyclopedia of the Social and Behavioral Sciences*, ed. N.J. Smelser and P.B. Baltes, 428–31. 2nd edition. New York: Elsevier Science.

Bird-David, Nurit, and Daniel Naveh. 2008. Relational Epistemology, Immediacy, and Conservation: Or, What Do the Nayaka Try to Conserve? *Journal for the Study of Religion, Nature and Culture* 2 (1): 55–73.

Birdwell-Pheasant, Donna, and Denise Lawrence-Zuniga, eds. 1999. *House Life: Space, Place and Family in Europe*. Oxford: Berg.

Bisht, B.S. 1994. *Tribes of India, Nepal and Tibet Borderland: A Study of Cultural Transformation*. New Delhi: Gyan.

Blaser, Mario. 2009. The Threat of the Yrmo: The Political Ontology of a Sustainable Hunting Program. *American Anthropologist* 111 (1): 10–20.

————. 2013. Ontological Conflicts and the Stories of Peoples in Spite of Europe: Toward a Conversation on Political Ontology. *Current Anthropology* 54 (5): 547–68.

Bloch, Maurice. 1992. What Goes without Saying: The Conceptualization of Zafimaniry Society. In *Conceptualizaing Society*, ed. A. Kuper, 127–47. London: Routledge.

Blurton Jones, Nicholas B., Kristen Hawkes, and Patricia Draper. 1994. Differences between Hadza and !Kung Children's Work: Original Affluence or Practical Reason? In *Key Issues in Hunter-Gatherer Research*, ed. E.S. Burch and J.L. Ellana, 169–89. Oxford: Berg.

Boddy, Janice. 1989. *Wombs and Alien Spirits: Women, Men, and the Zar Cult in Northern Sudan*. Madison: University of Wisconsin Press.

————. 1994. Spirit Possession Revisited: Beyond Instrumentality. *Annual Review of Anthropology* 23: 407–34.

Bodenhorn, Barbara. 2000. "He Used to Be My Relative": Exploring the Bases of Relatedness among Inupiat of Northern Alaska. In *Cultures of*

Relatedness: New Approaches to the Study of Kinship, ed. J. Carsten, 128–48. Cambridge: Cambridge University Press.

Bodenhorn, Barbara, and Gabriele Vom Bruck, eds. 2006. *The Anthropology of Names and Naming*. Cambridge: Cambridge University Press.

Bodley, John H. 1996. *Anthropology and Contemporary Human Problems*. Mountain View, CA: Mayfield.

Bohannan, Paul. 1955. Some Principles of Exchange and Investment among the Tiv. *American Anthropologist* 57 (1): 60–70.

Bott, Elisabeth. 1957. *Family and Social Network: Roles, Norms and External Relationships in Ordinary Urban Families*. London: Tavistock.

Bouquet, Mary. 1993. *Reclaiming English Kinship: Portuguese Refractions of British Kinship Theory*. Manchester: Manchester University Press.

———. 1996. Family trees and Their Affinities: The Visual Imperative of the Genealogical Diagram. *Journal of the Royal Anthropological Institute* 1: 43–66.

Bourdieu, Pierre 1973 [1971]. The Berber House. In *Rules and Meanings: The Anthropology of Everyday Knowledge*, ed. M. Douglas, 98–110. Harmondsworth: Penguin Education.

———. 1977. *Outline of a Theory of Practice*. Cambridge: Cambridge University Press.

Bowlby, John. 1969. *Attachment*. New York: Basic Books.

Breeks, James W. 1873. *An Account of the Primitive Tribes and Monuments of the Nilagiris*. London: India Museum.

Briggs, Jean L. 1998. *Inuit Morality Play: The Emotional Education of a Three-Year-Old*. New Haven, CT: Yale University Press.

Brightman, Robert. 1993. *Grateful Prey: Rock Cree Human-Animal Relationships*. Berkeley: University of California Press.

———. 1996. The Sexual Division of Foraging Labor: Biology, Taboo, and Gender Politics. *Comparative Studies in Society and History* 38 (4): 687–729.

Brubaker, Rogers. 2004. *Ethnicity without Groups*. Cambridge, MA: Harvard University Press.

Brubaker, Rogers, and Frederick Cooper. 2000. Beyond "Identity." *Theory and Society* 29 (1): 1–47.

Bryant, Rebecca. 2002. The Purity of Spirit and the Power of Blood: A Comparative Perspective on Nation, Gender and Kinship in Cyprus. *Journal of the Royal Anthropological Institute*, n.s., 8 (3): 509–30.

Buchanan, Francis (aka Francis Buchanan Hamilton). 1807. *A Journey from Madras through the Countries of Mysore, Canara and Mulubur*. London: W. Bulmer.

Burch, Ernest S., Jr. 1975. *Eskimo Kinsmen: Changing Family Relationships in Northwest Alaska*. New York: West.

Cashdan, Elizabeth A. 1985. Coping with Risk: Reciprocity among the Basarwa of Northern Botswana. *Man* 20 (3): 454–74.

Carsten, Janet. 1995. Houses in Langkawi: Stable Structures or Mobile Momes? In *About the House: Lévi-Strauss and Beyond*, ed. Janet

Carsten and Stephen Hugh-Jones, 105–28. Cambridge: Cambridge University Press.

———. 2000. "Knowing Where You've Come From": Ruptures and Continuities of Time and Kinship in Narratives of Adoption Reunions. *Journal of the Royal Anthropological Institute* 6 (4): 687–703.

———. 2004. *After Kinship*. Cambridge: Cambridge University Press.

Carsten, Janet, and Stephen Hugh-Jones, eds. 1995. *About the House: Lévi-Strauss and Beyond*. Cambridge: Cambridge University Press.

Chance, Norman A. 1966. *The Eskimo of North Alaska*. New York: Holt, Rinehart and Winston.

Chen, Paul C. Y. 1990. *Penans: The Nomads of Sarawak*. Petaling Jaya: Pelanduk.

Chudacoff, Howard P. 1992. *How Old Are You? Age Consciousness in American Culture*. Princeton, NJ: Princeton University Press.

Cohen, Anthony. 2000. Introduction. In *Signifying Identities: Anthropological Perspectives on Boundaries and Contested Values*, ed. A. Cohen, 1–13. London: Routledge.

Collier, Jane F., and Michelle Z. Rosaldo. 1981. Politics and Gender in Simple Societies. In *Sexual Meanings: The Cultural Construction of Gender and Sexuality*, ed. S. B. Ortner and H. Whitehead, 275–329. Cambridge: Cambridge University Press.

Colloredo-Mansfeld, Rudolf. 1994. Architectural Conspicuous Consumption and Economic Change in the Andes. *American Anthropologist* 96 (4): 845–65.

Comaroff, Jean. 1985. *Body of Power, Spirit of Resistance: The Culture and History of a South African People*. Chicago: University of Chicago Press.

Cormier, Loretta A. 2003. *Kinship with Monkeys: The Guaja Foragers of Eastern Amazonia*. New York: Columbia University Press.

Csikszentmihalyi, Mihaly, and Eugene Rochberg-Halton. 1981. *The Meaning of Things: Domestic Symbols and the Self*. Cambridge: Cambridge University Press.

Csordas, Thomas J. 1983. The Rhetoric of Transformation in Ritual Healing. *Culture, Medicine and Psychiatry* 7: 333–75.

Dahlberg, Frances. 1981. *Woman the Gatherer*. New Haven, CT: Yale University Press.

Damas, David, ed. 1969. *Contributions to Anthropology: Band Societies—Proceedings of the Conference on Band Organization, Ottawa, August 30 to September 2, 1965*. Bulletin 228. Ottawa: National Museums of Canada.

Daniel, E. Valentine. 1984. *Fluid Signs: Being a Person the Tamil Way*. Berkeley: University of California Press.

Davis-Floyd, Robbie E. 1992. *Birth as an American Rite of Passage*. Berkeley: University of California Press.

Delaney, Carol 1995. Father State, Motherland, and the Birth of Modern Turkey. In *Naturalizing Power: Essays in Feminist Cultural Analysis*, ed. S. Yanagisako and C. Delaney, 177–99. New York: Routledge.

Demmer, Ulrich. 1997. Voices in the Forest. The Field of Gathering among the Jenu Kurumba: Gatherer/Hunters of South India. In *Blue Mountains*

Revisited: Cultural Studies on the Nilgiri Hills, ed. P. Hockings, 164–91. Delhi: Oxford University Press.

———. 2001. Always an Argument: Persuasive Tools in the Death Rituals of the Jenu Kurumba. *Anthropos* 96: 475–90.

———. 2007. Memory, Performance and the Regeneration of Society among the Koya. In *Time in India: Concepts and Practices*, ed. A. Maliner, 185–205. New Delhi: Manohar.

———. 2014. The Poetics and Politics of Practical Reason: Indigenous Identity, Ritual Discourse, and the Post Colonial State in Northern Nilgiris (South India). *Asian Ethnology* 73 (1–2): 111–37.

———. 2015. "Agent Plus" and "Practical Reasoner": A Comparative Study of the Ethical Person. *Ethnos* 80 (1): 91–116.

Derevenski, J. Sofaer. 1994. Where Are the Children? Accessing Children in the Past. *Archaeological Review from Cambridge* 13 (2): 7–20.

Descola, Philippe. 1994. *In the Society of Nature: A Native Ecology in Amazonia*. Cambridge: Cambridge University Press.

———. 1996. Constructing Natures: Symbolic Ecology and Social Practice. In *Nature and Society: Anthropological Perspectives*, ed. P. Descola and G. Pálsson, 82–102. London: Routledge.

———. 2006. Beyond Nature and Culture (Radcliffe-Brown Lecture in Social Anthropology, 2005). *Proceedings of the British Academy* 139: 137–55.

———. 2013 [2005]. *Beyond Nature and Culture*. Chicago: Chicago University Press.

Douglas, Mary. 1991. The Idea of a Home: A Kind of Space. *Social Research* 58 (1): 287–307.

Dow, James. 1986. Universal Aspects of Symbolic Healing: A Theoretical Synthesis. *American Anthropologist* 88 (1): 56–69.

Dubois, J.A. 1897. *Hindu Manners, Custom and Ceremonies*, trans. H.K. Beauchamp. Oxford: Clarendon Press. (Indian reprint 1973.)

Dunbar, Robin. 1993. Coevolution of Neocortical Size, Group Size and Language in Humans. *Behavioral and Brain Sciences* 16 (4): 681–735.

———. 1998. *Grooming, Gossip, and the Evolution of Language*. Cambridge, MA: Harvard University Press.

Dussart, Françoise. 1988. Notes on Warlpiri Women's Personal Names. *Journal de la Société des Océanistes* 86 (1): 53–60.

———. 2000. *The Politics of Ritual in an Aboriginal Settlement: Kinship, Gender, and the Currency of Knowledge*. Washington, DC: Smithsonian Institution Press.

Edwards, Jeanette, and Marilyn Strathern. 2000. Including Our Own. In *Cultures of Relatedness: New Approaches of Study of Kinship*, ed. J. Carsten, 149–66. Cambridge: Cambridge University Press.

Ehrenfels, U.R. 1952. *Kadar of Cochin*. Anthropological Series, 1. Madras: University of Madras.

Ellen, Roy. 1993. *The Cultural Relations of Classification*. Cambridge: Cambridge University Press.

———. 2006. *The Cultural Relations of Classification: An Analysis of Nuaulu Animal Categories from Central Seram.* Cambridge: Cambridge University Press.

Endicott, Karen L. 1999. Gender Relations in Hunter-Gatherer Societies. In *The Cambridge Encyclopedia of Hunters and Gatherers*, ed. R.B. Lee and R. Daly, 411–19. Cambridge: Cambridge University Press.

Endicott, Kirk M. 1979. *Batek Negrito Religion: The World View and Rituals of a Hunting and Gathering People of Peninsular Malaysia.* Oxford: Clarendon Press.

Endicott, Kirk M., and Karen L. Endicott. 2008. *The Headman Was a Woman.* Long Grove, IL: Waveland Press.

Estioko-Griffin, Agnes, and P. Bion Griffin. 1981. Woman the Hunter: The Agta. In *Woman the Gatherer*, ed. F. Dahlberg, 121–51. New Haven, CT: Yale University Press.

Evans-Pritchard, Edward Evan. 1940. *The Nuer.* Oxford: Clarendon Press.

Everett, Daniel L. 2005. Cultural Constraints on Grammar and Cognition in Pirahã: Another Look at the Design Features of Human Language. *Current Anthropology* 46 (4): 621–46.

Fabian, Johannes. 1983. *Time and the Other: How Anthropology Makes Its Object.* New York: Columbia University Press.

Fei Xiaotong. 1992. *From the Soil: The Foundations of Chinese Society.* A Translation of Fei Xiaotong's Xiangtu Zhongguo with an Introduction and Epilogue by Gary G. Hamilton and Wang Zheng. Berkeley: University of California Press.

Feit, Harvey. 1994. Dreaming of Animals: The Waswamipi Cree Shaking Tent Ceremony in Relation to Environment, Hunting, and Missionization. In *Circumpolar Religion and Ecology: An Anthropology of the North*, ed. Takashi and Y. Takako. Tokyo: University of Tokyo Press.

Ferguson, James, and Akhil Gupta. 2002. Spatializing States: Toward an Ethnography of Neoliberal Governmentality. *American Ethnologist* 29 (4): 981–1002.

Fine, Gary Alan. 2012. *Tiny Publics: Idiocultures and the Power of the Local.* New York: Russell Sage Foundation.

Fine, Gary Alan, and Brooke Harrington. 2004. Tiny Publics: Small Groups and Civil Society. *Sociological Theory* 22 (3): 341–56.

Fleischer, Friederike. 2007. "To Choose a House Means to Choose a Lifestyle": The Consumption of Housing and Class-Structuration in Urban China. *City and Society* 19 (2): 287–311.

Fortier, Jana. 2009a. The Ethnography of South Asian Foragers. *Annual Review of Anthropology* 38: 99–114.

———. 2009b. *Kings of the Forest: The Cultural Resilience of Himalayan Hunter-Gatherers.* Honolulu: University of Hawai'i Press.

Foster, George M. 1988 [1967]. *Tzintzuntzan: Mexican Peasants in a Changing World.* Prospect Heights, IL: Waveland Press.

Fox, James J., ed. 2006. *Inside Austronesian Houses: Perspectives on Domestic Designs for Living.* Canberra: Australian National University Press.

Francis, W. 1908. *Madras District Gazetteers: The Nilgiris.* Madras: Government Press.

Fürer-Haimendorf, Christof von. 1943. *The Chenchus: Jungle Folk of the Deccan.* London: Macmillan.

———. 1950. Youth Dormitories and Community Houses in India. *Anthropos* 45 (1): 119–44.

———. 1952. Ethnographic Notes on Some Communities of the Wynad. *Eastern Anthropology* 6: 18–36.

Gaonkar, Dilip Parameshwar. 2002. Toward New Imaginaries: An Introduction. *Public Culture* 14 (1): 1–19.

Gardner, Peter M. 1966. Symmetric Respect and Memorate Knowledge: The Structure and Ecology of Individualistic Culture. *Southwestern Journal of Anthropology* 22 (4): 389–415.

———. 1985. Bicultural Oscillation as a Long-Term Adaptation to Cultural Frontiers: Cases and Questions. *Human Ecology* 13 (4): 411–32.

———. 1991a. Foragers' Pursuit of Individual Autonomy. *Current Anthropology* 31: 543–72.

———. 1991b. Pragmatic Meanings of Possessions in Paliyan Shamanism. *Anthropos* 86: 367–84.

———. 2000. *Bicultural Versatility as a Frontier Adaptation among Paliyan Foragers of South India.* Lewiston, NY: Edwin Mellen Press.

———. 2013. Understanding Anomalous Distribution of Hunter-Gatherers: The Indian Case. *Current Anthropology* 54 (4): 510–13.

Gellner, Ernest. 2008. *Nations and Nationalism.* Ithaca, NY: Cornell University Press.

Gibson, James J. 1979. *The Ecological Approach to Visual Perception.* Boston: Houghton Mifflin.

Gibson, Thomas. 1995. Having Your House and Eating It: Houses and Siblings in Ara, South Sulawesi. In *About the House: Levi-Strauss and Beyond*, ed. Janet Carsten and Stephen Hugh-Jones, 129–48. Cambridge: Cambridge University Press.

Giesbrecht, Melissa, Valorie A. Crooks, and Allison Williams. 2010. Scale as an Explanatory Concept: Evaluating Canada's Compassionate Care Benefit. *Area* 42 (4): 457–67.

Gingrich, André, and Richard Gabriel Fox., eds. 2002. *Anthropology, by Comparison.* London: Routledge.

Goodale, Jane C. 1980. Gender, Sexuality and Marriage: A Kaulong Model of Nature and Culture. In *Nature, Culture and Gender*, ed. C. MacCormack and M. Strathern, 119–42. Cambridge: Cambridge University Press.

———. 1999. Tiwi. In *The Cambridge Encyclopedia of Hunters and Gatherers*, ed. R.B. Lee and R. Daly, 353–57. Cambridge: Cambridge University Press.

Gordon, Peter. 2004. Numerical Cognition without Words: Evidence from Amazonia. *Science* 306 (5695): 496–99.

Grigg, H.B., ed. 1880. *A Manual of the Nilagiris District in the Madras Presidency.* Madras: Government Press.

Grinker, Roy Richard. 1994. *Houses in the Rain Forest: Ethnicity and Inequality among Farmers and Foragers in Central Africa.* Berkeley: University of California Press.

Hacking, Ian. 1990. *The Taming of Chance.* Cambridge: University of Cambridge Press.

Hallowell, A. Irving. 2000 [1960]. Ojibwa Ontology, Behavior, and World View. In *Readings in Indigenous Religions,* ed. H. Graham, 17–49. London: Continuum.

———. 2012 [1955]. *Culture and Experience.* Whitefish, MT: Literary Licensing.

Hareven, Tamara K. 1991. The Home and the Family in Historical Perspective. *Social Research* 58 (1): 253–87.

Harvey, Graham, ed. 2013. *The Handbook of Contemporary Animism.* Durham: Acumen.

Hawkes, Kristen. 2004. Human Longevity: The Grandmother Effect. *Nature* 428 (6979): 128–29.

Heal, Felicity. 1990. *Hospitality in Early Modern England.* Oxford: Clarendon Press.

Heidegger, Martin. 1971. *Poetry, Language, Thought.* New York: Harper Collins.

Herzfeld, Michael. 1997. *Cultural Intimacy: Social Poetics in the Nation-State.* New York: Routledge.

Hewlett, Barry. 1991. *Intimate Fathers: The Nature and Context of Aka Pygmy Paternal Infant Care.* Ann Arbor: University of Michigan Press.

Hewlett, Barry S., and Michael E. Lamb. 2005a. Emerging Issues in the Study of Hunter-Gatherer Children. In *Hunter-Gatherer Childhoods: Evolutionary, Developmental, and Cultural Perspectives,* ed. B.S. Hewlett and M.E. Lamb. 3–19. New Brunswick, NJ: Aldine Transaction.

Hewlett, Barry S., and Michael E. Lamb, eds. 2005b. *Hunter-Gatherer Childhoods: Evolutionary, Developmental, and Cultural Perspectives.* New Brunswick, NJ: Aldine Transaction.

Hewlett, Barry S., Michael E. Lamb, Birgit Leyendecker, and Axel Schölmerich. 2000. Parental Investment Strategies among Aka Foragers, Ngandu Farmers, and Euro-American Urban-Industrialists. In *Adaptation and Human Behavior: An Anthropological Perspective,* ed. L. Cronk, N. Chagnon, and W. Irons, 155–78. Hawthorne, NY: Aldine de Gruyter.

Hewlett, Barry S., and Steve Winn. 2014. Allomaternal Nursing in Humans. *Current Anthropology* 55 (2): 200–29.

Hewlett, Bonnie L. 2005. Vulnerable Lives: The Experience of Death and Loss among the Aka and Ngandu Adolescents of the Central African Republic. In *Hunter-Gatherer Childhoods: Evolutionary, Developmental and Cultural*

Perspectives, ed. B.S. Hewlett and M.E. Lamb, 322–42. New Brunswick, NJ: Aldine Transaction.

Hiatt, Betty. 1970. Woman the Gatherer. *Australian Aboriginal Studies* 32: 2–9.

Hill, Kim, and A. Magdalena Hurtado. 1996. *Ache Life History: The Ecology and Demography of a Foraging People*. Hawthorne, NY: Aldine de Gruyter.

Hirasawa, Ayako. 2005. Infant Care among the Sedentarized Baka Hunter-Gatherers in Southeastern Cameroon. In *Hunter-Gatherer Childhoods: Evolutionary, Developmental and Cultural Perspectives*, ed. B.S. Hewlett and M.E. Lamb, 365–84. New Brunswick, NJ: Aldine Transaction.

Hirschfeld, Lawrence A. 2002. Why Don't Anthropologists Like Children? *American Anthropologist* 104 (2): 611–27.

Hockings, Paul. 1978. *A Bibliography for the Nilgiri Hills of Southern India*. Vols. 1–2. New Haven, CT: HRAF Press.

———. 1996. *A Comprehensive Bibliography for the Nilgiri Hills of Southern India, 1603–1996*. Bordeaux: Université Michel de Montaigne.

Holbraad, Martin, Morten Axel Pedersen, and Eduardo Viveiros de Castro. 2014. The Politics of Ontology: Anthropological Positions. *Cultural Anthropology Online*, January 13. http://culanth.org/fieldsights/462-the-politics-of-ontology-anthropological-positions, accessed February 16, 2015.

Hollander, John. 1991. It All Depends. *Social Research* 58 (1): 31–51.

Holston, James. 1991. Autoconstruction in Working-Class Brazil. *Cultural Anthropology* 6 (4): 447–65.

Holý, Ladislav, ed. 1987. *Comparative Anthropology*. Oxford: Blackwell.

Howell, Nancy. 1979. *Demography of the Dobe !Kung*. New York: Academic Press.

Howell, Signe. 1984. *Society and Cosmos: Chewong of Peninsular Malaysia*. Oxford: Oxford University Press.

———. 2011. Sources of Sociality in a Cosmological Frame: Chewong, Peninsular Malaysia. In *Anarchic Solidarity: Autonomy, Equality, and Fellowship in Southeast Asia*, ed. T. Gibson and K. Sillande, 40–62. New Haven, CT: Yale University Press.

———. 2013. Metamorphosis and Identity: Chewong Animistic Ontology. In *The Handbook of Contemporary Animism*, ed. G. Harvey. 101–12. Durham: Acumen.

Howitt, Richard. 2002. Scale and the Other: Levinas and Geography. *Geoforum* 33 (3): 299–313.

Hrdy, Sarah Blaffer. 2009. *Mothers and Others: The Evolutionary Origins of Mutual Understanding*. Cambridge, MA: Harvard University Press.

Hugh-Jones, Christine. 1979. *From the Milk River: Spatial and Temporal Processes in Northwest Amazonia*. Cambridge: Cambridge University Press.

Hugh-Jones, Stephen. 1979. *The Palm and the Pleiades: Initiation and Cosmology in Northwest Amazonia*. Cambridge: Cambridge University Press.

Humphrey, Caroline. 1974. Inside a Mongolian Tent. *New Society*, October 31, 273–75.

Ikeya, Kazunobu, Hidefumi Ogawa, and Peter Mitchell, eds. 2009. *Interactions between Hunter-Gatherers and Farmers: From Prehistory to Present.* Osaka: National Museum of Ethnology.

Ingold, Tim. 1980. *Hunters, Pastoralists and Ranchers.* Cambridge: Cambridge University Press.

———. 1983. The Significance of Storage in Hunting Societies. *Man*, n.s., 18 (3): 553–71.

———. 1999. On the Social Relations of the Hunter-Gatherer Band. In *The Cambridge Encyclopedia of Hunters and Gatherers*, ed. R.B. Lee and R. Daly, 399–411. Cambridge: Cambridge University Press.

———. 2000. *The Perception of the Environment: Essays in Livelihood, Dwelling and Skill.* Abingdon: Routledge.

Ingold, Tim, ed. 1994. *Companion Encyclopedia of Anthropology: Humanity, Culture and Social Life.* London: Routledge.

Ivey, Paula K. 2000. Cooperative Reproduction in Ituri Forest Hunter-Gatherers: Who Cares for Efe Infants? *Current Anthropology* 41 (5): 856–66.

Ivry, Tsipy. 2010. *Embodying Culture: Pregnancy in Japan and Israel.* New Brunswick, NJ: Rutgers University Press.

Jackson, Jean Elizabeth. 1983. *The Fish People: Linguistic Exogamy and Tukanoan Identity in Northwest Amazonia.* Cambridge: Cambridge University Press.

James, Paul. 1996. *Nation Formation: Towards a Theory of Abstract Community.* London: Sage.

Janzen, John M. 1992. *Ngoma: Discourses of Healing in Central and Southern Africa.* Berkeley: University California Press.

Jiménez, Alberto Corsín. 2005. Changing Scales and the Scales of Change: Ethnography and Political Economy in Antofagasta, Chile. *Critique of Anthropology* 25 (2): 157–76.

Johnson, Allen. 2003. *Families of the Forest: The Matsigenka Indians of the Peruvian Amazon.* Berkeley: University of California Press.

Jones, Katherine T. 1998. Scale as Epistemology. *Political Geography* 17 (1): 25–28.

Kakkoth, Seetha. 2005. The Primitive Tribal Groups of Kerala: A Situational Appraisal. *Studies of Tribes and Tribals* 3 (1): 47–55.

Kamp, Kathryn A. 2001. Where Have All the Children Gone? The Archaeology of Childhood. *Journal of Archaeological Method and Theory* 8 (1): 1–34.

Kane, Sergei, ed. 2001. *Strangers to Relatives: The Adoption and Naming of Anthropologists in Native North America.* Lincoln: University of Nebraska Press.

Kapferer, Bruce. 1979a. Mind, Self, and Other in Demonic Illness: The Negation and Reconstruction of Self. *American Ethnologist* 6 (1): 110–33.

———. 1979b. Entertaining Demons: Comedy, Interaction and Meaning in a Sinhalese Healing Ritual. *Social Analysis* 1: 108–52.

Kapila, Kriti. 2008. The Measure of a Tribe: The Cultural Politics of Constitutional Reclassificatiion in North India. *Journal of the Royal Anthropological Society* 14 (1): 117–34.

Kaplan, David. 2000. The Darker Side of the "Original Affluent Society." *Journal of Anthropological Research* 56 (3): 301–24.

Kaplan, Hillard, and Heather Dove. 1987. Infant Development among the Ache of Eastern Paraguay. *Developmental Psychology* 23 (2): 190–98.

Kaplan, Joanna Overing. 1975. *The Piaroa, a People of the Orinoco Basin: A Study of Kinship and Marriage.* Oxford: Clarendon Press.

Kapp, Dieter B. 1978a. Childbirth and Name Giving among the Alu Kurumbas of South India. In *Aspects of Tribal Life in South Asia 1: Strategy and Survival,* ed. R. R. Moser and M. K. Gautam, 167–80. Berne: University of Berne.

———. 1978b. Alu Kurumba Riddles: Specimens of a South Dravidian Tribal Language. *Bulletin of the School of Oriental and African Studies* 41 (3): 512–22.

Karlsson, G. Bengt. 2003. Anthropology and the "Indigenous Slot": Claims to and Debates about Indigenous Peoples' Status in India. *Critique of Anthropology* 23 (4): 403–23.

Keane, Webb. 1995. The Spoken House: Text, Act, and Object in Eastern Indonesia. *American Ethnologist* 22 (1): 102–24.

Kelly, Robert L. 1995. *The Foraging Spectrum: Diversity in Hunter-Gatherers' Lifeways.* Washington, DC: Smithsonian Institution Press.

Khilnani, Sunil. 1997. *The Idea of India.* London: Hamish Hamilton.

Kipp, Rita Smith. 1986. Terms of Endearment: Karo Batak Lovers as Siblings. *American Ethnologist* 13 (4): 632–45.

Kirk, R. L., L. Y. C. Lai, G. H. Vos, and L. P. Vidyarthi. 1962. A Genetical Study of the Oraons of the Chota Nagpur Plateau (Bihar, India). *American Journal of Physical Anthropology* 20 (3): 375–85.

Kohli, Atul, ed. 2001. *Success of India's Democracy.* Cambridge: Cambridge University Press.

Konner, Melvin. 2005. Hunter-Gatherer Infancy and Childhood: The !Kung and Others. In *Hunter-Gatherer Childhoods: Evolutionary, Developmental and Cultural Perspectives,* ed. B. S. Hewlett and M. E. Lamb, 19–64. New Brunswick, NJ: Aldine Transaction.

Kuper, Adam. 1992. *Conceptualizing Society.* London: Routledge.

Lambek, Michael. 1993. *Knowledge and Practice in Mayotte: Local Discourses of Islam, Sorcery, and Spirit Possession.* Toronto: University of Toronto Press.

Lamont, Michèle, and Virág Molnár. 2002. The Study of Boundaries in the Social Sciences. *Annual Review of Sociology* 28: 167–95.

Latour, Bruno. 2005. *Reassembling the Social: An Introduction to Actor-Network-Theory.* Oxford: Oxford University Press.

Lavi, Noa. 2012. At Home in a Changing World: External Changes and Cultural Continuity in the Life of the Nayaka (a Hunter-Gatherer Group) in South India. MA thesis, Department of Sociology and Anthropology, University of Haifa.

Lavi, Noa, and Nurit Bird-David. 2014. At Home under Development: A Housing Project for the Hunter-Gatherers Nayaka of the Nilgiris. *Eastern Anthropologist* 67 (3–4): 401–27.

Lee, Richard B. 1968. What Hunters Do for a Living. Or, How to Make Out on Scarce Resources. In *Man the Hunter,* ed. R.B. Lee and I. DeVore, 30–48. Chicago: Aldine.

———. 1979. *The !Kung San: Men, Women, and Work in a Foraging Society.* New York: Columbia University Press.

Lee, Richard B., and Richard Daly, eds. 1999. *The Cambridge Encyclopedia of Hunters and Gatherers.* Cambridge: Cambridge University Press.

Lee, Richard B., and Irven DeVore, eds. 1968. *Man the Hunter.* Chicago: Aldine.

Leinaweaver, Jessaca B. 2009. Raising the Roof in the Transnational Andes: Building Houses, Forging Kinship. *Journal of the Royal Anthropological Institute* 15 (4): 777–96.

Levinson, David, ed. 1991–2001. *Encyclopedia of World Cultures.* Boston: G.K. Hall.

Lévi-Strauss, Claude. 1961. *A World on the Wane.* London: Hutchinson.

———. 1962. *Totemism.* Boston: Beacon Press.

———. 1969 [1949]. *The Elementary Structures of Kinship.* Boston: Beacon Press.

———. 1973 [1952]. *Tristes Tropiques,* trans. J.W. Weightman and D. Weightman. London: Jonathan Cape.

———. 1987. *Anthropology and Myth: Lectures 1951–1982.* Oxford: Blackwell.

Lewis, Jerome. 2013. A Cross-Cultural Perspective on the Significance of Music and Dance to Culture and Society. In *Language, Music, and the Brain: A Mysterious Relationship,* ed. M.A. Arbib, 45–65. Cambridge, MA: MIT Press.

Lindholm, Charles. 1997. Does the Sociocentric Self Exist? Reflections on Markus and Kitayama's "Culture and the Self." *Journal of Anthropological Research* 53 (4): 405–22.

Locke, John. 1900 [1689?]. *An Essay Concerning Human Understanding.* London: Ward, Lock.

Macfarlane, Alan. 1986. *Marriage and Love in England: Modes of Reproduction 1300–1840.* Oxford: Basil Blackwell.

Mailhot, Jose. 1999. Innu. In *The Cambridge Encyclopedia of Hunters and Gatherers,* ed. R.B. Lee and R. Daly, 51–56. Cambridge: Cambridge University Press.

Malkin, Irad. 2011. *A Small Greek World: Networks in the Ancient Mediterranean.* Oxford: Oxford University Press.

Mallett, Shelley. 2004. Understanding Home: A Critical Review of the Literature. *Sociological Review* 52 (1): 62–89.

Markus, Hazel R., and Shinobu Kitayama. 1991. Culture and the Self: Implications for Cognition, Emotion, and Motivation. *Psychological Review* 98 (2): 224–53.

Marriott, McKim. 1976. Hindu Transactions: Diversity without Dualism. In *Transaction and Meaning: Directions in the Anthropology of Exchange and Symbolic Behavior,* ed. B. Kapferer, 109–42. Philadelphia: Institute for the Study of Human Issues.

————. 1990. Constructing an Indian Ethnosociology. In *India through Hindu Categories*, ed. M. Marriott, 1–39. New Delhi: Sage.

Marshall, Lorna. 1962. !Kung Bushmen Religious Belief. *Africa* 32 (3): 221–25.

Marshall, Mac, ed. 1979. *Siblingship in Oceania: Studies in the Meaning of Kin Relations*. Ann Arbor: University of Michigan Press.

Mason, Alan. 1997. The Sibling Principle in Oronao's Residence. *Ethnology* 36 (4): 351–66.

Masuda, Jeffrey R., and Valorie A. Crooks. 2007. Introduction: (Re)Thinking the Scales of Lived Experience. *Area* 39 (3): 257–58.

Mathur, P. R. G. 1977. The Cholanaickans of Kerala. In *Primitive Tribes: The First Step*, ed. S. C. Sinha and B. D. Sharma, 141–49. New Delhi: Government of India, Ministry of Home Affairs.

McKinley, Robert. 1981. Cain and Abel on the Malay Peninsula. *Siblingship in Oceania: Studies in the Meaning of Kin Relations*, ed. M. Marshall, 335–87. Lanham, MD: University Press of America.

Middleton, C. Townsend. 2011a. Across the Interface of State Ethnography: Rethinking Ethnology and Its Subjects in Multicultural India. *American Ethnologist* 38 (2): 249–66.

————. 2011b. Ethno-logics: Paradigms of Modern Identity. In *Modern Makeovers*, edited by S. Dube. Oxford: Oxford University Press.

————. 2013. Scheduling Tribes: A View from Inside India's Ethnographic State. *Focaal* 65: 13–22.

Middleton, C. Townsend, and Sara Shneiderman. 2008. Reservation, Federalism and the Politics of Recognition in Nepal. *Economic and Political Weekly*, May 10.

Miller, Daniel. 2010. *Stuff*. Cambridge: Polity.

Misra, P. K. 1977. Social Transformation among Food-Gatherers: A Case Study. In *Dimensions of Social Change in India*, ed. M. N. Srinivas, S. Seshaiah, and V. S. Parthasarathy, 429–38. Bombay: Allied.

Moodie, Megan. 2015. *We Were Adivasis: Aspiration in an Indian Scheduled Tribe*. Chicago: University of Chicago Press.

Moore, Adam. 2008. Rethinking Scale as a Geographical Category: From Analysis to Practice. *Progress in Human Geography* 32 (2): 203–25.

Morris, Brian. 1975. An Analysis of the Economy and Social Organization of the Malapanatram. PhD diss., London School of Economics and Political Science.

————. 1976. Whither the Savage Mind? Notes on the Natural Taxonomies of a Hunting and Gathering People. *Man*, n s., 11 (4): 542–57.

————. 1981. Hill Gods and Ecstatic Cults: Notes on the Religion of a Hunting and Gathering People. *Man in India* 61 (3): 203–36.

————. 1982. *Forest Traders: A Socio-Economic Study of the Hill Pandaram*. London: Athlone Press.

Myers, Fred R. 1986. *Pintupi Country, Pintupi Self: Sentiment, Place, and Politics among Western Desert Aborigine*. Washington, DC: Smithsonian Institution Press and Australian Institute of Aboriginal Studies.

Nabokov, Isabelle. 2000. *Religion against the Self: An Ethnography of Tamil Ritual*. Oxford: Oxford University Press.

Nadasdy, Paul. 2012. Boundaries among Kin: Sovereignty, the Modern Treaty Process, and the Rise of Ethno-Territorial Nationalism among Yukon First Nations. *Comparative Studies in Society and History* 54 (3): 499–532.

Nader, Laura. 1994. Comparative Consciousness. In *Assessing Cultural Anthropology*, ed. R. Borofski, 84–94. New York: McGraw-Hill.

Nancy, Jean-Luc. 1991. *The Inoperative Community*. Minneapolis: University of Minnesota Press.

———. 2000. *Being Singular Plural*. Stanford, CA: Stanford University Press.

Naveh, Daniel. 2007. Continuity and Change in Nayaka Epistemology and Subsistence Economy: A Hunter Gatherer Case from South India. PhD diss., Department of Sociology and Anthropology, University of Haifa.

Naveh, Daniel, and Nurit Bird-David. 2013. On Animisms, Conservation and Immediacy. In *A Handbook on Contemporary Animism*, ed. G. Harvey, 27–37. Durham: Acumen.

———. 2014. How Persons Become Things: Economic and Epistemological Changes among Nayaka Hunter-Gatherers. *Journal of the Royal Anthropological Institute* 20 (1): 74–92.

Nisbett, Richard. 2004. *The Geography of Thought: How Asians and Westerners Think Differently . . . and Why*. New York: Free Press.

Norström, Christer. 2003. *"They Call for Us": Strategies for Securing Autonomy among the Paliyans, Hunter-Gatherers of the Palni Hills, South India*. Stockholm: Stockholm University.

Nuckolls, Charles W., ed. 1993. *Siblings in South Asia: Brothers and Sisters in Cultural Context*. New York: Guilford Press.

Nuttall, Mark. 1992. *Arctic Homeland: Kinship, Community and Development in Northwest Greenland*. Toronto: University of Toronto Press.

———. 2000. Choosing Kin: Sharing and Subsistence in a Greenlandic Hunting Community. In *Dividends of Kinship: Meanings and Uses of Social Relatedness*, ed. P. P. Schweitzer, 33–60. London: Routledge.

Ong, Aihwa. 1987. *Spirits of Resistance and Capitalist Discipline: Factory Women in Malaysia*. Albany: State University New York Press.

Overing, Joanna, and Alan Passes, eds. 2000. *The Anthropology of Love and Anger: The Aesthetics of Conviviality in Native Amazonia*. London: Routledge.

Pader, J. Ellen. 1993. Spatiality and Social Change: Domestic Space Use in Mexico and the United States. *American Ethnologist* 20 (1): 114–37.

Pandya, Vishvajit. 1993. *Above the Forest: A Study of Andamanese Ethnoanemology, Cosmology and the Power of Ritual*. Delhi: Oxford University Press.

Peterson, Nicolas. 1993. Demand Sharing: Reciprocity and the Pressure for Generosity among Foragers. *American Anthropologist* 95 (4): 860–74.

Philips, Susan U. 2013. Scale and Scaling in Powerful Institutions: Higher and Lower Court Levels in Tonga. Paper presented at the 112th Annual Meeting of the American Anthropological Association, Chicago, November 20–24.

Pinker, Steven. 2007. *The Stuff of Thought: Language as a Window into Human Nature*. New York: Viking.

Polanyi, Karl. 1957. The Economy as Instituted Process. In *Trade and Market in the Early Empires: Economies in History and Theory*, ed. K. Polanyi, C.M. Arensberg, and H.W. Pearson, 243–69. Glencoe, IL: Free Press.

Povinelli, Elizabeth A. 2001. Radical Worlds: The Anthropology of Incommensurability and Inconceivability. *Annual Review of Anthropology* 30: 319–34.

———. 2002. *The Cunning of Recognition: Indigenous Alterities and the Making of Australian Multiculturalism*. Durham, NC: Duke University Press.

Praet, Istvan. 2013. *Animism and the Question of Life*. London: Routledge.

Pyyhtinen, Olli. 2009. Being-With: Georg Simmel's Sociology of Association. *Theory, Culture and Society* 26 (5): 108–28.

Rabinow, Paul. 2007. *Reflections on Fieldwork in Morocco*. Berkeley: University of California Press.

Raghavan, M.D. 1929. Jain-Kurumbers: An Account of Their Life and Habits. *Man in India* 9 (1): 54–65.

Ramos, Alcida Rita. 2012. The Politics of Perspectivism. *Annual Review of Anthropology* 41: 481–94.

Rapport, Nigel, and Joanna Overing. 2000. *Social and Cultural Anthropology: The Key Concepts*. London: Routledge.

Rival, Laura M. 2002. *Trekking through History: The Huaorani of Amazonian Ecuador*. New York: Columbia University Press.

Rivers, W.H.R. 1968 (1910). *Kinship and Social Organization (Together with "The Genealogical Method of Anthropological Enquiry" with Commentaries by Raymond Firth and David M. Schneider)*. Edited by A. Forge. London School of Economics Monographs on Social Anthropology, 34. London: Athlone Press.

Robben, Antonius C.G.M. 1989. Habits of the Home: Spatial Hegemony and the Structuration of House and Society in Brazil. *American Anthropologist* 91 (3): 570–88.

Rosaldo, Renato. 1980. *Ilongot Head Hunting: 1883–1974*. Stanford, CA: Stanford University Press.

Roseman, Marina. 1991. *Healing Sounds from the Malaysian Rainforest: Temiar Music and Medicine*. Berkeley: University of California Press.

Rudolph, Lloyd I., and Susanne Hoeber Rudolph. 2002. Living with Multiculturalism: Universalism and Particularism in an Indian Historical Context. In *Engaging Cultural Differences: The Multicultural Challenge in Liberal Democracies*, ed. R. Shweder, M. Minow, and H. Markus, 43–58. New York: Russell Sage Foundation.

Rykwert, Joseph. 1991. House and Home. *Social Research* 58 (1): 51–65.

Sahlins, Marshall David. 1972. *Stone Age Economics*. London: Tavistock.

———. 1985. *Islands of History*. Chicago: University of Chicago Press.

———. 2013. *What Kinship Is—and Is Not*. Chicago: University of Chicago Press.

Saint-Exupéry, Antoine de. 1943. *The Little Prince*. New York: Reynal and Hitchcock.

Schieffelin, Edward L. 1985. Performance and the Cultural Construction of Reality. *American Ethnologist* 30 (1): 707–25.

———. 1996. On Failure and Performance: Throwing the Medium Out of the Trance. In *The Performance of Healing*, ed. C. Laderman and M. Roseman, 59–90. New York: Routledge.

Schneider, David M. 1968. *American Kinship: A Cultural Account*. Englewood Cliffs, NJ: Prentice-Hall.

———. 1969. Kinship, Nationality and Religion in American Culture: Toward a Definition of Kinship. In *Forms of Symbolic Action: Proceedings of the 1969 Annual Spring Meeting of the American Ethnological Society*, ed. R. Spencer, 116–25. Seattle: University of Washington Press.

Schneider, David M., and G.C. Homans. 1955. Kinship Terminology and the American Kinship System. *American Anthropologist* 57 (1): 1195–208.

Schrire, Carmel. 1980. An Inquiry into the Evolutionary Status and Apparent Identity of San Hunter-Gatherers. *Human Ecology* 8 (1): 9–27.

Scott, James C. 1998. *Seeing Like a State: How Certain Schemes to Improve the Human Condition Have Failed*. New Haven, CT: Yale University Press.

Seitz, Stefan. 2007. Game, Pets and Animal Husbandry among Penan and Penan Groups. In *Beyond the Green Myth: Hunter-Gatherers of Borneo in the Twenty-First Century*, ed. P.G. Sercombe and B. Sellato, 177–91. Copenhagen: Nordic Institute of Asian Studies Press.

Seligman, Cecil G., and Brenda Z. Seligman. 1911. *The Vedas*. Cambridge: Cambridge University Press.

Service, Elman R. 1966. *The Hunters*. Englewood Cliffs, NJ: Prentice Hall.

Shani, Ornit. 2011. The Politics of Communalism and Caste. In *A Companion to the Anthropology of India*, ed. I. Clark-Deces, 297–312. Oxford: Wiley-Blackwell.

Shapiro, Judith. 1985. The Sibling Relationship in Lowland South America: General Considerations. In *The Sibling Relationship in Lowland South America*, ed. K.M. Kesinger, 1–7. Working Papers on South American Indians, 7. Bennington, VT: Bennington College.

Shneiderman, Sara. 2009. Ethnic (P)reservations: Comparing Thangmi Ethnic Activism in Nepal and India. In *Ethnic Activism and Civil Society in South Asia*, ed. D. Gellner, 115–41. Delhi: Sage.

Shostak, Marjorie. 1981. *Nisa: The Life and Words of a !Kung Woman*. London: Allen Lane.

Singh, Kumar Suresh. 1994. *The Scheduled Tribes*. Delhi: Oxford University Press.

Skultans, Vieda. 1987. The Management of Mental Illness among Maharashtrian Families: A Case Study of a Mahanubhav Healing Temple. *Man*, n.s., 22 (4): 661–79.

Slocum, Sally. 1975. Woman the Gatherer: Male Bias in Anthropology. In *Toward an Anthropology of Women*, ed. R.R. Reiter, 36–50. New York: Monthy Review Press.

Smith, Eric Alden. 1988. Risk and Uncertainty in the "Original Affluent Society": Evolutionary Ecology of Resource-Sharing and Land Tenure. In *Hunters and Gatherers.* Vol. 1, *History, Evolution, and Social Change,* ed. T. Ingold, D. Riches, and J. Woodburn, 222–51. Oxford: Berg.

Smith, Eric Alden, and Mark Wishnie. 2000. Conservation and Subsistence in Small-Scale Societies. *Annual Review of Anthropology* 29: 493–524.

Smole, William J. 1976. *The Yanomama Indians: A Cultural Geography.* Austin: University of Texas Press.

Sneath, David, Martin Holbraad, and Morten Axel Pedersen. 2009. Technologies of the Imagination: An Introduction. *Ethnos* 74 (1): 5–30.

Solway, Jacqueline S., and Richard B. Lee. 1990. Foragers, Genuine or Spurious? Situating the Kalahari San in History. *Current Anthropology* 31 (2): 109–46.

Sontag, Susan. 1978. *Illness as Metaphor.* New York: Farrar, Strauss and Giroux.

Spielmann, Katherine A. 2002. Feasting, Craft Specialization, and the Ritual Mode of Production in Small-Scale Societies. *American Anthropologist* 104 (1): 195–207.

Spielmann, Katherine A., and James F. Eder. 1994. Hunters and Farmers: Then and Now. *American Review of Anthropology* 23: 303–23.

Spruhan, Paul. 2006. A Legal History of Blood Quantum in Federal Indian Law to 1935. *South Dakota Law Review* 51 (1): 1–50.

Stange, Mary Zeiss. 1997. *Woman the Hunter.* Boston: Beacon Press.

Steward, Julian H. 1936. The Economic and Social Basis of Primitive Bands. In *Essays in Anthropology Presented to A. L. Kroeber,* ed. R. H. Lowie, 311–50. Berkeley: University of California Press.

———. 1969. Observations on Bands. In *Contribution to Anthropology: Band Societies,* ed. D. Damas, 1–10. Ottawa: National Museum of Canada.

Stewart, Henry, Alan Barnard, and Jiro Tanaka, eds. 2002. *Self- and Other-Images of Hunter-Gatherers.* Senri Ethnological Studies, 60. Osaka: National Museum of Ethnology.

Stoller, Paul. 1989. *Fusion of the Worlds: An Ethnography of Possession among the Songhay of Niger.* Chicago: University of Chicago Press.

Stolte, John F., Gary Alan Fine, and Karen S. Cook. 2001. Sociological Miniaturism: Seeing the Big through the Small in Social Psychology. *Annual Review of Sociology* 27: 387–413.

Strathern, Marilyn. 1988. *The Gender of the Gift: Problems with Women and Problems with Society in Melanesia.* Berkeley: University of California Press.

———. 1991. *Partial Connections.* Savage, MD: Rowman and Littlefield.

———. 1992a. *After Nature: English Kinship in the Late Twentieth Century.* Cambridge: Cambridge University Press.

———. 1992b. Parts and Wholes: Refiguring Relationships in a Post-Plural World. In *Conceptualizing Society,* ed. A. Kuper, 75–104. London: Routledge.

———. 1995. *The Relation: Issues in Complexity and Scale.* Cambridge: Prickly Pear Press.

————. 2004. The Whole Person and Its Artifacts. *Annual Review of Anthropology* 33: 1–19.

Strum, S. S., and Bruno Latour. 1987. Redefining the Social Link: From Baboons to Humans. *Social Science Information* 26 (4): 783–802.

Svensson, Tom G. 1999. Ainu. In *The Cambridge Encyclopedia of Hunters and Gatherers*, ed. R. B. Lee and R. Daly, 269–73. Cambridge: Cambridge University Press.

Taylor, Charles. 2002. Modern Social Imaginaries. *Culture* 14 (1): 91–124.

————. 2004. *Modern Social Imaginaries*. Durham, NC: Duke University Press.

Testart, Alain. 1982. The Significance of Food Storage among Hunter-Gatherers: Residence Patterns, Population Densities, and Social Inequalities. *Current Anthropology* 23 (5): 523–31.

Thurston, Edgar 1909. *Castes and Tribes of Southern India*, vol. 4. Madras: Government Press.

Tronick, Edward Z., Gilda A. Morelli, and Paula K. Ivey. 1992. The Efe Forager Infant and Toddler's Pattern of Social Relationships: Multiple and Simultaneous. *Developmental Psychology* 28 (4): 568–77.

Tronick, Edward Z., Gilda A. Morelli, and Steve Winn. 1987. Multiple Caretaking of Efe (Pygmy) Infants. *American Anthropologist* 89 (1): 96–106.

Tsing, Anna Lowenhaupt. 1993. *In the Realm of the Diamond Queen*. Princeton, NJ: Princeton University Press.

————. 2005. *Friction: An Ethnography of Global Connections*. Princeton, NJ: Princeton University Press.

Tuck-Po, Lye. 2004. Changing Pathways: Forest Degradation and the Batek of Pahang, Malaysia. Lanham, MD: Lexington Books.

Turnbull, Colin M. 1965. *Wayward Servants: The Two Worlds of the African Pygmies*. Garden City, NY: Natural History Press.

Turner, Terry S. 2009. The Crisis of Late Structuralism, Perspectivism and Animism: Rethinking Culture, Nature, Spirit, and Bodiliness. *Tipití: Journal of the Society for the Anthropology of Lowland South America* 7 (1): 3–40.

Tylor, E. B. 1958 [1871]. *Primitive Culture*. 2 vols. New York: Harper and Row.

Urry, John. 2007. *Mobilities*. Cambridge: Polity.

Valkonon, Jarno, Sanna Valkonen, and Timo Koivurova. 2016. Groupism and the Politics of Indigeneity: A Case Study on the Sámi Debate in Finland. *Ethnicities* 16 (3): 1–20. Van Den Abbeele, Georges. 1991. Introduction. In *Community at Loose Ends*, ed. Miami Theory Collective, ix–xxvi. Minneapolis: University of Minnesota Press.

Vanderbilt, Amy. 1954. *Amy Vanderbilt's Complete Book of Etiquette: A Guide to Gracious Living*. Garden City, NY: Doubleday.

Vigh, Henrik Erdman, and David Brehm Sausdal. 2014. From Essence Back to Existence: Anthropology beyond the Ontological Turn. *Anthropological Theory* 14 (1): 49–73.

Viveiros de Castro, Eduardo. 1992 [1986]. *From the Enemy's Point of View: Humanity and Divinity in an Amazonian Society*. Chicago: University of Chicago Press.

———. 1998. Cosmological Deixis and Amerindian Perspectivism. *Journal of the Royal Anthropological Institute* 4 (3): 469–88.

———. 2009. The Gift and the Given: Three Nano-Essays on Kinship. In *Kinship and Beyond: The Genealogical Method Reconstructed,* ed. S. Bamford and J. Leach, 237–68. New York: Berghahn.

———. 2012. *Cosmological Perspectivism in Amazonia and Elsewhere.* Manchester: HAU Network of Ethnographic Theory.

Walker, Harry. 2013. *Under a Watchful Eye: Self, Power, and Intimacy in Amazonia.* Berkeley: University of California Press.

Waterson, Roxana. 1990. *The Living House: An Anthropology of Architecture in South-East Asia.* Singapore: Oxford University Press.

Wazir-Jahan, Karim. 1981. *Ma'Betisek Concepts of Living Things.* London: Athlone Press.

Weiner, Annette B. 1988. *The Trobrianders of Papua New Guinea.* New York: Holt, Rinehart and Winston.

Whitelaw, Todd M. 1994. Order without Architecture: Functional Social and Symbolic Dimensions in Hunter-Gatherer Settlement Organization. In *Architecture and Order: Approaches to Social Space,* ed. M.P. Pearson and C. Richards, 217–43. London: Routledge.

Widlok, Thomas. 2000. Names That Escape the State: Hai//om Naming Practices versus Domination and Isolation. In *Hunters and Gatherers in the Modern World,* ed. P.P. Schweitzer, M. Biesele, and R.K. Hitchcock, 361–79. Oxford: Berghahn.

Wiessner, Polly. 1982. Risk, Reciprocity and Social Influences on !Kung San Economics. In *Politics and History in Band Societies,* ed. E. Leacock and R.B. Lee, 61–84. Cambridge: Cambridge University Press.

Willerslev, Rane. 2007. *Soul Hunters: Hunting, Animism, and Personhood among the Siberian Yukaghirs.* Berkeley: University of California Press.

Williams, Raymond. 1976. *Keywords: A Vocabulary of Culture and Society.* New York: Oxford University Press.

Wilmsen, Edwin N. 1989. *Land Filled with Flies.* Chicago: University of Chicago Press.

Wilmsen, Edwin N., and James R. Denbow. 1991. Paradigmatic History of San-Speaking People and Current Attempts at Revision. *Current Anthropology* 31 (5): 489–524.

Wilson, Peter J. 1988. *The Domestication of the Human Species.* New Haven, CT: Yale University Press.

Wimmer, Andreas, and Nina Glick Schiller. 2002. Methodological Nationalism and Beyond: Nation-State Building, Migration and the Social Sciences. *Global Networks* 2 (4): 301–34.

Wolfram, Sybil. 1987. *In-laws and Outlaws: Kinship and Marriage in England.* London: Croom Helm.

Woodburn, James. 1968a. Stability and Flexibility in Hadza Residential Grouping. In *Man the Hunter,* ed. R.B. Lee and I. DeVore, 103–10. Chicago: Aldine.

———. 1968b. An Introduction to Hadza Ecology. In *Man the Hunter*, ed. R.B. Lee and I. DeVore, 49–56. Chicago: Aldine.

———. 1980. Hunters and Gatherers Today and Reconstruction of the Past. In *Soviet and Western Anthropology*, ed. E. Gellner, 95–117. London: Duckworth.

———. 1982. Social Dimensions of Death in Four African Hunting and Gathering Societies. In *Death and the Regeneration of Life*, ed. M. Bloch and J. Parry, 187–210. Cambridge: Cambridge University Press.

———. 1997. Indigenous Discrimination: The Ideological Basis for Local Discrimination against Hunter-Gatherer Minorities in Sub-Saharan Africa. *Ethnic and Racial Studies* 20 (2): 345–61.

Worthman, Carol M., and Melissa K. Melby. 2002. Toward a Comparative Developmental Ecology of Human Sleep. In *Adolescent Sleep Patterns: Biological, Social, and Psychological Influences*, ed. M.A. Carskadon, 69–117. Cambridge: Cambridge University Press.

Xiang, Biao. 2013. Multi-scalar Ethnography: An Approach for Critical Engagement with Migration and Social Change. *Ethnography* 14 (3): 282–99.

Yuval-Davis, Nira. 1997. *Gender and Nation*. London: Sage.

Zihlman, Adrienne. 1989. Woman the Gatherer: The Role of Women in Early Hominid Evolution. In *Gender and Anthropology: Critical Reviews for Research and Teaching*, ed. S. Morgan, 21–40. Washington, DC: American Anthropological Association.

Index

Page references followed by *fig.* indicate an illustration, and *t* indicates a table.

author's study group, categorical
  identification of *(continued)*
  Particularly Vulnerable Tribal
  Group, or PTG (state designation),
  24, 208–9; as Scheduled Tribe, or ST
  (state designation), 203, 206–7, 209–
  16, 220; as South Asian forager
  people (in anthropology of hunter-
  gatherers), 25

band societies: anthropology of, 22,
  184–85; and scale, debates on, 68–69;
  sociality of, 233n24; and visiting,
  68–69
Barth, Fredrik, 187, 201
Bateson, Gregory, 50
batha. See illnesses/misfortunes *(batha)*
"being many," modes of, 12–14, 22,
  226–27, 232nn14,15,16; vs. "being
  one" and "being two" modes, 14,
  16–21; concept of, 12–14, 226–27;
  "many-as-One" as, 12, 16, 19–20,
  98, 114; "many huts," as
  ethnographic demonstration of,
  55–60; ontological options of
  foragers, migrants, and the state
  compared, 198–200, 209–16;
  "pluripresence" as, 16–21; scalability
  of, 224–25
being-with: as being, x–xii, 15–16, 40,
  218; vs. being in, 15, 16, 37; vs. being
  like, 158, 172–76; vs. being one, 17,
  19, 88, 216; of more than two, 19;
  Nancy on, 15–16; scalability of, 22,
  39, 216
belongings: absent storage of, 49–55;
  and being-with, 53, 59; inventories
  of, 51–52; multiple usage of, 53–54;
  relational system of, 53; untidiness
  of, 50–51, 53–54
"big (animistic) visits": burial ritual
  during, 87–88; celebration of
  pluripresence during, 164–66; dance
  and music during, 128, 162, 167;
  Gorge dwellers' participation in, 87,
  197, 235n10; mediums'/spirits'
  involvement in, 152 *fig.*, 158–59,

162–63, 190–91; nonhumans'
  participation in, 128, 161–66,
  239n10; "parents-and-children"
  frame of, 128; preparations for, 115,
  158–62, 197–98; reversal husband-
  wife ritual/playact in, 126–128, 127
  fig.; sharing and pluralogues during,
  161–62, 166–68; terms for, 158
birthing, as social: case study, 77–82;
  pluripresence during, 78–81; of
  relative (vs. individual), 82
Bomi and her relatives: situational
  designator of author's study group,
  28–29, 93 *fig.*
Botanical Survey of India (BSI) and
  botanists, 146–48, 173, 175
boundary: absence of in *sime* concept,
  22, 55–60; absence of in *sonta*
  concept, 193, 201, 225; as cultural
  model, 187–88, 201, 225; and group,
  10, 186–187; "new Nayaka word,"
  187–89
Bowlby, John, 124, 135
Briggs, Jean, 139
budi (skill of being-with), 142, 167–68,
  200. *See also* morality
burial. *See* death

categorization: absent/limited in
  hunter-gatherer cultures, 165, 172,
  146–53; plurirelational grouping vs.,
  173; taxonomy and nomenclature
  vs. (Howell), 172
census of India, 24–25, 178, 210
Center for Rural Development Trust
  (CTRD), 219
Chathen (case study): "big visit"
  preparations by, 159–61; children of,
  108; family history of, 193; marriage
  of, 107–9; and Mathew (plantation
  bookkeeper), 195–96, 200; as
  modale, 115, 159, 193
Chathen and his relatives: situational
  designator of author's study group,
  28–29, 93 *fig.*
Chewong, 158, 168; cross-species
  kinship myths of, 170–72;

ethnonyms *(continued)*
(Trobrianders and Chewong
examples), 3, 11–12; indigenous
terms used as, 9–10; "many-ones-
and-One" logic of, 10; in
multiculturalist India, 204–5, 208–
12; Nayaka case study, 177–80;
peoples without, 26; scale-blind
universal use of, 3; as subject of
ethnographic inquiry, 28–29; upscale
travel of, 203

Fabian, Johannes, 6, 227
face-to-face: vs. abstract other, 18;
posture rare in intimate community,
xiv, 18, 98, 112, 139
family. *See* sib family (*kudumba*)
fishing, 118 *fig.*, 129–30, 182 *fig. See
also* hunting-gathering
footpaths: as constitutive of habitat,
55, 58, 70; mapping social
connections, 73; as metaphor for
social structures, 98, 104, 116, 133,
200–202; as scalar perspective
(after Latour), 203–4, 206, 210,
220, 224
forager intimate communities: as
context of everyday life, 2;
oversighted in anthropological
analysis, 2, 32
foragers' belongings/possessions. *See*
belongings
foragers' dwellings/huts. *See*
dwellings
The Foraging Spectrum (Kelly), 22, 69
Fürer-Haimendorf, Christoph von,
178, 209

Gardner, Peter: Paliyans studied by, 25,
68–69, 113, 140, 238n12; on South
Asian foragers, 233–34nn33,34
gender: and anthropology of hunter-
gatherers' division of labor, 120–23;
foragers' disinterest in, 122–23;
imagined communities of, assumed,
120–23; overgenderizing, 122–23.
See also husband-wife pair

Gorge (fictive name of author's study-
group habitat): census in, 61–65, 62
t; development projects in (since
1990s), 42, 218–20; dynamic
contours of, 107, 109–11; history of
contact with incomers/outsiders,
194–98, 217–18; large-scale horizons
enter into (in 2000s), 203, 217–20;
maps of fieldwork locales, 32–37, 33
figs., 36 *figs.*; topography of, 35
grandmother hypothesis, 124
Grinker, Roy Richard, 185
groupism, as paradigm and language,
xiv, 15, 20, 183–84, 186, 217–18, 227
group size. *See* population size/scale
growing up: developing *budi* (skill of
being-with) during, 142 (*see also*
morality); helping relatives during,
142, 144–45; "leaving parents" for
visiting relatives, 140–42. *See also*
infants (*kusu*); parents and children;
sib family (*kudumba*)
Gudalur (India), 34, 35, 219, 237n7
(ch 3)

Hallowell, Irving, 155–56
hamlets: "crawling" of, 70, 115;
distance between, 23; history of,
109–11; moving between/visiting,
67–89; names of 57, 62 *t*, 64; and
satellite-hamlets , 23, 104–5; size of,
23, 62 *t*
Heidegger, Martin, 15, 40
Hewlett, Barry, 138
Hobbes, Thomas, 16–17
home (*sime*): dwelling-with, in, 44–46,
49, 58–60; hamlet and, 55–60;
horizons of, 32–35, 36 *figs.*, 58; life
inside/outside of huts, 45–46;
meanings of, 58–60, 188, 193–94;
plurirelationally performed, 60; as
setting and mind-setting, 39–60
honey collecting, *xvi*, 113, 115, 131,
132 *fig. See also* hunting-gathering
horizons of imagination (of Gorge
foragers), 23–24, 34–35
Howell, Nancy, 6–7, 99–100

Howell, Signe, 11–12, 72–73, 76, 155, 164–65, 170, 172–73

hunter-gatherers: anthropology of, 21–22; changing perspectives on, 26, 154; definition of, 22; importance of, in modern social thought, 4, 26; other terms for, 4; tiny communities of, 4. *See also* scalar slippage in studies of hunter-gatherers

hunting-gathering (in Gorge): collecting *sikai*, 130–31; digging roots, 131, 133; fishing, 118 *fig.*, 129–30, 182 *fig.;* foraging as "bringing home," 147; gathering animals, 133, 237n7 (ch 4); honey collecting, *xvi fig.*, 113, 115, 131, 132 *fig.;* by parties of couples and children, 128–35

husband-wife pair: bipresence of (vs. unity and division of labor) 121, 123–25, 128–35, 143–44; conjugal attachment of (case studies), 135–38; in cosmology, 126–27, 127 *fig.;* as nuclei of groupings, 111, 119, 130, 137

illnesses/misfortunes (*batha*): being-with the ill, 86, 143–44; dialogue with spirits on, 153, 166–68; social disruption, as sign of, 81

imagination, conceptions of, 232n14

Imagined Communities (Anderson), 12–14

imagined community, 12–13, 20–21, 223–28

"incommensurate," as disproportion, 226–27

indigenous people as radical alterity, *xvii*, 5, 226. *See also* hunter-gatherers

indigenous/hunter-gatherer-cultivator people. *See* hunter-gatherers; *specific people under regional categories*

indigenous we-designations, 9–11; as identity categories, 3, 9, 10–11; Levi-Strauss and Viveiros de Castro on

Amerindian "real people," 9–10; *sonta*, a forager case, 224–25; as term instead of auto-ethnonyms and self-designations, 9–11; used as ethnonyms, 9–10; understudied cross-cultural phenomenon, 8–9. *See also* ethnonyms; *sonta* (us, relatives)

individual: pregiven singular being, *xii*, 14; subversive concepts of, 14, 17–18; in theorizing society, 14, 16–17

individualism/individualistic, as paradigm and language: English, 140–41; and groupism, 20, 68; in hunter-gatherer studies, 68, 238n12; limits of redressed by relational approach, *xiv*, 15, 17, 18, 68. *See also* plurirelational; relation/relational

infants (*kusu*): absence of cooing and play dialogue with, 139; assessing development of, by interactive capacity, 139; carrying of, compared with modern slings, 139; constant holding of, compared with African foragers and Americans, 138; turning into children (*makalo*), 139–40

Ingold, Tim, 4, 35, 39–41, 239n2

Institute for Development Alternatives (IDA), 219–20

interpersonal names, 64

Kalliyani (case study): birth of her son, 78–82; death of, 105; kinship terms used by, 103; marriage to Kalan, 104–5, 189–91; siblings/cousins of, 97, 111–13

Kalliyani and her relatives: situational designator of author's study-group, 28–29, 93 *fig.*

Kattunayaka: claims for identity in India, 202, 205, 208–17; compared with *sonta*, as embodying clashing modes of being-many, 210–17, 224–25; population explosion of in India, 214–15; as PTG (Particularly

ethnonymically constituted group, 223–28; extending to diverse present beings, *x*, 158, 183–84, 196–201; vs. group, 201; low scalability of, 225; meanings of, *x*, 8–9, 22, 215–16, 231n1 (prologue); pluripresent-and-diverse character of (overview), 60; subversive of "same-and-separate" basis of nation, 225–26, 228

sonta (we-designation): endurance of, 220; translation as "relatives," 15, 232n11. *See also* author's study group, appellatory identification of; indigenous we-designations

sonta kudumba: sonta as first person plural possessive, 97, 236n1 (ch 3). *See also* sib family (*kudumba*)

South American peoples: Achuar, 155; Amazonian cosmology of, 2, 101, 154, 157–58, 160, 176, 186, 233n25, 238n14; Arawete, 157; Oronao', 100; Piraha, 235n5; Urarina, 143, 238n15

South Asian foragers: Andaman Islanders, 233–34n33; Birhor, 233–34n33; Chenchu, 233–34n33; estimated population of, 25, 233–34nn33,34, 240n2; Hill Pandaram, 25, 113, 133, 140, 146, 166, 172; Jenu Kurumba, 25, 167, 233-34n33, 238n13, 239n11; Kadar, 233-34n33; as major subdivision of world's hunter-gatherers, 25; Raute, 233–34n33; Vedda, 233–34n33. *See also* Nayaka; Nilgiri foraging/forest peoples; Nilgiri tribal peoples; Paliyan

South Asian peoples: Dhanka, 207; Gaddis, 207; Gorkha, 207. *See also* Nilgiri foraging/forest peoples; Nilgiri tribal peoples

Southeast Asian peoples: Batek, 9, 122, 168; Ilongot, 9; Meratus, 70, 204–5, 218; Orang Asli, 168. *See also* Chewong

spirit possession. *See under* "big (animistic) visits"; nonhuman kin

State Level Scrutiny Committee (SLTC), 211, 241n6. *See also*

multiculturalist policy of distributive justice in India

Steward, Julian, 68

Strathern, Marilyn: on English kinship/ontology, 102–3, 121, 124, 141, 191; on gender 2, 120–21; on large-scale/scaling, 3, 6, 8, 44, 232n10; on person, individual, relation, and society, 14, 15, 18, 57, 82, 141, 233nn22,24

STs (Scheduled Tribes), 203, 206–7, 209–16, 220

Tamil Nadu (India), 24–25, 41–42, 45, 163, 188–89, 209

tapu (fault upsetting coeval), 167–68. *See also* morality

tininess/tiny scale of forager-cultivator communities, as phenomenological condition: conspicuous diversity under, 225–26; invalid statistical analysis under, 7; lacking smoothing effect of "law of large numbers," 7, 56, 65; as nonfactor in anthropology, 1–3; surveying problems under, 2, 210–12, 214–15, 238n15

tininess/tiny scale of forager-cultivator communities, size of specific groups: Arawete (136), 157; Batek (about 800), 122; Chewong (131), 72; Eastern Hadza (about 400), 77; Nilgiris Kattunayaka (1,245), 210

tribal/indigenous peoples of India, 24, 27, 218–19

Tsing, Anna Lowenhaupt, 70, 204–5, 218

Us-ing vs. Othering: in-marrying non-kin, 191–94, 240n9; in-marrying relatives, 189–91; newcomers (ethnographer, migrants, and others), *ix–xii*, 194–98, 218; overview of, 183–84; plurirelational work of, 198; *sonta* discourse and, 183–84, 196–201